A HANDBOOK FOR SUPPORTING TODAY'S
GRADUATE STUDENTS

A HANDBOOK FOR SUPPORTING TODAY'S GRADUATE STUDENTS

Edited by David J. Nguyen and Christina W. Yao

Foreword by Ann E. Austin

STERLING, VIRGINIA

COPYRIGHT © 2022 BY STYLUS PUBLISHING, LLC.

Published by Stylus Publishing, LLC.
22883 Quicksilver Drive
Sterling, Virginia 20166-2019

Library of Congress Cataloging-in-Publication Data
The CIP data for this title has been applied for.

13-digit ISBN: 978-1-64267-064-6 (cloth)
13-digit ISBN: 978-1-64267-065-3 (paperback)
13-digit ISBN: 978-1-64267-066-0 (library networkable e-edition)
13-digit ISBN: 978-1-64267-067-7 (consumer e-edition)

Printed in the United States of America

All first editions printed on acid-free paper
that meets the American National Standards Institute
Z39-48 Standard.

Bulk Purchases

Quantity discounts are available for use in workshops and for staff development.

Call 1-800-232-0223

First Edition, 2022

We dedicate this volume to graduate students everywhere and all who support grad students, especially to our advisor Dr. Roger Baldwin, who supported us through our doctoral journey.

CONTENTS

PART TWO: ADDRESSING ACADEMIC AND PROFESSIONAL SKILL DEVELOPMENT

PART THREE: SUPPORTING GRADUATE STUDENTS BEYOND THE CLASSROOM

This book is timely and important because the experiences and education of today's graduate students relate directly to the future of our country and the broader world—to the innovation, insight, creativity, health, collaborative skill, and imagination that graduates bring to the work that they will do for many decades, in education and across a wide range of other sectors. As this book explains, graduate education involves the academic study, research, and teaching in which students are involved—as well as the lives they live outside the classroom and laboratory. How graduate education is organized and how students are supported and guided in their journey impact graduate students' individual experiences and lives, the likelihood of their degree completion, and the attitudes and aspirations they take forward as they continue their careers.

Preparing the next generation of leaders, teachers, and researchers who will work in academe as well as in business, industry, nonprofits, government, social services, and other sectors is part of the core mission of American universities. Nguyen and Yao, along with their colleagues who have authored chapters in this book, provide fresh as well as compassionate perspectives on the experiences of graduate students as well as probing insights and pointed reminders of the responsibilities of faculty, administrators, and other stakeholders in higher education to ensure high-quality, comprehensive, multifaceted graduate education. I see two major purposes motivating this book. The first is to provide a picture of today's graduate students, the nature of their experiences, and the challenges they face as they prepare for meaningful, varied, and productive careers. The second purpose is to provide guidance, ideas, and practical suggestions to key stakeholders within U.S. universities who shape the graduate experience—institutional leaders, faculty members serving as advisors and mentors, and graduate students themselves.

The characteristics of graduate students today reflect changing demographics, including great diversity in the range of racial and ethnic backgrounds, national origins, and personal identities among the body of graduate students. In many fields where White male students have historically been the norm, current demographics show increased involvement of students from groups previously less represented. Arguably, the major project of graduate education is to develop a scholarly identity and related skills that serve as preparation for meaningful, varied, and productive careers. To pursue this goal in meaningful ways, students should be encouraged and supported to reflect and build on their own rich cultures and heritages, as they also decipher and negotiate the multiple cultures, values, and assumptions of their disciplines, their specific departments and institutions, and the overall U.S. and international higher education system. The institutional cultures in which graduate students pursue their degrees have complex and sometimes conflicting norms in terms of their processes, expectations, and traditions. They include what is called the "hidden curriculum" in which expectations and habits are often simultaneously unspoken and powerful. For example, how students are expected to interact with faculty members, what is considered excellent writing, how to handle authorship issues, who participates in various institutional meetings or decisions, and what is considered acceptable behavior within courses, research teams, and at conferences are norms that are often unclear and unexplained to graduate students.

Negotiating these cultural mysteries is made even more challenging by the structural racism and assumptions of White privilege embedded deeply within American society, including its universities, which create inhospitable institutional cultures for many students in U.S. higher education institutions. As the academy becomes more diverse and as members of the academic community commit to challenging structural and systemic barriers to equity, graduate education is a particularly important site for reform. Graduate education is where universities prepare those who will create the future of academe and of society. Finding ways to support the full array of students so that they can succeed in meeting their individual goals and are prepared to contribute their expertise to the broader society should be a central commitment within higher education.

Many graduate students, especially those who identify with groups historically less represented in academe and those who are first-generation higher education students, face the challenge of feeling that they don't belong; this can manifest in a sense of imposter syndrome ("I don't belong in this academic environment") or traitor syndrome ("I have left my family and life experiences behind"). Such feelings can be exacerbated by daily microaggressions, interactions with advisors with different backgrounds from their own and little understanding of the student's own background, and absence of culturally relevant curriculum. In response, graduate students often report feeling lonely and isolated and may find it hard to express their authentic selves. In fact, in recent years, across institutions, deans and faculty have been very concerned about the rise in mental health issues among graduate students, including depression and fear of stigma around seeking help.

External pressures add to the burden of worry affecting many graduate students. Increasing debt loads and a very competitive employment market in many fields are daily concerns for many students. Furthermore, students are often unaware of the range of employment options related to their knowledge and skills. Graduate students may also have family responsibilities, and many balance full-time or part-time work, along with their studies, to provide necessary income. Concerns about being pulled in multiple directions and simply not having enough time to fulfill all responsibilities compete with the press of moving efficiently through a graduate program and minimizing time to degree.

At the same time that individual students are wrestling with competing demands and pressures, the shortcomings of graduate education are becoming more apparent to many observers, faculty members, leaders, researchers, and students. Critiques emphasize that graduate education typically does not acquaint students with the array of possible careers they might consider, minimal attention is given to teaching preparation and refinement of writing skills, and students usually are not encouraged to be collaborative and reflective about their development and ways to connect their interests to a wide array of employment options. Furthermore, recognizing that all graduates do not enter academic work, voices across academe and in the employment sector are calling for more explicit attention in graduate study to helping students identify and cultivate competencies that are applicable to many sectors of work. For example, graduate experiences can nurture leadership, teamwork, and communication skills, as well as a range of analytical abilities. Excellent ideas are being shared and implemented across the country—and are discussed in this book—concerning professional development for teaching, strategies to help graduate students develop a range of writing skills, strategies for facilitating graduate student engagement in international opportunities, paths for student participation in scholarly organizations, approaches to addressing and supporting graduate student mental health, and options for providing comprehensive career development. The chapters in this volume discuss a number of the skills and abilities that those calling for reform in doctoral education encourage leaders and faculty to address.

In addition to describing noteworthy features of today's graduate students and graduate education, another goal of this book is to provide guidance to key stakeholders focused on enhancing the quality of graduate education. Across the chapters, readers will find a considerable array of suggestions. In my reading, I began to organize them into recommendations for institutional leaders of universities that provide graduate education, the faculty members who advise and mentor graduate students, and the students themselves. The suggestions for institutional leaders fit into four categories. First, those involved with graduate education need to recognize and acknowledge the diversity of identities, experiences, and social capital that students bring to their graduate programs. Creating environments explicitly committed to diversity, equity, and inclusion requires going beyond general statements to impactful actions that ensure that students' experiences are characterized by respect, appreciation, and support for their unique and often intersecting identities. As emphasized throughout this volume, this approach involves integrating culturally appropriate approaches into curricula, and celebrating the ways of knowing that Graduate Students of Color bring to their graduate study. Institutions need to develop culturally sensitive mentor models that help prepare and guide faculty members to serve as effective advisors and mentors for each of their graduate students, including students whose identities and backgrounds may differ from those of their faculty advisors. The basic principle should be that support cannot be generic but rather should be designed to fit individual needs.

A second priority for institutional leaders should be to foster supportive communities of practice for graduate students in both the in-person and the online contexts. The graduate student experience is enriched through opportunities for peer engagement, such as via workshops and collaborative work. Boot camps for new students to acquaint them with resources, expectations, and processes, and spaces for students to meet across fields for conversation and interaction are examples of the kinds of structures that institutional leaders can encourage and support.

A third area for institutional attention pertains to the implicit and explicit messages conveyed to graduate students. Expressions of welcome and information about resources and relevant opportunities help students feel supported. Universities are large entities so highlighting cross-institutional opportunities can help transitions and can foster occasions for students to meet their counterparts across departments. When institutional and departmental information is available about a range of career outcomes, and when the institution highlights the diverse pathways that can be pursued through graduate education, students receive the message that success can have different meanings depending on individuals' goals, circumstances, interests, and aspirations. Institutions can help normalize the idea of career exploration by providing an array of examples of various career paths and offering for-credit internships as part of the graduate curriculum. Furthermore, a particularly important message for institutional leaders to convey is their support for the well-being and mental health of graduate students, and the availability of mental health resources and people to support student needs.

Fourth, institutional leaders, especially those serving as graduate deans and department chairs, can stay abreast of innovative programmatic opportunities and find ways to integrate effective options into their institutional offerings. Some ideas, highlighted in chapters in this volume, include focused support for the development of writing skills, providing opportunities for integrating international experiences into graduate education, explicitly encouraging involvement in student organizations, and organizing programming around financial planning. Even better than stand-alone, unconnected programming to address specific needs is an approach that creates and encourages the development of an ecosystem that draws on resources, opportunities, and information from departments, campus units such as career services, and employers.

As important as institutional leaders are in shaping graduate education, faculty members are probably the key people in the academic lives of most graduate students, as they advise, mentor, facilitate research teams, and supervise teaching assistants. While faculty members are most likely influenced in their interactions with graduate students by their memories of their own experiences in graduate school, ideas found in this book can help them consider the specific needs of today's students and enrich their repertoire of support strategies. One idea is to develop a learner-centered approach to advising and mentoring in which the faculty member purposely explores the values and goals, and cultural, epistemological, and ontological perspectives of the student in order to individualize support. Faculty members can also be alert to linking graduate students to specific resources and opportunities that are relevant to their particular circumstances and needs. Knowing that a faculty member is taking the time to support the student in ways that are especially pertinent and meaningful in the context of a student's life conveys a message that the student "matters." Feeling that one is valued and that a faculty member cares also helps students feel a sense of belonging, which counteracts the feelings of isolation and loneliness that students often report. Faculty members can also learn more about systemic racism, develop skills as allies, and learn more about how to be culturally knowledgeable and responsible in interactions with a diverse group of students. They can engage in initiatives that challenge and dismantle systemic racism and help their universities rethink structures and policies that are barriers to open, supportive, and equitable environments.

Developing a scholarly identity is a particularly important part of the graduate experience, and a process where faculty members could find ways to be more involved with graduate students. They can encourage their students to participate in conversations, conferences, and projects that foster deeper understanding of the discipline, the issues and questions that scholars within the field pursue, and the habits of thinking and doing that characterize scholarly work. Supporting students as they explore their own scholarly identities also requires humility and openness on the part of the faculty member—that is, a commitment not to replicate oneself but to walk with students as they find their own voice, positionality, and commitments within their fields. Another role a faculty member can play in helping students deal with the complexities and challenges of the graduate experience is to help make explicit the hidden curriculum and messages being conveyed in academe. They can also strive to recognize the multiple pressures that students experience, model strategies to balance and manage both professional and personal responsibilities, and encourage attention to well-being and positive mental health. In many fields, faculty members have traditionally focused only on the academic development of their students; in the complexity of graduate education today, there are compelling reasons for faculty members to take a comprehensive approach to supporting students, that is, an approach that recognizes the multiple dimensions of students' lives.

In addition to the roles and responsibilities of institutional leaders and faculty members, graduate students themselves can be proactive in creating the kind of graduate experience that they believe will most fully help them achieve their goals. Woven throughout this book are ideas for students to consider. One of the most important steps is to consciously examine their goals, motivations, and hopes, and then to be proactive in identifying, finding, mapping, and pursuing opportunities to pursue those aspirations. Graduate students should not wait and hope that they will have the experiences, receive the support, and find the opportunities they imagine. Rather, they can be purposeful in seeking out and creating occasions to advance their goals. They can approach their faculty and ask for guidance, they can request resources, they can press institutional leaders to respond to their requests. Several strategies stand out: creating networks with peers and providing support and encouragement to each other; taking the time to participate in events, conversations, workshops, and conferences available at their university or in professional and scholarly associations; investing time in conversations that help sharpen a sense of professional identity; participating in professional development activities such as writing workshops; and finding resources and experiences that help develop skills and abilities in leadership, mentoring, teamwork, communication, analytical thinking, and adaptability. Graduate students also can work on reframing their experiences in ways that prepare them for a myriad of employment options; that is, they can practice identifying their strengths and attributes and presenting those as competencies that are relevant to many contexts in the work sector as well as in academe.

It is an honor for me to write this foreword as the editors, David Nguyen and Christina Yao, are two colleagues who were, several years ago, doctoral students in the graduate program at Michigan State where I teach.

As graduate students, they were actively engaged in our program, distinguishing themselves not only in their academic work but also in their contributions to their peers and to the overall culture and climate of our graduate program and the broader college and university communities. They have been very successful as they have pursued their careers and established themselves as faculty members guiding, teaching, and working with their own students. As a scholar who has studied doctoral education and collaborated with others to create institutional and national strategies to support those pursuing graduate work, I am very pleased to see these colleagues whom I admire also choose to make a contribution as researchers and writers to strengthening graduate education.

As I write this foreword, we are all in the midst of the COVID-19 pandemic, in which everyone in the academic community is grappling with how best to fulfill the educational, research, and service missions of higher education institutions in the current situation. Graduate students are experiencing the full force of the implications of this daunting and unusual period. Those who are teaching assistants are often being asked to become more adept at teaching in remote learning contexts. Many universities are adjusting budgets and thus have less flexibility to provide financial support to graduate students. Those students approaching the conclusion of graduate study face uncertain employment contexts, and, furthermore, many are far from home and loved ones. Finding ways to support graduate students is more important than ever. Emphasizing the many dimensions of graduate education, this volume provides innovative and practical ideas for the kinds of holistic approaches that promote the well-being and success of graduate students. I hope university leaders, faculty members, and graduate students themselves will commit to their shared responsibility to ensure a robust graduate experience and will tap into the thoughtful ideas shared in this book.

—Ann E. Austin
Michigan State University, East Lansing, MI
August 2021

ACKNOWLEDGMENTS

First, we would like to acknowledge the thoughtfulness of our chapter authors in creating practical solutions to support the academic, personal, and social well-being of graduate students.

Second, we would like to acknowledge the work of doctoral students—Salome Aluso (Ohio University) and Reena Patel (University of South Carolina)—for their editorial support of this volume.

Last but certainly not least, we would like to acknowledge David Brightman's editorial support of and patience with this idea from inception to publication. His thoughtful and insightful feedback has helped us to make this work accessible and practical for audiences.

INTRODUCTION

Christina W. Yao and David J. Nguyen

Graduate education is an increasingly important aspect of higher education as it can provide opportunities for career advancement, career changes, or academic career access. In fall of 2019, over three million students enrolled in postbaccalaureate programs across the United States, which included students in master's, doctoral, and professional degree programs (National Center for Educational Statistics [NCES], 2021). The number of master's and doctoral degrees conferred grew significantly between the 2009–2010 and 2018–2019 academic years, with all signs pointing to increased graduate enrollment each year (NCES, 2021). Overall, graduate education is a significant component of U.S. higher education, which necessitates increased attention to student learning and development while enrolled in graduate programs.

Higher education in the United States has faced increased scrutiny in recent years, with multiple calls for accountability, affordability, and relevance to general society (see Cassuto, 2015). Affordability and convenience contribute to the growth in online and distance education over the past 15 years (Seaman et al., 2018). In addition, more students from diverse backgrounds (e.g., gender, race, ethnicity, national origin, socioeconomic) are enrolling in higher education, necessitating a shift in pedagogy, curriculum, and socialization toward more culturally responsive ways. Yet, the emphasis in shifts in higher education tend to focus primarily on undergraduate students, with little attention given to the increasing graduate student population. How can U.S. higher education better support, train, and socialize graduate students for their professions in ways that are societally and culturally responsive?

Despite the continued growth in numbers, graduate program attrition rates are of great concern to academic program coordinators and have persisted over time, especially as the world starts to emerge from the COVID-19 pandemic. Although specific numbers are not easily accessed, the Council of Graduate Schools (2004) stated that "conventional wisdom holds that only 40 to 50 percent of students who begin PhD programs in the United States

1

actually complete their degrees" (p. 3). The attrition and completion rates of master's students is more difficult to target due to the variation in time, format, and relation to doctoral programs (Council of Graduate Schools, 2010). Overall, the attrition and departure of all graduate students may be affected by a variety of factors. Current studies on graduate education noted that advising, finances, student preparation, test scores, loneliness, lack of community, mental health challenges, and socialization experiences contribute to why graduate students lengthen time to degree completion or leave their programs altogether (Abedi & Benkin, 1987; Berelson, 1960; Bowen & Rudenstine, 2014; Ehrenberg & Mavros, 1995; Gardner, 2009; Gururaj et al., 2010; Lovitts, 2002; Nettles & Millett, 2006).

Many of these attrition factors relate to activities beyond the classroom that may impede academic progress. For example, in spring of 2020, the COVID-19 pandemic upended educational practices all over the world. Graduate students were heavily affected, citing mental health concerns such as depression, anxiety, and fear as they tried to navigate the sudden shifts to online classes amidst safety concerns for self and family within a racialized pandemic (Kee, 2021; Koo et al., 2021; Patias et al., 2021). In addition, studies on graduate education tend to focus on unwinding the attrition puzzle, with an emphasis on factors leading to departure rather than persistence and completion (see Lovitts, 2002; Nettles & Millett, 2006).

Yet understanding graduate student persistence necessitates an emphasis on successful programs, initiatives, and interventions that lead to overall student success. Thus, the purpose of this book is to provide contemporary practices and programs that may provide a comprehensive approach to supporting graduate student success and completion. For the purpose of this book, we focus on graduate education, which includes both master's and doctoral programs. We chose to exclude professional doctorates (i.e., law, medicine, and dental) as professional programs have unique contexts, outcomes, and structure. We also acknowledge that the chapters in this book are not intended to be a "one-size-fits-all" approach to graduate student success. Rather, it is our hope that readers can and will adapt the authors' suggestions for practice to individuals' unique environmental contexts.

This book is divided into three distinct sections: navigating contexts and identities, addressing academic and professional skill development, and supporting graduate students beyond the classroom. In the Navigating Contexts and Identities section, we highlight the shifting demographics and contextual factors shaping graduate education over the past 20 years. Acknowledging and addressing these shifting demographics are critical for supporting graduate students. David J. Nguyen's chapter highlights key trends in graduate education as educators begin considering how they are supporting graduate students. Christina W. Yao and Crystal E. Garcia's chapter 2 discusses how institutions can support graduate students participating in virtual and online contexts. In chapter 3, Francena Turner, HyeJin Tina Yeo, and Eboni M. Zamani-Gallaher explore the role of power, intracultural, and cross-cultural communications alongside Brown et al.'s (1999) exploration of myths affecting graduate mentor/and mentees of color. Sonja Ardoin and Maria Erb's chapter 4 highlights the unique challenges first generation students face when they enter graduate education and offers suggestions how institutions can help first generation graduate students' transition. In chapter 5, Colin Ben and Jessica Solyom address different ways of knowing that graduate students may bring with them, with an emphasis on American Indian/Native American students. Finally, Chelsea H. Lyles, Natali Huggins, and Claire K. Robbins discuss the hidden curriculum embedded within graduate education and share tips for understanding the culture of graduate school.

The section on Addressing Academic and Professional Skill Development describes institutional practices to develop the requisite academic and professional development necessary to succeed in master's and doctoral programs. A key ingredient for graduate students is to learn what is valued within their discipline and to develop the requisite skill required for degree completion. In the skill development section, we address different ways institutions can support academic and professional adroitness. In chapter 7, Lucas B. Hill shares his findings on how institutions can use teaching programs for graduate instructors to train student teachers across a range of career interests. OiYan Poon, Josefina Carmona, Carmen Rivera, and Kim Nehls's chapter 8 addresses the ways institutions can create supportive writing programs and environments. In chapter 9, Kim Nehls shares how institutions can support skill development through participating in professional organizations and associations. Finally, Meggan Madden and Jennifer Donaghue conclude this section with recommendations for how institutions can support students with international engagement interests.

In the Supporting Graduate Students Beyond the Classroom section, we curate a conversation about different ways institutions can support graduate students beyond the classroom. In chapter 11, Carmen M. McCallum, Sarah Kurz, Emily Boerman, and Allison Boone address how institutions can support graduate student mental health. Jake Livengood's chapter calls attention to myriad career paths for graduate students. In chapter 13, Phil Schuman and Salome Aluso share ways for students to tackle financial stress and avoid financial mismanagement. Matthew M. Couch and Kerry M. Hodak address how institutions can create student organizations to help students find community beyond their graduate program. Finally, in chapter 15, A. Emiko Blalock, Katy B. Mathuews, and Nicole Lor discuss ways for graduate students to create work–life balance.

This edited volume brings together scholars and practitioners for a dialogue on how best to support graduate students in contemporary contexts while developing requisite skills and finding support beyond the classroom. In particular, this book addresses the needs of today's changing student demography and offers ways to address challenges they may face inside and outside of the classroom. Within this edited book, a talented mixture of administrators and scholars offers new insights on supporting graduate students and encourages institutions to have a dialogue about how to best support students during both in-class and out-of-class academic experiences. We are still grappling with the effects of the COVID-19 pandemic, yet we know that graduate education has shifted over the years and we must be ready to support students within contemporary contexts of higher education. It is our hope that readers, especially graduate school administrators, student affairs professionals, faculty, and researchers, find this edited book useful in reimagining ways to better support today's graduate student population.

References

Abedi, J., & Benkin, E. (1987). The effects of students' academic, financial, and demographic variables on time to the doctorate. *Research in Higher Education*, *27*(1), 3–14.

Berelson, B. (1960). *Graduate education in the United States*. McGraw-Hill.

Bowen, W. G., & Rudenstine, N. L. (2014). *In pursuit of the PhD*. Princeton University Press.

Brown, M. C., II, Davis, G. L., & McClendon, S. A. (1999). Mentoring graduate students of color: Myths, models, and modes. *Peabody Journal of Education*, *74*(2), 105–118.

Cassuto, L. (2015). *The graduate school mess: What caused it and how we can fix it*. Harvard University Press.

Council of Graduate Schools. (2004). *PhD completion and attrition: Policy, numbers, leadership, and next steps*.

Council of Graduate Schools. (2010). *The role and status of the master's degree in STEM*.

Ehrenberg, R. G., & Mavros, P. G. (1995). Do doctoral students' financial support patterns affect their times-to-degree and completion probabilities? *Journal of Human Resources*, *30*(3), 581–609.

Gardner, S. K. (2009). Conceptualizing success in doctoral education: Perspectives of faculty in seven disciplines. *The Review of Higher Education*, *32*(3), 383–406.

Gururaj, S., Heilig, J. V., & Somers, P. (2010). Graduate student persistence: Evidence from three decades. *Journal of Student Financial Aid, 40*(1), 31–46.

Kee, C. E. (2021). The impact of COVID-19: Graduate students' emotional and psychological experiences. *Journal of Human Behavior in the Social Environment, 31*(1–4), 476–488.

Koo, K. K., Yao, C. W., & Gong, H. J. (2021, August 30). "It is not my fault": Exploring experiences and perceptions of racism among international students of color during COVID-19. *Journal of Diversity in Higher Education* [Advance online publication]. https://doi.org/10.1037/dhe0000343

Lovitts, B. E. (2002). *Leaving the ivory tower: The causes and consequences of departure from doctoral study.* Rowman & Littlefield. https://doi.org/10.1086/378426

National Center for Education Statistics. (2021). *Postsecondary certificates and degrees conferred.* https://nces.ed.gov/programs/coe/indicator_cts.asp

Nettles, M. T., & Millett, C. M. (2006). *Three magic letters: Getting to PhD.* Johns Hopkins University Press.

Patias, N. D., Von Hohendorff, J., Cozzer, A. J., Flores, P. A., & Scorsolini-Comin, F. (2021). Mental health and coping strategies in undergraduate and graduate students during COVID-19 pandemic. *Trends in Psychology*, 1–20.

Seaman, J. E., Allen, I. E., & Seaman, J. (2018). *Grade increase: Tracking distance education in the United States.* Babson Survey Research Group and Quahog Research Group.

PART ONE

NAVIGATING CONTEXTS
AND IDENTITIES

TRENDS IN GRADUATE EDUCATION BETWEEN 1998 AND 2018

David J. Nguyen

G aps in access and attainment have persisted throughout the history of higher education and graduate education. In this chapter, I examine the demography of graduate students and how this demography has changed during a 20-year period—1998 to 2018. To illustrate this point, in this chapter, I use National Center for Educational Statistics (NCES) data from the Digest of Educational Statistics to show the exponential growth in master's education and National Science Foundation's (NSF) Survey of Earned Doctorates to highlight key changing trends in doctoral education. Results from this trend analysis demonstrate the majority of graduate students completing degrees continue to be White; however, degree programs are seeing a range of racial/ethnic, socioeconomic, and gender diversity within graduate enrollments.

Master's Degrees

A primary challenge with highlighting trends within master's education is that these degrees are difficult to track institutionally and nationwide. For example, some master's degree programs take 1 year, many are completed in 2 years, while others are designed to be 3 to 4 years (e.g., Master of Divinity). Adding to these challenges is that some master's programs may be completed on a part-time basis, while others may require full-time attendance. Thus, record keeping for graduate education and master's students can be a challenging endeavor.

Despite these data challenges, NCES's Digest of Educational Statistics uses recorded data from Integrated Postsecondary Education Data System (IPEDS), which captures data from Title IV funded institutions. In this section, I highlight the following trends in master's data from 1998 to 2018: growth of master's degree completions in total and across degree programs, changing participation across sex, and participation variation across race/ethnicity.

Overall Master's Degree Production and Growth in Programs

Between 1998 and 2018, master-level degree attainment has substantially grown. In 1998, 429,296 total students completed a master's degree, while the number of degrees conferred grew more than 90% between 1998 and 2018 to 820,102. In looking at the aggregate number of degrees earned, key nuances would be missed. For example, degree conferrals grew modestly between 2013 and 2018, while more rapid growth occurred at the 10-year (2008, 195,079 more degrees earned) and 15-year (2003, 307,456 more degrees earned) intervals.

The six most popular master's degree programs in 1998 were education (114,691), business (102,171), health professions and related sciences (39,260), engineering (25,936), public administration and services (25,144), and social sciences and history (14,938). These six degree programs accounted for more than 322,000 or approximately 75% of all degrees awarded in 1998 (total 429,296 degrees earned). These same six degree programs accounted for more than 70%, or 581,666, master's degrees in 2018 (total degrees earned 820,102); however, the magnitude of some programs grew considerably and a new discipline climbed into the top six (computer science displaced history). The top six in 2018 were business (192,184), education (146,367), health professions and related sciences (125,216), engineering (51,721), computer and information sciences (46,468), and public administration and services (46,294).

Certain degree programs witnessed significant volume and percentage growth. With respect to number of degrees awarded, business awarded an additional 90,000 master's degrees and grew 88.1%. While not originally in the top six degree granting programs, computer and information sciences increased in popularity by awarding 46,468 degrees in 2018, while in 1998, 11,246 master's degrees in this field were awarded. This 20-year increase represents 313.2% growth. Not all degree programs saw steady growth. Although education grew as a field, the 2018 total represents a substantial decrease from its 2008 peak of 175,880 master's degrees conferred. Library science saw an 11.7% decline overall, but similar to education saw a peak in 2008 that has steadily declined over the last 10 years.

Sex and Race/Ethnicity

Table 1.1 shows that females by proportion and number earned more master's degrees than males between 1998 and 2018. Throughout the past 20 years, the proportion of females hovered around 60%, peaking in 2008 at 60.6%. Similarly, the number of females doubled over the last 20 years to slightly less than 500,000 females earning a master's degree in 2018.

Table 1.2 shows the percentage changes of White students participating in master's education has steadily declined from a high of 71.6% in 1998 to 53.5% in 2018. The decline in White student proportions gave way to the growing numbers of Black, Non-Hispanic, Hispanic, and Nonresident Alien students participating in master's education. Asian/Pacific Islander and American Indian/Alaskan Native proportions remained consistent during this time period. When considering race/ethnicity and gender together, Black, Non-Hispanic females and males, Hispanic females and males, and Nonresident alien females and males grew substantially.

Doctoral Degrees

Overall, doctoral education enrollments and degree completion have continued to increase over the last 20 years. In 1998, 42,636 doctoral degrees were conferred across all fields. In 2018, 55,195 degrees were conferred. This represents an almost 12,500 degree increase, or a 29% increase.

Across major fields of study, engineering and life sciences together account for more than a 67% increase in the number of doctoral degrees conferred in 2018. In 1998, these two fields accounted for approximately 31% (life sciences: 8,611 and 12,780 in 1998 and 2018 respectively; engineering: 5,922 and 10,183 in 1998 and 2018 respectively). Another field seeing significant growth over the last two decades is the physical and earth sciences (4,566 in 1998 and 6,335 and in 2018). The proportion of degrees earned within this field has remained steady though the number of degrees awarded has increased nearly 150%.

Certain degree programs have driven much of the growth in doctoral degree attainment between 1998 and 2018. Many of these fields are concentrated in the STEM-related disciplines. For example, there have been significant upticks in the percentage of doctoral degrees awarded in biomedical and biomedical engineering (895% increase), material science engineering (285% increase), computer and information sciences (289% increase), and health sciences (189% increase). On the other hand, education-related doctoral degrees across subdisciplines were down over time (6,569 in 1998 and 4,834 in 2018, indicating a 24% drop in degrees earned), while many humanities and social science degree programs witnessed gains, including psychology (25%), anthropology (30%), and history (57%). Table 1.3 shows the changes in 5-year, 10-year, 15-year, and 20-year doctoral degree production.

TABLE 1.1
Master's Student Sex 1998–2018

Differences by Sex	1998		2003		2008		2013		2018	
Total Male	183,982.00	42.9%	211,381.00	41.2%	246,491.00	39.4%	301,552.00	40.1%	326,870.00	39.9%
Total Female	245,314.00	57.1%	301,264.00	58.8%	378,532.00	60.6%	450,166.00	59.9%	493,232.00	60.1%

Sources:

- Digest of Educational Statistics. (2005). "Table 266. Master's degrees conferred by degree-granting institutions, by sex, racial/ethnic group, and major field of study: 2002–03." https://nces.ed.gov/programs/digest/d05/tables/dt05_266.asp
- Digest of Educational Statistics. (2010). "Table 301. Master's degrees conferred by degree-granting institutions, by sex, race/ethnicity, and field of study: 2007–08." https://nces.ed.gov/programs/digest/d10/tables/dt10_301.asp
- Digest of Educational Statistics. (2015). "Table 323.30. Master's degrees conferred by postsecondary institutions, by race/ethnicity and field of study: 2012–13 and 2013–14." https://nces.ed.gov/programs/digest/d15/tables/dt15_323.30.asp
- Digest of Educational Statistics. (2015). "Table 323.40. Master's degrees conferred to males by postsecondary institutions, by race/ethnicity and field of study: 2012–13 and 2013–14." https://nces.ed.gov/programs/digest/d15/tables/dt15_323.40.asp
- Digest of Educational Statistics. (2015). "Table 323.50. Master's degrees conferred to females by postsecondary institutions, by race/ethnicity and field of study: 2012–13 and 2013–14." https://nces.ed.gov/programs/digest/d15/tables/dt15_323.50.asp
- Digest of Educational Statistics. (2019). "Table 323.30. Master's degrees conferred by postsecondary institutions, by race/ethnicity and field of study: 2016–17 and 2017–18." https://nces.ed.gov/programs/digest/d19/tables/dt19_323.30.asp
- Digest of Educational Statistics. (2019). "Table 323.40. Master's degrees conferred to males by postsecondary institutions, by race/ethnicity and field of study: 2016–17 and 2017–18." https://nces.ed.gov/programs/digest/d19/tables/dt19_323.40.asp
- Digest of Educational Statistics. (2019). "Table 323.50. Master's degrees conferred to females by postsecondary institutions, by race/ethnicity and field of study: 2016–17 and 2017–18." https://nces.ed.gov/programs/digest/d19/tables/dt19_323.50.asp

TABLE 1.2

Master's Student Sex and Race/Ethnicity Demographics 1998–2018

Field of Study	5-Year Change (2013–2018)	10-Year Change (2008–2018)	15-year Change (2003–2018)	20-Year Change (1998–2018)
All fields, total	9.1%	31.2%	60.0%	91.0%
White	–3.7%	7.3%	28.5%	42.7%
Black, Non-Hispanic	3.7%	40.3%	106.2%	203.3%
Hispanic	36.8%	96.9%	190.2%	346.9%
Asian/ Pacific Islander	11.5%	33.9%	83.9%	137.5%
American Indian / Alaskan Native	–10.2%	–11.7%	17.0%	61.9%
Two or more races	59.8%	–	–	–
Nonresident Alien	53.6%	99.6%	102.6%	177.6%
Differences by Sex				
Total Male	8.4%	32.6%	54.6%	77.7%
Total Female	9.6%	30.3%	63.7%	101.1%
Male				
White	–7.1%	6.2%	23.6%	31.4%
Black, Non-Hispanic	4.3%	50.1%	115.2%	186.1%

(Continued)

TABLE 1.2 *(Continued)*

Field of Study	5-Year Change (2013–2018)	10-Year Change (2008–2018)	15-year Change (2003–2018)	20-Year Change (1998–2018)
Hispanic	29.9%	93.4%	173.0%	288.6%
Asian/Pacific Islander	4.0%	23.5%	70.2%	107.8%
American Indian / Alaskan Native	–15.9%	–15.9%	5.3%	37.9%
Two or more races	48.9%	–	–	–
Nonresident Alien	53.7%	93.4%	88.7%	155.1%
Female				
White	–1.6%	7.9%	31.6%	50.5%
Black, Non-Hispanic	3.5%	36.4%	102.5%	211.4%
Hispanic	40.7%	98.9%	200.3%	386.0%
Asian/Pacific Islander	17.9%	42.8%	95.4%	165.6%
American Indian / Alaskan Native	–7.1%	–9.5%	23.5%	76.7%
Two or more races	66.5%	–	–	–
Nonresident Alien	53.4%	107.7%	123.1%	211.5%

Sources:

- Digest of Educational Statistics. (2000). "Table 269. Master's degrees conferred by degree-granting institutions, by racial/ethnic group, major field of study, and sex of student: 1997–98." https://nces.ed.gov/programs/digest/d00/dt269.asp
- Digest of Educational Statistics. (2005). "Table 266. Master's degrees conferred by degree-granting institutions, by sex, racial/ethnic group, and major field of study: 2002–03." https://nces.ed.gov/programs/digest/d05/tables/dt05_266.asp
- Digest of Educational Statistics. (2010). "Table 301. Master's degrees conferred by degree-granting institutions, by sex, race/ethnicity, and field of study: 2007–08." https://nces.ed.gov/programs/digest/d10/tables/dt10_301.asp
- Digest of Educational Statistics. (2015). "Table 323.30. Master's degrees conferred by postsecondary institutions, by race/ethnicity and field of study: 2012–13 and 2013–14." https://nces.ed.gov/programs/digest/d15/tables/dt15_323.30.asp
- Digest of Educational Statistics. (2015). "Table 323.40. Master's degrees conferred to males by postsecondary institutions, by race/ethnicity and field of study: 2012–13 and 2013–14." https://nces.ed.gov/programs/digest/d15/tables/dt15_323.40.asp
- Digest of Educational Statistics. (2015). "Table 323.50. Master's degrees conferred to females by postsecondary institutions, by race/ethnicity and field of study: 2012–13 and 2013–14." https://nces.ed.gov/programs/digest/d15/tables/dt15_323.50.asp
- Digest of Educational Statistics. (2019). "Table 323.30. Master's degrees conferred by postsecondary institutions, by race/ethnicity and field of study: 2016–17 and 2017–18." https://nces.ed.gov/programs/digest/d19/tables/dt19_323.30.asp
- Digest of Educational Statistics. (2019). "Table 323.40. Master's degrees conferred to males by postsecondary institutions, by race/ethnicity and field of study: 2016–17 and 2017–18." https://nces.ed.gov/programs/digest/d19/tables/dt19_323.40.asp
- Digest of Educational Statistics. (2019). "Table 323.50. Master's degrees conferred to females by postsecondary institutions, by race/ethnicity and field of study: 2016–17 and 2017–18." https://nces.ed.gov/programs/digest/d19/tables/dt19_323.50.asp

TABLE 1.3

Doctorate Recipients, by Major Field of Study: Selected Years, 1998–2018

Field of study	5-year change (2013–2018)	10-year change (2008–2018)	15-year change (2003–2018)	20-year change (1998–2018)
All fields	4.7%	13.2%	35.4%	29.5%
Life sciences	4.7%	15.3%	50.2%	48.4%
Physical sciences and earth sciences	13.4%	28.1%	59.5%	38.7%
Mathematics and computer sciences	10.1%	26.5%	116.8%	91.5%
Psychology and social sciences	3.7%	16.6%	25.4%	20.4%
Engineering	13.1%	29.5%	92.9%	72.0%
Education	−2.0%	−26.3%	−27.3%	−26.4%
Humanities and arts	−10.0%	8.6%	−2.4%	−3.9%
Other	−1.1%	8.2%	40.6%	40.8%

Note. Adapted from National Center for Science and Engineering Statistics (2019). *2018 Survey of Earned Doctorates* (Table 12).

Average Time-to-Degree

One area significantly related to the completion of a doctoral degree is time-to-degree. Overall trends in Table 1.4 suggest that time-to-degree since entering graduate school has been gradually reduced by nearly 1.5 (1.5=1.0) years since 1998. In the 2018 Survey of Earned Doctorates, students across all fields completed their doctoral degrees in 7.3 years. The most notable reduction in time-to-degree was the 3.1-year decrease (15.0 to 11.9 years) in education-related fields. Education-related fields also had the widest gap between when a person completed a bachelor's degree and started graduate school (4.6 years in education-related fields) while humanities and arts had the smallest gap (approximately 1.0 years).

Racial/Ethnic Diversity Among U.S. Citizens and Permanent Residents

Racial/ethnic diversity among U.S. citizens and permanent residents completing doctoral degrees has largely shifted over time. In 1998, approximately

TABLE 1.4

Median years to doctorate, by broad field of study: Selected years, 1998–2018

Field of study and time to degree	1998	2003	2008	2013	2018
All fields					
Since bachelor's	10.5	10.2	9.4	9.0	8.6
Since starting graduate school	8.3	8.5	7.7	7.5	7.3
Since Starting Graduate School					
Life sciences	7.5	7.2	6.9	6.9	6.8
Physical Sciences and Earth Sciences	6.7	6.7	6.4	6.3	6.3
Mathematics and computer sciences	7.4	7.7	7.0	6.9	6.8
Psychology and social sciences	7.9	8.2	7.7	7.7	7.8
Engineering	7.2	7.3	6.7	6.7	6.7
Education	15.0	13.2	12.7	11.7	11.9
Humanities and Arts	9.7	9.7	9.3	9.3	9.4

Note. Adapted from National Center for Science and Engineering Statistics. (2019). *2018 Survey of Earned Doctorates* (Table 31).

93% of all U.S. doctoral degree recipients held U.S. citizenship or permanent residency status. In 2018, 55% of doctoral degree recipients held U.S. citizenship or permanent residency status.

Racial/ethnic diversity increased in number among Hispanic or Latino, Asian, Black or African American, White, and "More than one race" during the previous 20 years. The most notable gain was among Hispanic or Latino (94%) and Black or African American (53%) doctoral degree recipients. Conversely, American Indian or Alaska Native, "Other race" or "Race not reported," and "Ethnicity not reported" saw observable declines over time.

One particular challenge with interpreting these percentage changes over time is just how few Students of Color are represented in doctoral education. Out of the 35,404 doctoral degree recipients in 1998, 24,951 (70.4%) identified as White. When considering different race/ethnicity classifications (e.g., "More than one race") used within the NSF data, small incremental increases or decreases can create large swings in the percentage of students. For example, between 2003 and 2018, there were 739 more doctoral degrees awarded to students identifying as more than one race. This increase represents approximately a 204% increase. Similarly, 75 fewer doctoral degrees were awarded to American Indian or Alaska Native students. This decrease represents an approximately 39% decrease.

Sex

Between 1998 and 2018, more males than females completed doctoral degrees. However, the proportion of degrees awarded to men has lessened during that time. For example, across all fields 58% (24,628) of all doctoral degrees were awarded to males; however, in 2018, 54% of recipients are males (29,798). In evaluating these numbers, these percentages across fields offer nuanced insight into places where fields have increased equitable participation. For example, within the life sciences during 1998, males (54.5%) completed doctoral degrees at a higher rate than females (45.5%); however, in 2018, these percentages have flipped to a point where more females (55.7%) than males (44.3%) earned doctoral degrees. While engineering and physical and earth sciences still disproportionately awards degrees to males, females have steadily made inroads by closing the gap by nearly 11%. Within education, females continue to widen the gap by percentage of degree earners, while within the humanities and arts, males and females earn doctoral degrees at similar rates.

So What Do These Trends Mean?

The preceding trends merit discussion. First, there has been significant growth in the proliferation of graduate degrees awarded between 1998 and 2018. These increases in degree production coincide with the cyclical oscillations within the U.S. economy. A healthy economy usually leads to fewer students returning to educational settings (Johnson, 2013). Conversely, some key economic downturns including the dot-com bust (circa 2001) and subprime mortgage crisis (circa 2007–2009) coincided with increases in educational enrollments (Altonji et al., 2016). Presumably individuals considered advanced degrees around each of these economic crisis moments. For example, consider this timeline for an engineering student—if an individual was involved in the dot-com bust, they likely would have applied for a graduate program in 2001 and entered in 2002. If this student completed their doctoral degree around the average time-to-degree in these fields of study, they would complete their degree around the reporting of the 2008 Survey of Earned Doctorates. Among master's degree students, engineering was a popular option during the dot-com economic recession, as evidenced by the number of people earning master's degrees at this point in time.

Second, the demographics of graduate education continue to evolve over time. Differences based on demographic characteristics, such as race/ ethnicity and sex, show a slow changing demography, but a closer look at the intersections of these demographics also indicate that much has changed. These results are simultaneously heartening and disheartening. Within some fields and disciplines, the focus of changing the student body composition is evident. Funding agencies like the National Science Foundation and Spencer Foundation are funding projects that seek to change the status quo and shake up who has access to postbaccalaureate education. Investments from these funding agencies are heartening. What makes these demographic trends disheartening is that some fields continue to perpetuate male dominance that can negatively shape a student's experience before and during the student's education (Posselt & Grodsky, 2017; Walton et al., 2015). This point becomes more evident in the lopsided nature of fields like engineering and physical sciences still having a substantial proportion of males earning doctoral degrees. These percentages continue to suggest a chilly climate for women in science, technology, engineering, and mathematics-related (STEM) fields (Cabay et al., 2018; Chan et al., 2019; De Welde & Laursen, 2011).

Third, this chapter not only shows the diversifying student population, but offers glances of the types of socialization that they may be receiving. During a doctoral program, students often engage in three socialization processes—"mastering the knowledge base of their disciplines and specialty areas, learning their discipline's theories and methods, and establishing relationships with peers, faculty, and their advisor" (Lovitts, 2005, p. 140; Weidman et al., 2001)—to develop an identity and commitment to the discipline. Doctoral student socialization guides students in their transformation from neophyte to emerging scholar (Walker et al., 2008; Weidman et al., 2001). The emphasis of much socialization is preparation for a singular academic career rather than a multitude of career options (see chapter 12 of this volume). In addition, considerations for the mentoring of this diversifying student body are necessary so that graduate students can thrive within unfamiliar contexts (see chapters 3, 4, and 6 of this volume).

Finally, the statistics in this chapter primarily represent only the "successful" students that have completed their doctoral degrees. Myriad studies continue to show the attrition rate in doctoral education to hover around 50%. Two main reasons why people do not complete doctoral degrees are lengthy time-to-degrees and the financial aspects. Abedi and Benkin (1987) restricted their analyses to the primary type of financial support. The study separated financial support into five categories—personal sources (e.g., savings, off-campus earnings), family and/or spouse, on-campus employment (e.g., teaching and research assistantships), fellowships and grants, and loans. The study results showed that doctoral students employed as a research or teaching assistant graduated in the shortest amount of time (7.68 years). Similarly, fellowship students graduated in 8.06 years. Students relying on family support (9.40 years), loans (9.52 years), and their own earnings (10.82 years) had the longest time to the doctorate. In other words, institutionally supported students had shorter enrollments than their self-financing peers.

For many people, the financial challenges of graduate school encourage them to ask the question of whether it's worth it. In Lovitts's (2001) study of doctoral student attrition, she found evidence of students "not having fellowship support; not being able to continue because support was cut off; and not having financial support in the dissertation stage; thus requiring the student to get a job, which in turn leads to insufficient time and energy to devote to the dissertation" (p. 21). Financial concerns remain a significant concern among graduate students (see chapter 13 of this volume). Indeed, financing doctoral education is a complex matter for many students (Nettles & Millet, 2006). Institutions are beginning to pay more attention to factors like money and finance that can affect graduate student success. Several reports have made note of this challenge. For example, the University of California *Graduate Student Happiness and Well-Being Report* (2015) noted that graduate students mentioned financial concerns in the written comments more than any other category. Institutional accounts and reports demonstrate and confirm the complex influence financial considerations have on the doctoral student experience from recruitment to degree completion. In short, financial challenges have prompted doctoral students to wonder "whether the financial reward [after completion] compensate[s] for the poor lifestyle" during doctoral education (Rogers et al., 2015, p.10).

Conclusion

In this chapter, I have highlighted trends among master's and doctoral degree recipients. These trends highlight the changing nature of who might be participating in graduate education while maintaining some of the status quo concerning demographics in certain fields. Taking a snapshot of these demographics can begin to inform graduate program leadership that the one-size-fits-all approach or socialization attempts may not resonate with students in the same ways that they traditionally have (Antony, 2002; Austin, 2002; Gardner, 2008). Furthermore, now more than ever graduate degree holders need to be more nimble in career aspirations because of the oversaturation of the academic labor market and the ways a student can parlay their graduate training into careers beyond academic posts (see chapters 7 and 12 in this volume).

References

Abedi, J., & Benkin, E. (1987). The effects of students' academic, financial, and demographic variables on time to the doctorate. *Research in Higher Education*, *27*(1), 3–14. https://doi.org/10.1007/bf00992302

Altonji, J. G., Kahn, L. B., & Speer, J. D. (2016). Cashier or consultant? Entry labor market conditions, field of study, and career success. *Journal of Labor Economics*, *34*(S1), S361–S401. https://doi.org/10.1086/682938

Antony, J. S. (2002). Reexamining doctoral student socialization and professional development: Moving beyond the congruence and assimilation orientation. In J. C. Smart, & W. G. Tierney, (Eds.), *Higher education: Handbook of theory and research* (Vol. 17, pp. 349–380). Springer. https://doi.org/10.1007/978-94-010-0245-5_8

Austin, A. E. (2002). Preparing the next generation of faculty: Graduate school as socialization to the academic career. *The Journal of Higher Education*, *73*(1), 94–122. https://doi.org/10.1353/jhe.2002.0001

Cabay, M., Bernstein, B. L., Rivers, M., & Fabert, N. (2018). Chilly climates, balancing acts, and shifting pathways: What happens to women in STEM doctoral programs. *Social Sciences*, *7*(2), 23. https://doi.org/10.3390/socsci7020023

Chan, M., Kwon, J., Nguyen, D. J., Saunders, K. M., Shah, N., & Smith, K. N. (2019). Indebted over time: Racial differences in student borrowing. *Educational Researcher*, *48*(8), 558–563. https://doi.org/10.3102/0013189X19864969

De Welde, K., & Laursen, S. (2011). The glass obstacle course: Informal and formal barriers for women PhD students in STEM fields. *International Journal of Gender, Science and Technology*, *3*(3), 571–595. http://genderandset.open.ac.uk/index.php/genderandset/article/viewFile/205/363

Gardner, S. K. (2008). Fitting the mold of graduate school: A qualitative study of socialization in doctoral education. *Innovative Higher Education*, *33*(2), 125–138. https://doi.org/10.1007/s10755-008-9068-x

Johnson, M. T. (2013). The impact of business cycle fluctuations on graduate school enrollment. *Economics of Education Review*, *34*, 122–134. https://doi.org/10.1016/j.econedurev.2013.02.002

Lovitts, B. E. (2001). *Leaving the ivory tower: The causes and consequences of departure from doctoral study*. Rowman and Littlefield. https://doi.org/10.1086/378426

Lovitts, B. E. (2005). Being a good course taker is not enough: A theoretical perspective on the transition to independent research. *Studies in Higher Education*, *30*(2), 137–154. https://doi.org/10.1080/03075070500043093

Posselt, J. R., & Grodsky, E. (2017). Graduate education and social stratification. *Annual Review of Sociology*, *43*, 353–378. https://doi.org/10.1146/annurev-soc-081715-074324

Rogers, M. E., Creed, P. A., Searle, J., & Nicholls, S. L. (2015). Coping with medical training demands: Thinking of dropping out, or in it for the long haul. *Studies in Higher Education*, *41*(9), 1715–1732. https://doi.org/10.1080/03075079.2014.999318

University of California Berkeley. (2015). *Graduate student happiness and well-being report*. http://ga.berkeley.edu/wp-content/uploads/2015/04/wellbeingreport_2014.pdf

Walker, G., Golde, C., Jones, L., Bueschel, A., & Hutchings, P. (2008). The formation of scholars: Rethinking doctoral education for the twenty-first century. *Higher Education*, *60*, 119–121. https://doi.org/10.1007/s10734-009-9287-9

Walton, G. M., Logel, C., Peach, J. M., Spencer, S. J., & Zanna, M. P. (2015). Two brief interventions to mitigate a "chilly climate" transform women's experience, relationships, and achievement in engineering. *Journal of Educational Psychology*, *107*(2), 468–485. https://doi.org/10.1037/a0037461

Weidman, J. C., Twale, D. J., & Stein, E. L. (2001). *Socialization of graduate and professional students in higher education: A perilous passage?* Jossey-Bass. https://doi.org/10.1080/00221546.2003.11780868

2

MOVING TOWARD CULTURALLY RESPONSIVE AND INCLUSIVE SUPPORT FOR ONLINE GRADUATE STUDENTS

Christina W. Yao and Crystal E. Garcia

Most of the literature prior to the COVID-19 pandemic related to graduate student success focused almost exclusively on students attending traditional, face-to-face graduate programs despite the growth in online graduate education (Allen et al., 2016). Fully online graduate students often experience lower sense of community than students in traditional face-to-face and hybrid courses (Rovai & Jordan, 2004), which could lead to program dissatisfaction and attrition. Thus, it is essential to identify challenges that online graduate students experience and provide strategies for promoting student success in online contexts.

The imperative of understanding the online context is driven by the continuous growth of online education, which was exacerbated by the increase in online offerings due to COVID-19 (Lederman, 2021). Studies estimated that nearly 75% of all college students were at least partially enrolled in online courses in the fall of 2020 (Lederman, 2021). Prior to COVID-19, graduate online learning modalities comprised a significant portion of overall distance education in 2014 with over 960,000 enrolled (Allen et al., 2016). Seaman et al. (2018) reported that enrollments in distance education increased for the 14th year in a row in their annual report on distance education based on enrollment through 2016. According to the

U.S. Department of Education National Center for Education Statistics (2021), 37.2% of all college students were enrolled in at least one distance education course with 17.6% being exclusively enrolled in online courses in fall 2019. Because of the growth in online education, "professional and graduate programs have been targeted for growth" (McClintock et al., 2013, p. 2), particularly because online graduate education may support working adults who "require flexible access to education" (p. 3).

Yet although online graduate education has grown in recent years, limited literature exists that offers insight considering how to best support online graduate students. Online graduate students must learn to simultaneously develop online learning competency while their identities shift into becoming graduate students (Yao et al., 2017). The support for graduate students is particularly important as these adult learners may have a variety of responsibilities (e.g., children, elder care, full-time jobs) that they must balance alongside student responsibilities (e.g., coursework, research, thesis). At the same time, a student who is considered successful is often labeled as a "self-motivated, independent, and self-directed learner; a critical thinker; a good time manager; and a highly organized individual" (Rovai & Ponton, 2005, p. 77). However, despite the flexibility of online education, how do online graduate learners balance various responsibilities, including their own learning? More importantly, how can teachers and administrators support graduate students enrolled in online programs to optimize learning?

In this chapter, we discuss the possibilities of how to support online graduate students by illuminating actions university administrators and faculty can take to better support graduate students and their academic socialization within online contexts. We specifically address the support process from a culturally responsive approach. Although online spaces may often be considered neutral or values-free spaces, we posit that neutrality never exists in teaching and learning, especially when content and pedagogy are laden with power dynamics and privilege certain knowledges. Thus, we recognize and highlight the many differences in thought, approach, and priorities that exist within online teaching and learning.

Conceptual Framework for Online Teaching and Learning

We frame our recommendations for supporting graduate student learning through two models related to online teaching and learning: Anderson's (2008) model of online learning and McLoughlin's (2000) framework for equity and participation in technology use. Anderson's (2008) work identifies components of an online course with an emphasis on structural considerations.

Anderson's (2008) model incorporates three major components—students, teachers, and content—for online learning. In this chapter, the students we refer to are graduate students. Teachers are those guiding and facilitating the learning, which may include full-time faculty, adjuncts, and teaching assistants/apprentices. Our recommendations are primarily focused on the students and teachers, and only to a lesser extent on the content. Though we recognize that content may be viewed differently across disciplines, content also reflects the human component as instructors make decisions on what content is chosen and how it should be engaged in the course. These decisions carry important implications as they determine whose voices and realities are heard and whose are silenced.

In addition to Anderson's (2008) model, we utilize McLoughlin's (2000) framework as our overarching lens for how we approach online teaching and learning. Specifically, the framework serves as a guide for how to infuse cultural responsiveness in instruction design, especially when considering the diversity of graduate students in distance education. McLoughlin (2000) built upon Henderson's (1996) multiple cultural model incorporating four dimensions that emphasize flexibility in course design and allow students to engage with diverse perspectives. These dimensions include cultural maintenance, ownership of learning, communities of practice, and provision of multiple perspectives. These dimensions honor students' culture and background while also promoting a "sense of place . . . [which] is critical to identity and belonging," (McLoughlin, 2000, p. 237) particularly for marginalized student populations. As a result, multiple perspectives are honored within the community of inquiry and practice.

The two frameworks are complementary as they both subscribe to a community of inquiry approach to online learning (Anderson, 2008; McLoughlin, 2000). Structurally, a community of inquiry includes the interactivity between the three major components (i.e., learners, teachers, and content) for online learning (Anderson, 2008). Interaction "serves a variety of functions in the educational transaction" (Anderson, 2008, p. 55), including communication, shared knowledge, and both dependent and independent work. Online classes may provide access to prospective graduate students as a result of flexibility and accessibility. As a result, more returning adults, who have a variety of daily responsibilities such as full-time employment and familial responsibilities, can gain access to graduate education. Because of the diverse backgrounds of graduate learners, culturally responsive approaches to learning are needed in online graduate education, which is highlighted by McLoughlin's (2000) model for equity and participation in online course design. "Culture pervades learning" (McLoughlin, 2001, p. 9), and therefore requires consideration of issues related to "the social and cultural dimensions of task design, communication channels, and structuring of information if the needs of culturally diverse learners are to be met" (p. 9).

Moving Toward Inclusive Support for Online Graduate Students

Although multiple topics affect distance education, we chose to focus on *student learning* as our guiding approach to this chapter. We consider learning to be "a way of interacting with the world" (Biggs, 1999, p. 13) and believe that "education is about conceptual change, not just the acquisition of information" (p. 13). Thus, we use the term *learning* as a consideration for the support of graduate students in online classes as learning occurs as a result of the interactions among content, peer exchanges, and teacher engagement. Learning also goes beyond content and engages in themes and topics that are particularly salient to graduate students, such as socialization into academic norms and disciplinary expectations (Weidman et al., 2001). Our suggestions are appropriate for consideration by multiple constituencies; however, our emphasis is primarily toward who we consider *teachers*—inclusive of course instructors, instructional designers, and program administrators.

In this section, we explore the human dynamics of online education and offer considerations for practice that do not ignore, but intentionally center, individual identities through learner–learner, teacher–learner, and teacher–teacher interactions (Anderson, 2008) with an emphasis on developing students' cultural maintenance, ownership of learning, communities of practice, and provision of multiple perspectives (McLoughlin, 2000).

Cultural Maintenance Through Culturally Responsive Teaching

Teachers have an important role in relation to the teaching and the content of a course. Specific interaction areas include "learning objects as well as units of study, complete courses, and associated learning activities" (Anderson, 2008, p. 59). Thus, teachers have a critical role in engaging with learners, especially related to honoring and accepting different ways of learning and knowing. We provide two specific areas for supporting students' cultural maintenance: scaffolding students' knowledge and continuous training for culturally responsive teaching.

Scaffolding knowledge through teaching. Although scaffolding has its roots in childhood education, the techniques are increasingly used in adult and graduate education. The use of scaffolding supports learning, which McLoughlin (2000) describes as learner support in distance education. Scaffolding assists learners by acknowledging learners from a constructive perspective by providing ample support and guidance, and then eventually removing the structures as learners gain confidence to manage the complexity of course context. Simply stated, scaffolding can be metaphorically represented by a person learning to ride a bicycle—scaffolding would include the use of training wheels until the individual learns to balance without the structures of the additional wheels. We suggest that as part of learner support, instructors provide ample structure in the first few weeks of a course that includes clear instructions and constant communication. For example, many graduate students may be unfamiliar with how to meaningfully engage with classmates on discussion boards. Thus, we recommend that teachers provide clear instructions, examples, and prompts for initial discussion board posts, yet still allow for flexibility of various knowledges and experiences. Another example could be assigning a research paper in parts—that is, the teacher could break down the parts of an academic research paper and have the parts due at different points of the semester. The instructor can schedule brief online check-ins with students (either individually or as a class) or peer check-ins to ensure they feel supported during the process. We piloted this assignment in an online doctoral seminar for first semester students and required students to work on different parts of a research paper that corresponded to course content throughout the semester. For example, students had to submit a literature review after a module on conducting literature reviews and engaging with theoretical frameworks. The next part that was due was related to researcher positionality after reading through a module on researcher reflexivity and positionality. Overall, students found the scaffolding of the research project helpful in understanding the course concepts while simultaneously reading and conducting the research, all of which contributed to their overall scholarly identity development (Garcia & Yao, 2019).

While it is essential that learners scaffold their content knowledge development, at the same time, students and their experiences must not be stifled by teacher expectations and programmatic norms. Most importantly, knowledge development should be based on students' prior experiences and knowledges because of the specialized content of graduate programs. McLoughlin (2000) recommends that teachers allow for flexibility from students toward achieving the course learning objects. As such, teachers provide a range of activities and assignments that demonstrate learning. For example, Christina taught an online Critical Race Theory in Education course. In the course, the discussion boards have focused prompts that reflect the content and readings of the module. However, the prompts always allow for personal reflection that asks students to build on their own knowledge and experiences. In doing so, students can engage in complex theoretical content and build upon their own understandings of the world.

In the final assignment, students are asked to describe what they learned in the course that they will apply to their own professional careers and/or future research. Students are told that they can use any format that they would like, including spoken word, song, paper, poem, or video—as long as it meets the goal of the assignment. By providing this open-ended assignment, Christina engages in the spirit of critical race theory by asking for storytelling and critical race praxis, all of which engages students in their own sense making of the content, yet also reflects some of the tenets discussed in course readings.

An essential component of culturally responsive teaching includes content selection. When considering course content, the teachers must question, "whose stories and voices are centered in the course?" And perhaps just as important, "whose stories and voices are absent?" The need to adapt course content to culturally diverse students is a necessity as graduate students, especially those in online courses, come from a variety of backgrounds, experiences, and ways of knowing. Culturally responsive approaches to online teaching are important as "online programs are becoming ubiquitous across traditional institutions of higher education and their core faculty are teaching an increasingly diverse student body" (Heitner & Jennings, 2016, p. 54). Thus, the decisions related to content are also extremely important in online education and must be combined with pedagogical aspects.

Learning and training for culturally responsive teachers. We would be remiss not to mention the importance of continued learning and development for instructors to improve their practices in online education for graduate students. Anderson (2008) articulated the importance of "professional development and support through supportive communities" (p. 59). Further, we assert that developing content expertise and knowledge of approaches to engage students in learning are important, but they are incomplete without considering ways these practices move forward equity within online spaces (McLoughlin, 2000).

Many colleges and universities assume that faculty and instructors automatically know how to teach. However, several universities are making efforts toward effective pedagogy with the establishment of teaching and learning centers. We strongly encourage teachers to take advantage of teaching workshops and informal discussions that are available on their campuses. We also suggest that teachers participate in other campus programs such as LGBTQ+ resource center trainings, Safe Zone and Safe Harbor Training, undocumented student sessions and others as a way to gain some knowledge on supporting the needs of today's students. Further, as instructors attend these sessions, if it is not addressed directly, ask how supports for these students may be implemented in an online setting. A word of caution is that although campus programs are helpful in gaining awareness of diverse students' needs, the programmatic outcomes are typically insufficient for truly developing an equitable learning space in online courses. Additional trainings would be needed, and they may have to come from teachers' own initiatives in reading and gaining such knowledge.

We encourage educators to build supportive communities by having conversations with colleagues about their equitable practices engaging online graduate students. Faculty may consider starting online teaching groups similar to writing groups in which individuals can meet and discuss course format and approaches that have been more or less effective in serving online graduate students. Finally, we recommend that individuals connect with others through professional development opportunities at the regional or national level through professional and academic associations and learning communities. Associations such as the Online Learning Consortium or EDUCAUSE may be a good start for developing networks of other teachers who are interested in developing and sustaining culturally responsive online courses.

Developing Ownership of Learning in Online Graduate Learners

Learners' engagement with content has always been a primary aspect of education, and with online education, the internet "provides a host of new opportunities, such as immersion into micro-environments, exercises in virtual labs, and online computer-assisted learning tutorials" (Anderson, 2008, p. 58). Although student engagement with content may be perceived as an expected aspect of learning, teachers cannot assume that deep learning automatically occurs in online settings. More importantly, teachers cannot expect graduate students to automatically have the skills to successfully navigate online classes. Thus, we have two suggestions for teachers to consider for better supporting online graduate learners' engagement and ownership of their individual learning.

Academic skill development. One of the greatest strengths and at the same time the greatest challenge of online learning is the independent nature of online classes. Online courses, especially those that are primarily asynchronous, require independent learning from students. The independent nature of online learning may be challenging for graduate students, especially when considering the need for effective time management and navigating new learning management systems. We suggest that instructors spend ample time early in their courses to prepare graduate students for the independent nature of online courses. If possible, we strongly recommend putting together an orientation or transition program/module prior to the start of graduate students' coursework (Yao et al., 2017).

The orientation and transition program can introduce important aspects of online graduate learning, such as tips on time management and suggestions for how to engage with course materials. Online students need focused assistance in understanding the assumptions and expectations of graduate education, including citation rules and academic norms (Garcia & Yao, 2019). We suggest that what may be seemingly basic and fundamental skills must be addressed early on in an online course for graduate students. For example, do all new graduate students know how to read and accurately cite research articles? Or do all students understand the difference between refereed articles and opinion blogs? Thus, providing time and information about how to engage with the independent aspects of online learning and content would benefit graduate students as they transition to graduate education.

Connections to campus services for distance students. One often forgotten aspect of distance learning is how online students access campus resources. For example, do online students know what library services are available to them at a distance? Or do distance students have access to the on-campus writing center? If the campus offers basic needs resources such as a food pantry, are there opportunities for students to use these outside of typical office hours? Engaging with campus partners and developing a relationship is the first step to ensuring a supportive learning environment for graduate students in online classes. Many campus departments often focus primarily on in-person, undergraduate students and at times may be less aware and prepared for the varying needs of adult graduate students. Thus, establishing collaborations across campus would be extremely beneficial for graduate students who must navigate various aspects of online learning.

Some considerations would be to ensure that student services are available to graduate students in online classes in ways that meet their specific needs. For example, how can graduate students capitalize on using interlibrary book loans and get books delivered closer to their physical location? How do graduate students know what journals and search engines are typically most useful for members of a specific discipline? Also, new graduate students may need to learn and adjust to new ways of academic writing—so how do students access the on-campus writing center? Are the hours varied enough for adult learners who may also be working full-time? At the University of Nebraska-Lincoln, we coordinated with the on-campus Writing Center to establish virtual consultations to meet students' writing needs. This process took some time for the program to develop as we had to think outside of the traditional confines of a physical center, but distance students were able to take advantage of the flexible hours and virtual meeting times. Thinking beyond the traditional confines of on-campus support during typical business hours would ensure better support for graduate students in online courses.

Most importantly, collaborating with various campus departments and student support services will ensure that the needs of online graduate students can be met on your campus.

Creating Online Communities of Practice

The literature on distance education and graduate student experiences have pointed to the importance of building a sense of community among adult learners, particularly for those with marginalized identities (Du et al., 2015; Du et al., 2016; Hyun et al., 2006; Nadal et al., 2010; Rovai & Wighting, 2005). This notion is further reflected in McLoughlin's (2000) dimensions—particularly by way of building communities of practice and engaging multiple perspectives. Yet, an emphasis on the convenience of asynchronous methods over peer interactions may cause instructors may overlook the value of peer interactions within online graduate course settings. We assert that an important component for instructors to consider within any educational environment is how student learners engage with one another. In this section, we discuss some approaches and considerations for online instructors to cultivate a sense of community for graduate students.

Introductory activities. Peer relationships can be built from the start with introductory activities similar to what many adopt in face-to-face courses. As Anderson (2008) articulated, teachers "must make time at the commencement of their learning interactions to provide incentive and opportunity for students to share their understandings, their culture, and the unique aspects of themselves" (p. 48). While students can be prompted to share a written paragraph of themselves at the beginning of the semester, we recommend that instructors adopt more creative and interactive introductory activities. For instance, students can create infographics that highlight aspects of their identities and experiences that they would like to share with their peers. Students may also record a short video introduction (we recommend no longer than 2–3 minutes in length) for their peers. Instructors can guide these activities by providing students a list of prompts to include in their introductions.

Another option is engaging students in a cultural artifacts activity where they discuss items that hold meaning for them based on their identities/backgrounds. Regardless of the format, an important component of these activities is that members of the learning community can share their academic and personal interests. Furthermore, these activities can communicate expectations around creating an inclusive environment by requiring that students check their submissions for accessibility and giving students the option to share aspects of themselves such as their pronouns, which we recommend instructors consider modeling.

Creating low-stakes discussion spaces. Discussion spaces are another area in which online graduate students can build a sense of community. However, teachers must recognize that discussion spaces in which students engage in authentically are not always developed organically and may take some work to construct. Therefore, we recommend that online teachers intentionally consider ways to develop these spaces for their graduate students. To begin, instructors can form the foundation for these spaces by clearly communicating the nature and purpose of these discussions as well as by communicating guidelines and expectations for respectful dialogue and productive interactions with the course material. Teachers can further develop a sense of community among students by including low-stakes synchronous and asynchronous opportunities for students to interact with one another.

In a recent study by Garcia and Yao (2019), they found that graduate students in an online seminar valued interaction with their peers through both asynchronous methods, such as online interactions discussion boards, and synchronous methods, such as "live sessions." Students appreciated the informal format of the discussion board. The prompts and readings posted in the discussion boards allowed students to engage in a conversational way as opposed to constructing scholarly, APA-formatted responses. Adopting this low-stakes approach allowed students the freedom to express their thoughts similarly to the ways they would within a face-to-face setting, without fears around monitoring their "correct" use of language. We recognize there are several other platforms on which students can engage in dialogue beyond institutional platform discussion boards such as by using WebEx, VoiceThread, social media platforms, or Jamboards to name a few. Regardless of the platform, instilling the sense that these spaces are not overly regulated with academic guidelines may enhance students' ability to connect with their peers through more honest and genuine dialogue.

Within a graduate course setting, teachers may also falsely assume that the students will more naturally engage in course material and in learning with their peers without the instructor's presence. In contrast, we suggest that teachers develop an active presence within these spaces. Some ways they can do so without dominating the discussion and intimidating students to post include redirecting students with a prompt that connects back to the course content when conversations become unproductive. In addition, teachers should encourage students to engage further with the course material by responding to posts with additional questions and considerations for thought.

Synchronous opportunities for peer engagement. Furthermore, while asynchronous formats allow for flexibility, including some synchronous elements provides the opportunity for students to develop familiarity and comfort with the individuals in the course that may contribute to their ability to be more open to these discussions. Planning synchronous sessions and inviting guest speakers while leaving some time at the end or beginning of each synchronous session for questions about the course and discussion among the class can be a simple way to create these opportunities. Faculty can mirror these initiatives for informal interactions in out-of-class experiences for online learners as well. For instance, graduate programs can create online professional development workshops hosted through video chat platforms like Zoom or Google Hangouts. While these types of social opportunities are typically only afforded to on-campus students, academic programs and student organizations such as graduate student associations can consider ways to bridge these initiatives to distance students. Instructors must also use caution with planning too many synchronous sessions and should be clear about dates and times of these commitments from the start of the semester.

An additional way teachers can build community within online graduate student spaces is to be intentional about engaging students in collaborative work. Research has pointed to differences in ways students view and experience working with peers in online learning spaces. For instance, Du et al. (2015, 2016) found that African American female graduate students generally preferred to work in racially mixed groups, asserting their peers often added perspectives that were useful to their learning. However, Du et al. (2016) also noted that students experienced frustrations when working with peers who did not contribute to the work in meaningful ways. This is a common experience for students working collaboratively with their peers. Keeping this in mind, instructors should be cognizant of the work balance to ensure the work is collaborative and not one-sided. One option for doing so is to have students construct a group contract outlining member responsibilities, deadlines, and ramifications for not completing assigned tasks as well as opportunities for students to submit evaluations of their peers.

Facilitating Sharing of Multiple Perspectives
Similar to face-to-face educational settings, the student and teacher are central components of Anderson's (2008) model for online learning environments. Importantly, these relationships not only define who is involved in these interactions, but also the nature of those interactions. Yet there are nuances in how these interactions are made and ways they affect the educational space for online graduate students that are distinct from a typical face-to-face classroom. Furthermore, just as in face-to-face educational settings, students' identities play an important role in how these spaces are constructed and experienced. Contrary to scholarship that asserts the usefulness of online environments as colorblind spaces (Enger, 2006), research has found ways that demographic factors play a role in how students perceive online learning environments as well as their success within those spaces (Ashong & Commander, 2012; Du et al., 2015; Du et al., 2016;

González-Gómez et al., 2012; Johnson, 2011; Kumi-Yeboah et al., 2017; Okwumabua et al., 2011; Palacios & Wood, 2016). This is a primary reason why instructors should intentionally consider students' identities when facilitating sharing of multiple perspectives.

While much of the findings on hostile environments for marginalized student populations point to important implications for educational practice for undergraduate students on campus, they also carry considerations for educators working with distance graduate students. For instance, similar to face-to-face environments, online graduate students' identities can be rendered invisible and they can be made to feel as if their contributions do not matter. When Graduate Students of Color perceive a lack of culturally diverse views within the content of their courses, it can be difficult for them to feel engaged in the course and connect to the content (Kumi-Yeboah et al., 2017). In contrast, we recommend that instructors explicitly acknowledge that students possess different identities and carry various forms of cultural capital, perspectives, and experiences along with those identities. This should be done through multiple avenues such as in the syllabus, an introductory video, and synchronous sessions as applicable.

Once instructors have openly acknowledged the value students bring to the course, they should construct assignments and activities that facilitate the sharing of these perspectives. McLoughlin's (2000) framework as well as other campus climate research (Bowman, 2013; Hurtado et al., 1998; Milem et al., 2005) point to the importance of not only having a diverse group of individuals within an educational setting, but also intentionally engaging these individuals in interactions across and about difference. Instructors can also think about the format in which students share these perspectives, whether through writing, visual representations, or audio and video recordings. Instructors can create written opportunities by having students construct online journals or blogs to be shared with the class, or through online discussion boards, creating closed Facebook groups, or generating a Twitter series. Students can create infographics to share information using free online platforms such as Piktochart and Canva or audio and visual recordings using TechSmith Relay, YouTube, and Zoom.

As students share their perspectives, it is also up to the instructor to monitor how students are engaging in those discussions. Instructors should be cautious of students making discriminatory statements under the guise of hearing "different sides of an issue." This problem can largely be avoided by communicating clear expectations for students to engage with their peers in a respectful manner. For instance, in Crystal's courses, she encourages her students to engage in discussion around different sides of a topic, but also makes it clear to students that discriminatory or hostile comments targeted around individual identities will not be tolerated. She emphasizes that aspects of individuals' identities, who they are as a person, are not political issues and are not up for debate. Regardless of how instructors choose to set the parameters for respectful discussion, they should consider how they communicate these statements such as by including a statement on diversity and mutual respect within syllabi.

Finally, when students are active in the course it is also important for students to feel as if their instructors recognize their efforts. This may seem obvious, but it can easily be overlooked by instructors teaching graduate students in online courses. For instance, instructors can make specific comments on students' discussion points and thank them for sharing their perspectives within the course when grading assignments.

Conclusion

Online teaching has both its benefits and drawbacks, which can be challenging for both teachers and learners. However, with the growth in online programs for graduate education, higher education stakeholders must invest in the necessary support structures for online graduate student success. Most importantly, a culturally responsive approach should be developed as a way to incorporate and address the needs of the growing diversity of adult learners. Effective online graduate student learning should center around learner, teacher, and content interactions (Anderson, 2008), with an emphasis on developing students' cultural maintenance, ownership of learning, communities of practice, and provision of multiple perspectives (McLoughlin, 2000). In doing so, higher education stakeholders can identify the unique needs of online graduate students and enact strategies for promoting student success in online contexts.

References

Allen, E., Seaman, J., Poulin, R., & Straut, T. (2016). *Online report card: Tracking online education in the United States.* Babson Survey Research Group and Quahog Research Group. http://webmedia.jcu.edu/institutionaleffectiveness/files/2016/06/onlinereportcard.pdf

Anderson, T. (2008). Towards a theory of online learning. In T. Anderson (Ed.), *Theory and Practice of Online Learning* (2nd ed., pp. 45–74). Athabasca University Press.

Ashong, C. Y., & Commander, N. E. (2012). Ethnicity, gender, and perceptions of online learning in higher education. *MERLOT Journal of Online Learning and Teaching, 8*(2). https://jolt.merlot.org/vol8no2/ashong_0612.pdf

Biggs, J. B. (1999). *Teaching for quality learning at university: What the student does.* Society for Research into Higher Education and Open University Press.

Bowman, N. (2013). The conditional effects of interracial interactions on college student outcomes. *Journal of College Student Development, 54*(3), 322–328. https://doi.org/10.1353/csd.2013.0026

Du, J., Ge, X., & Xu, J. (2015). Online collaborative learning activities: The perspectives of African American female students. *Computers & Education, 82,* 152–161. https://doi.org/10.1016/j.compedu.2014.11.014

Du, X., Zhou, M., Xu, J., & San Lei, S. (2016). African American female students in online collaborative learning activities: The role of identity, emotion, and peer support. *Computers in Human Behavior, 63,* 948–958. https://doi.org/10.1016/j.chb.2016.06.021

Enger, K. B. (2006). Minorities and online higher education. *EDUCAUSE Quarterly, 29*(4), 7–8. https://er.educause.edu/articles/2006/11/~/media/c9836d0c-512941568c5764f2bdeb9911.ashx

Garcia, C. E., & Yao, C. W. (2019). The role of an online first-year seminar in higher education doctoral students' scholarly development. *The Internet and Higher Education, 42,* 44–52. https://doi.org/10.1016/j.iheduc.2019.04.002

González-Gómez, F., Guardiola, J., Rodríguez, Ó. M., & Alonso, M. Á. M. (2012). Gender differences in e-learning satisfaction. *Computers & Education, 58*(1), 283–290. https://doi.org/10.1016/j.compedu.2011.08.017

Heitner, K. L., & Jennings, M. (2016). Culturally responsive teaching knowledge and practices of online faculty. *Online Learning, 20*(4), 54–78. https://doi.org/10.24059/olj.v20i4.1043

Henderson, L. (1996). Instructional design of interactive multimedia: A cultural critique. *Educational Technology Research and Development, 44*(4), 85–104. https://doi.org/10.1007/bf02299823

Hurtado, S., Milem, J. F., Clayton-Pedersen, A. R., & Allen, W. R. (1998). Enhancing campus climates for racial/ethnic diversity: Educational policy and practice. *The Review of Higher Education, 21*(3), 279–302. https://doi.org/10.1353/rhe.1998.0003

Hyun, J. K., Quinn, B. C., Madon, T., & Lustig, S. (2006). Graduate student mental health: Needs assessment and utilization of counseling services. *Journal of College Student Development, 47*(3), 247–266. https://doi.org/10.1353/csd.2006.0030

Johnson, R. D. (2011). Gender differences in e-learning: Communication, social presence, and learning outcomes. *Journal of Organizational and End User Computing, 23*(1), 79–94. https://doi.org/10.4018/joeuc.2011010105

Kumi-Yeboah, A., Yuan, G., & Dogbey, J. (2017). Online collaborative learning activities: The perceptions of culturally diverse graduate students. *Online Learning, 21*(4), 5–28. https://doi.org/10.24059/olj.v21i4.1277

Lederman, D. (2021, September 16). Detailing last fall's online enrollment surge. *Inside Higher Ed.* https://www.insidehighered.com/news/2021/09/16/new-data-offer-sense-how-covid-expanded-online-learning

McClintock, C., Benoit, J., & Mageean, D. (2013). *Online graduate education.* Council of Graduate Schools.

McLoughlin, C. (2000). Cultural maintenance, ownership, and multiple perspectives: Features of web-based delivery to promote equity. *Journal of Educational Media, 25*(3), 229–241. https://doi.org/10.1080/1358165000250306

McLoughlin, C. (2001). Inclusivity and alignment: Principles of pedagogy, task and assessment design for effective cross-cultural online learning. *Distance Education, 22*(1), 7–29. https://doi.org/10.1080/0158791010220102

Milem, J. F., Chang, M. J., & Antonio, A. L. (2005). *Making diversity work on campus: A research-based perspective.* Association of American Colleges and Universities.

Nadal, K. L., Pituc, S. T., Johnston, M. P., & Esparrago, T. (2010). Overcoming the model minority myth: Experiences of Filipino American graduate students. *Journal of College Student Development, 51*(6), 694–706. https://doi.org/10.1353/csd.2010.0023

Okwumabua, T. M., Walker, K. M., Hu, X., & Watson, A. (2011). An exploration of African American students' attitudes toward online learning. *Urban Education, 46*(2), 241–250. https://doi.org/10.1177/0042085910377516

Online Learning Consortium. (2019). *About.* https://onlinelearningconsortium.org/about/olc-2/

Palacios, A. M., & Wood, J. L. (2016). Is online learning the silver bullet for men of color? An institutional-level analysis of the California community college system. *Community College Journal of Research and Practice, 40*(8), 643–655. https://doi.org/10.1080/10668926.2015.1087893

Rovai, A. P., & Jordan, H. (2004). Blended learning and sense of community: A comparative analysis with traditional and fully online graduate courses. *The International Review of Research in Open and Distributed Learning, 5*(2). https://doi.org/10.19173/irrodl.v5i2.192

Rovai, A. P., & Ponton, M. K. (2005). An examination of sense of classroom community and learning among African American and Caucasian graduate students. *Journal of Asynchronous Learning Networks, 9*(3), 77–92. https://doi.org/10.24059/olj.v9i3.1786

Rovai, A. P., & Wighting, M. J. (2005). Feelings of alienation and community among higher education students in a virtual classroom. *The Internet and Higher Education, 8*(2), 97–110. https://doi.org/10.1016/j.iheduc.2005.03.001

Seaman, J. E., Allen, I. E., & Seaman, J. (2018). *Grade increase: Tracking distance education in the United States.* Babson Survey Research Group and Quahog Research Group.

U.S. Department of Education National Center for Education Statistics. (2021). *Distance learning.* https://nces.ed.gov/fastfacts/display.asp?id=80

Weidman, J. C., Twale, D. J., & Stein, E. L. (2001). *Socialization of graduate and professional students in higher education: A perilous passage? ASHE-ERIC Higher Education Report,* (Vol. 28, no. 3). Jossey-Bass.

Yao, C., Wilson, B., Garcia, C., DeFrain, E., & Cano, A. (2017). Helping graduate students join an online learning community. *EDUCAUSE Review.* https://er.educause.edu/articles/2017/5/helping-graduate-students-join-an-online-learning-community

3

MENTORING DOMESTIC AND INTERNATIONAL GRADUATE STUDENTS OF COLOR

Francena Turner, HyeJin (Tina) Yeo, and Eboni M. Zamani-Gallaher

While access to college is critical in today's global knowledge economy, completing postbaccalaureate education has become increasingly necessary for career advancement. College degrees allow for greater earning potential; however, graduate study generally offers significant opportunities for career and economic upward mobility. In fact, increases in jobs requiring master's degrees and doctoral degrees for entry-level and advanced positions are projected to grow. According to the U.S. Bureau of Labor Statistics (2019) growth in postbaccalaureate degrees between 2018 and 2028 is expected to increase 13.7% for master's and 9.0% for doctoral degrees. Across degree completers, graduate degree holders earn a median income of $80,000, reflecting the highest earnings of any group (Carnevale et al., 2017). It is not surprising that trends in graduate school enrollment illustrate growth in master's degree (+1.4%) and doctoral degree programs (+4.1%) between 2017–2018, yet the number of international graduate students has declined during this same period (-4% in applications and -1% enrollments; Okahana & Zhou, 2019). Okahana and West (2019) contend although enrollment growth in master's and doctoral programs is modest, the U.S. labor market demand for graduate degree holders is steady.

International students compose 5.5% of all U.S. higher education student populations. Out of the total 1,094,792 international students from 223 countries, 43% (382,953) are graduate students (Institute of International Education, 2018). The majority of international students are from non-White, non-Eurocentric, and non-English-speaking countries. These students boost financial revenues, exchange knowledge/skills, and promote global competence. They bring a wide and valuable worldview, contributing to linguistic, social, cultural, political, religious, and ethnic diversity (Greenblatt, 2005; NAFSA, 2017). However, there has been little examination of the mentoring experiences of international Graduate Students of Color (GSoC). Hence, this chapter endeavors to include international graduate students into the broader consideration of mentoring GSoC.

Overall, the graduate school attendance patterns for racially minoritized students have increased, including a significant increase in the number of participating Women of Color. According to the Council of Graduate Schools (CGS), there was notable growth in the number of underrepresented racialized minorities (URM) though they remain proportionally underrepresented. Little over one-fifth (22.5%) of first-time U.S. citizens and permanent resident graduate students in fall 2015 were underrepresented minorities (i.e., 0.5% American Indian/Alaska Native, 11.8% Black/African American, 0.2% Native Hawaiian/Other Pacific Islander, and 10% Hispanic/Latino; Okahana et al., 2016).

For the purposes of this chapter, the term *racially minoritized* is used to reflect GSoC. More specifically, *GSoC* refers to those graduate students who have historically experienced race and ethnicity-based marginalization, isolation, and erasure while trying to pursue graduate degrees. The term *GSoC* arguably could include international Students of Color from countries outside the United States with various racial/ethnic, historical, social, cultural, political, linguistic, and religious backgrounds (Yeo et al., 2018). However, international GSoC may not be underrepresented but in fact overrepresented and de-minoritized in higher education, whereas the term *racially minoritized* primarily addresses U.S.-born, non-Asian (with the exception of Southeast Asians) racial/ethnic minoritized groups that have been historically underserved and continue to be underrepresented (Yeo et al., 2018).

Typically, Black/African American, Indigenous Native American/American Indian, Hispanic/Latinx, and Asian/Asian American students constitute the GSoC demographic though the distinction of being underrepresented generally does not apply across the board with Asian American students (e.g., overrepresentation in science, technology, engineering, and mathematics—STEM fields, underrepresentation in the humanities). Due to historical discrimination and its present-day effects, many GSoC are first-generation college graduates and/or the first in their family to pursue graduate degrees. Their age, gender, sexual identity, nationality, economic status, and (dis)ability status also further complicate their identities. Since U.S. higher education was created for the sons of White, wealthy men (Zamani-Gallaher et al.,

2016), GSoC deal with many layers of political, cultural, social, linguistic, and educational differences. Add to this being first-generation U.S. citizens or being an international GSoC, as well as other intersectional identities and nuances such as lack of familiarity with the context of U.S. schooling that disrupts navigating graduate study. Thus, the barriers facing GSoC necessitate a further discussion on the importance of mentoring to support GSoC in graduate education.

Issues in Mentoring

Some scholars and practitioners erroneously conflate advising and mentoring. *Mentoring* is a reciprocal process (Chan et al., 2015) by which "a student or mentee is positively socialized by a faculty or mentor for the purpose of learning the traditions, practices, and frameworks of a profession, association, or organization" (Brown et al., 1999, p. 106). In contrast, *advising* focuses on ensuring that students meet academic requirements and milestones. Montgomery et al. (2014) posit that mentoring of graduate students includes advising but advising does not equate to mentoring. Advisors often think they are mentoring their graduate students, but are not providing the "psychosocial support, career support, and role modeling inherent in mentoring" (Jones et al., 2013, p. 328). Eby et al. (2000) argue that "[c]urrent conceptualizations of mentoring may be too narrowly focused on the positive aspects of the relationship rather than considering the full scope of experiences, both positive and negative, that are likely to occur" (p. 14). This refusal to discuss negative experiences has the potential to adversely affect future mentoring experiences. GSoC may enter graduate school with myriad ways of knowing, backgrounds, and skills that do not readily align with the institutional culture, graduate school processes, or their individual colleges and academic departments (Antony, 2002). Graduate mentoring aids in socializing GSoC into graduate school culture and, eventually, the professoriate—both of which are Western-oriented and White normed.

Similar to racially minoritized U.S. born graduate students, international students also struggle with identity formation and concepts of self, due to racial, cultural, and linguistic conflicts in their academic and social spheres given the lack of familiarity and experiences with the U.S. sociopolitical context (Knox et al., 2013; Yeo et al., 2018; Zhang, 2016). Dealing with different academic and social cultures, international graduate students may face challenges in forming a scholarly identity, building rapport with an advisor, and/or establishing a mentoring relationship with persons most likely from a different background (Kim, 2007; Nguyen & Larson, 2017;

Zhang, 2016). In addition, international graduate students encounter difficulties of interaction and socialization with American advisors due to different communication and social relationship culture. For example, Korean, Chinese, and Japanese students influenced by Confucianism frequently practice a high-context communication style that employs delicate indirect verbal and nonverbal cues rather than direct literal speech (Park & Kim, 2008). This communication style could be complicated with professors or mentors lacking understanding of non-Western communication styles and the hierarchical relationship culture (Kim, 2007; Zhang, 2016).

GSoC who do not want to assimilate or who have a hard time assimilating into graduate school culture are often tacitly deemed unreceptive to mentoring. These students can go through their entire graduate school experience without one meaningful mentoring experience (Brunsma et al., 2017). We mention this point with caution as there are certainly GSoC who navigate graduate school terrains well-mentored and without problem and we do not wish to essentialize struggles with mentoring to all GSoC.

As previously stated, both domestic and international GSoC are often *first-generation graduate students.* This term means there are generally no family members with whom to discuss the rules governing graduate studies, navigating graduate school expectations, how to secure funding, or access to necessary informal networks that lead to mentorship (Mackey & Shannon, 2014). Most GSoC attempt to find mentors who look like them or share their racial, gender, cultural, or international background, but GSoC outnumber both domestic and international Faculty of Color (Brunsma et al., 2017; Dancy & Brown, 2011; Harris & Lee, 2019; Jones et al., 2013; Pope & Edwards, 2016; Tillman, 2018). Subsequently, Faculty of Color are taxed with advising and mentoring disproportionate numbers of GSoC.

Mentoring is considered service within the tenure and promotion hierarchy, but service trails behind research and teaching in importance. The tenure and promotion process minimizes the time, effort, and energy involved in mentoring students (Montgomery et al., 2014). While Faculty of Color may want to aid GSoC, they often have to make tough choices to protect their time during pre-tenure stages (Brunsma et al., 2017; Pope & Edwards, 2016). Moreover, junior Faculty of Color may not yet have access to informal mentoring networks and thus the social capital they are expected to share with GSoC (Tillman, 2018). *Social capital* refers to the social networks and connections developed as one progresses in the academy (Yosso, 2005). White male tenured faculty members have more access to important professional networks, and therefore power. Mentoring—as currently constructed—favors those (usually White male graduate students) mentored by a similar race and gender faculty demographic (Mackey & Shannon, 2014).

Herein lies the equity imperative in establishing effective formal mentoring opportunities for GSoC. Studies have found that White faculty, staff, and administrators simply do not possess the skills and culturally relevant knowledge to provide holistic mentoring of GSoC and in some cases may refuse to mentor therm (Luedke, 2017; Park-Saltzman et al., 2012).

Mainstream graduate students see themselves as viable parts of the academy or as future knowledge producers in fields outside the academy through their mentoring experiences (Brunsma et al., 2017). As such, White domestic and international students rarely have to divide themselves to be accepted into the fold (Lewis, 2016). Domestic and international GSoC may not enter graduate school with working knowledge of how the U.S. academy functions, but they do not enter as empty vessels. Instead, they arrive with a host of life experiences, academic experiences, and worldviews. Regardless of the salient identities of available mentors, GSoC must have access to formal mentoring experiences that allow them to gain access to the inner workings and varied cultures of their future career fields without having to deny parts of who they are (Chan et al., 2015; Mackey & Shannon, 2014; Park-Saltzman et al., 2012; Zhang, 2016).

Cross-Cultural GSoC Mentoring Experiences

GSoC come from cultures that value communal or collective ways of being that are in direct contrast to the solitary and individualistic nature of mentoring in graduate school (e.g., cultural values, racial/gender norms, and power dynamics that moderate cross-cultural mentoring relationships; Triandis, 2018). Hence, there is variation in mentoring and the extent to which equitable student outcomes are realized within and across cultures for GSoC (Park-Saltzman et al., 2012; Ramaswami et al., 2014). The cultural mismatch and lack of mentoring leads to students feeling like imposters (Chan et al., 2015; Dancy & Brown, 2011; Mackey & Shannon, 2014), feeling disconnected, confused, and uninformed (Pope & Edwards, 2016; Tillman, 2018), or feeling disillusioned with their chances of successfully completing their graduate degrees or procuring work in the academy (Brunsma et al., 2015).

GSoC often experience difficulty finding mentors who can help them develop research agendas and frameworks that are not marginalized in the academy (Grant & Ghee, 2015; Kochan, 2015; Luedke, 2017; Welton et al., 2015). Mentoring provides socialization and normalization into academia, and given the hyper-focus on publishing, power dynamics and issues of supervision embedded in advising relationships also shape mentoring in significant ways, some of which are to the detriment of graduate students' preparation (Mackey & Shannon, 2014; Manathunga, 2007). Finding an understanding, accessible, and caring mentor who is knowledgeable of their unique needs and challenges is difficult for international graduate students as nation of origin further complicates their experiences (Zhang, 2016).

GSoC experiences are consistently oversimplified and referred to as *imposter syndrome.* Clance and Imes (1978) define *imposter syndrome* as "deep feelings of intellectual and professional phoniness in high achieving individuals" characterized by GSoC, "maintaining thoughts and feelings of phoniness despite much evidence that they are outstanding academics and professionals" (as cited in Dancy & Brown, 2011, p. 616). However, imposter syndrome and recognizing systemic inequity are nuanced and not comparable concepts.

Race Matters

Even though studies show that GSoC are inclined to seek out mentors who share their racial identity, there are not enough domestic or international Faculty of Color to meet the demand (Turner & Gonzalez, 2014). Race and national origin do not always signify relatedness between GSoC and Faculty of Color. If not careful, Faculty of Color can reinscribe the same systemic inequities that the academy already inflicts on GSoC. It is unfair to both GSoC and the Faculty of Color to make the work of mentoring GSoC the job of an already overtaxed and underappreciated faculty member. Overworked mentors become ineffective mentors and GSoC deserve to work with faculty who have the time, energy, training, and desire to help them achieve their highest potential.

All faculty (the default should not be Faculty of Color) need to be open to mentoring the GSoC in their departments. Hence, majority faculty especially have to do the internal work it takes to expose their implicit biases and discomfort working closely with GSoC, and the research agendas and frameworks GSoC choose to explore during their studies. Whereas organically formed mentoring relationships are most desirable, arbitrary or forced assignment of a mentor to a student should not occur, though is found to be routine (Tillman, 2018). All students deserve to have a mentor who welcomes working with them. Administrators and faculty should reevaluate the departmental culture if faculty members readily seek to opt out of mentoring and examine that culture alongside their admissions decisions, especially when assigning advisors and mentors for GSoC in historically White contexts.

Even as the extant literature acknowledges varying mentoring experiences by race, ethnicity, and nationality as well as power differences in mentoring relationships, less research has interrogated whiteness, White privilege, and race matters relative to mentorship (McIntyre & Lykes, 1998; Powell, 2000). Research has demonstrated that White mentors are often uncomfortable discussing issues of race, gender, power, and privilege—issues that materially affect GSoC's daily experiences and their approaches to knowledge production (Harris & Lee, 2019; McCoy et al., 2015). Because of this discomfort, White mentors of domestic and international GSoC often focus on academics and neglect the other facets of mentoring (Luedke, 2017).

The passivity, explicit and conscious racial colorblindness, and ideology of avoidance hamper the ability to develop relationships between GSoC and White mentors and can adversely influence their outcomes in terms of program satisfaction and career advancement given the necessary conditions to produce sufficient mentoring situations were inhibited. The powerlessness of GSoC and superficial mentoring offered is often exacerbated by nationality. Domestic and international students experience racial microaggressions when working with American students and faculty members. However, international GSoC also experience microinsults due to their accents, frequently feel ignored for their academic contributions, or find their needs and values are deemed invalid (Kim & Kim, 2010; Yeo et al., 2019). By not appreciating the individual differences of their GSoC mentees, introducing their mentees to their professional networks, offering them collaborative copublishing projects, or working to provide them aid in securing funding, these mentors allow their implicit or explicit biases to limit the career possibilities and career trajectories of GSoC (McCoy et al., 2015). Such mentor neglect was the single most frequently reported negative experience among the mentees in the existing literature (Eby et al., 2000; Park-Saltzman et al., 2012; Zhang, 2016). Such benign neglect affects the interpersonal relationships among GSoC and between GSoC and White graduate students (Tillman, 2018).

Strategies for Improving Mentoring Experiences for GSoC

Effective mentoring is too important a component of the graduate school experience to leave to chance. As such, formal mentoring programs are needed to ensure that no GSoC completes their graduation education without mentoring. However, just merely assigning students to a faculty member does not equate to effective mentoring. Tillman (2018) provides a framework for such a program for Faculty of Color with steps for each level of governance to ensure that a culture of data-supported mentoring—based in the experiences of GSoC and the expectations of the careers in knowledge production—is established and supported at the institutional, college, and department level. In the next section, we adapt her framework for GSoC with added recommendations at the faculty level as well.

Institutional and College Level

Each institution of higher education's central administration must evaluate the mentoring experiences and needs of GSoC and collect demographic and cultural information before creating a mentoring philosophy or plan. Interested parties must (a) conduct needs analysis of GSoC, (b) review and examine the current institutional policies and practices, and (c) develop or revise policies and practices in a data-informed manner. At the very minimum, a formal mentoring plan should include implicit and explicit bias training, mentor/mentee training workshops, and mentoring handbooks for faculty and graduate students. Such handbooks should explicitly address differences in cultural and academic practices between the United States and the sending countries for international students and between the academy and GSoC for domestic students, using strengths-based perspectives. A mentoring plan should also include a funding commitment to ensure that a lack of fiscal resources does not allow GSoC to go without mentorship (Park-Saltzman et al., 2012; Tillman, 2018).

At the campus level, there should be active aligning of the informed mentoring philosophy established by central administration. At the college and department level, faculty should receive credit for their mentoring work in the tenure and promotion process (Montgomery et al., 2014). Next, colleges should strongly consider providing substantive funding for one major conference per year as a part of mentoring practice. Conference presentations and attendance are important in aiding GSoC in finding additional mentoring, networking, collaboration, and publishing opportunities (Tillman, 2018). Lastly, offering for-credit seminars or courses about U.S. racial inequity and racism will help international GSoC have a better understanding of a racialized learning environment, cope with their experiences within one of the minoritized groups in the United States, and seek out adequate support mechanisms.

Department Level

The two most important actions a department might take toward the improvement of mentoring experiences for GSoC are to develop a culturally sensitive mentoring model to fit their context and culture and to teach mentor training as dedicated courses. Culturally sensitive mentoring begins with acknowledging diverse backgrounds of GSoC and understanding the cultural values and norms of the mentor and the mentee (Park-Saltzman et al., 2012). Without a consistent, long-term method for culturally sensitive mentoring, the quality of mentor/mentee relationships would vary solely based on an individual mentor's capacity. Part of the reason so many GSoC have unfulfilling mentoring experiences is that there is little formal training in how to mentor graduate students, much less GSoC.

Each department should make a commitment to providing mentoring opportunities to each GSoC it admits (e.g., offer mentoring seminars, networking socials, handbooks, etc. to both faculty and students). More specifically, formal and informal opportunities for newly admitted domestic and international GSoC could provide a more customized and personalized experience at the master's and doctoral level. In addition, any formal mentoring plan should have a protocol for ending mentoring relationships that are not working for either the mentor or the mentee.

Faculty Level

An effective mentor recognizes their limitations as a mentor. Faculty members should examine their capacity to mentor GSoC. If the reasons they may find mentoring GSoC to be difficult relate to the student's race, gender, sexual identity, nation of origin, or other parts of the student's salient identities, the faculty member should make use of racial equity and intersectional consciousness training and scholarship. Seeking out other mentors or resources both in the United States and abroad for mentees could be an active effort to meet graduate students' needs. Likewise, faculty mentors need to be amenable to open and direct communication that allows them to learn from and about GSoC during the mentoring process.

Advocate-Mentors

Harris and Lee (2019) argue that GSoC need more than mentors; they need advocates. *Advocate-mentors* are tenured faculty who "commit to challenging the department or institution to be accountable for and to their increasingly diverse student body, subsequently promoting equity, inclusivity, and systemic change" (p. 107). An advocate-mentor would fight for their students in closed-door decision-making processes and in public by introducing their students to their networks and providing them with publishing and copublishing opportunities. This advocate-mentoring is exceedingly vital for international GSoC because of their sociocultural barriers and vulnerabilities related to the realities of their foreign national status (e.g., losing a visa and power relationships as a form of economic colonization or cultural imperialism between the United States and the home countries of international students).

Learner-Centered Mentoring
Developed from an evaluation of an urban teacher preparation program, *learner-centered mentoring* (LCM) could be adapted to GSoC and would require vulnerability and reflexivity on the part of the GSoC and the faculty mentor. According to Kolman et al. (2017), a department commitment to LCM when used with GSoC:

1. focuses on [GSoC] needs, readiness, and purposes for learning,
2. understands the [GSoC] within a developmental trajectory,
3. provides conditions for [GSoC] development and autonomy,
4. positions the [faculty mentor] as learner, observer, & supporter, and
5. draws on observations of each [GSoC] to develop [research, teaching, and service] experiences meant to foster individual growth (p. 94)

At regular intervals, a GSoC and their mentor would collaboratively develop plans centering the GSoC's diverse culture, needs, and skill sets.

Curriculum Homeplacing. Pope and Edwards (2016) offered a mentoring philosophy based in Black feminist thought as a way to provide culturally sensitive mentoring spaces for Black women graduate students and their Black women faculty mentors. We argue that such spaces could also be created in formal department-supported peer mentoring networks among Black women graduate students or GSoC. Specifically, *curriculum homeplacing* "[p]laces Black women and Black women's ways of knowing at the center. Curriculum homeplacing further asserts the humanity of Black women and consciously resists institutional frames that would seek to invalidate their position as knowers, theorists, and scholars" (p. 770). When adapted to GSoC, this conceptualization of mentoring would involve creating counterspaces where domestic and international GSoC and their cultural ways of knowing, research frameworks, and knowledge production are nurtured and celebrated.

Mentors who follow this framework would, instead of shying away from discussing seemingly obscure research methodologies, devote time to helping GSoC develop a thorough understanding of the research questions that they are grappling with while developing a means for answering or addressing these questions. Such a mentor might introduce the GSoC to scholars who are working with the same frameworks, methodologies, or global contexts. They would support their GSoC who may not want to enter the academy and find them effective mentors to help them navigate nontraditional career paths. The unique needs of the GSoC would take center stage. In terms of peer mentoring, advanced GSoC could mentor incoming GSoC in literal and figurative spaces that are more welcoming to their ways of knowing and being than the academy, thereby strengthening and preparing them to advocate for themselves and effectively assert their autonomy in formal academic spaces.

Critical Collective Community. Montgomery et al.'s (2014) conceptualization of *critical collective community* (CCC) refers to "a collective of individuals similarly dedicated to providing honest structured guidance and supporting opportunities to enhance their individual cultural capital to sustain and expand all members for their future careers" (p. 5). Similarly, *cultural capital* is considered the abilities, skills, and knowledge one has accumulated often passed from one generation to the next, generally inherited by privileged groups but not solely possessed by dominant members of society (Yosso, 2005). GSoC often construct such communities among themselves on an informal basis, but there is merit in considering establishing and introducing GSoC to a department-supported version as a part of orientation. With a knowledgeable faculty member present, GSoC could ask any questions they may have and gain answers from both faulty and advanced GSoC. A department-supported CCC would eradicate the idea that only certain GSoC deserve time, effort, and care while others do not. CCCs have roles that the mentor would shift in and out of depending on the needs of the GSoC, to include: confronter, clarifier, comforter, and collaborator. Ultimately, departments should reconsider any faculty mentoring practices that impede GSoC's cultural desire to collaborate and commune with their fellow graduate students. Such practices make for poor interpersonal relations even as those GSoC become faculty members.

Graduate Student Level

GSoC should perform the same reflexive work that we suggest for potential faculty mentors. GSoC should identify their needs and examine their ability to approach mentors. For example, they should ask themselves questions such as, "How do I need to be treated for me to have the best experience in my mentoring relationships?" "What do I want to gain from mentorship?" "What do I want to feel in the presence of my mentor?" and "What can I commit to bringing to my mentoring relationships?" At the beginning phase of the mentoring relationship, GSoC should explicitly discuss their needs and expectations with their mentors. This helps avoid future dissonance due to a mismatch between mentors and mentees' role expectations, especially due to a different culture of socialization. When formal mentoring networks are available, GSoC should take advantage of them as well as informal peer mentoring opportunities such as reading and writing groups.

It is never too early to begin developing a collaborative view of knowledge production. While mentoring training is not currently a consistent part of graduate education, GSoC might want to consider taking any workshops their campus holds on mentoring as well as electing to effectively mentor at least one Undergraduate Student of Color. Lastly, GSoC should consider mentoring opportunities outside their institution. Professional organizations often offer preconference mentoring opportunities during their annual meetings and GSoC could gain access to publishing opportunities and other forms of professionalization and networks by taking part in these activities.

Conclusion

This chapter sought to explore some issues related to the mentoring experiences of historically and racially minoritized graduate students (i.e., domestic and international GSoC), and strategies for creating effective, culturally responsive mentoring programs for GSoC. The terms *advising* and *mentoring* are not synonyms. Though there may be overlap in some of the activities involved the function and depth within each role differ as the assignment of a graduate faculty advisor occurs as one enters their postbaccalaureate program, which is typically based on student research and career interests that are matched with faculty expertise. Both faculty advisors and mentors can be formally assigned to a student, however advisors and not necessarily mentors are responsible for successfully guiding students through their graduate program. For example, mentors may not be expected to share course scheduling and discuss offerings, know deadlines for registration, course drop dates, approved internships, processes for filing theses/dissertations, or required forms to participate in commencement (Blanchard & Haccoun, 2019). Graduate faculty mentoring, like advising, involves an academic-centered relationship, however mentors serve as a sounding board and resource supporting the student developmentally both in and out of coursework which includes cultural and mental supports (Lunsford, 2012) to navigate both academic and nonacademic challenges.

The essence of mentoring involves an interactive process whereby faculty members engage in layered ways through multiple roles with protégés centering and concerned about their personal and professional growth. When entering graduate school, GSoC have to make meaning of different cultural norms, the unwritten rules of the academy, and the academic culture of their departments (often quite homogenous and centering Westernized, Eurocentric standards). History shows that whiteness and White privilege are justified and authorized by America's essential principles of prosperity and individualism (Alvarado, 2010; McIntyre & Lykes, 1998; Powell, 2000). Indeed, the culture of the academy is racialized and subscribes to meritocratic principles that further whiteness and individualism (Gusa, 2010; Posselt, 2018). In turn, academic and social failures of GSoC are regarded as individual problems rather than institutionalized and systemic.

Culturally responsive mentoring requires reciprocal efforts. The institution and college should take the lead in creating and facilitating a culturally responsive mentoring practice by reforming policy, hiring more domestic and international Faculty/Staff of Color, and providing mentor training and development resources across the institution. In addition, a contextualized mentoring model should be developed and provided consistently at the department level. Each department can provide formal and informal networking events and faculty training. Faculty should be aware of the different communication styles of GSoC. Mentors should avoid assuming what domestic and international GSoC know or do not know about graduate school experiences or that international GSoC with high English proficiency do not experience cultural dissonance.

Developing culturally responsive and equity-conscious mentoring programs should require faculty to acknowledge cultural differences and identify the needs and mentoring expectations of GSoC, understanding that graduate school socialization is not race-neutral and effective mentoring seeks to advance racially equitable student outcomes (Williams et al., 2018). Finally, peer-mentoring opportunities offer another way to take advantage of mentoring. Mentoring without intentional attention to cultural differences results in the maintenance of the status quo, White, Westernized culture which does not advance anti-racist education at the graduate level (Welton et al., 2018) or the urgency of addressing institutional culture and transforming practices in the mentorship of GSoC.

References

Alvarado, L. A. (2010). Dispelling the meritocracy myth: Lessons for higher education and student affairs educators. *The Vermont Connection, 31*(1), 10–20. https://scholarworks.uvm.edu/tvc/vol31/iss1/2/

Antony, J. S. (2002). Reexamining doctoral student socialization and professional development: Moving beyond the congruence and assimilation orientation. In J. C. Smart & W. G. Tierney (Eds.), *Higher education: Handbook of theory and research, Vol. 17,* (pp. 349–380). Springer.

Blanchard, C., & Haccoun, R. R. (2019). Investigating the impact of advisor support on the perceptions of graduate students. *Teaching in Higher Education, 25*(8), 1010–1027. https://doi.org/10.1080/13562517.2019.1632825

Brown, M., Davis, G. L., & McClendon, S. A. (1999). Mentoring graduate students of color: Myths, models, and modes. *Peabody Journal of Education, 74*(2), 105–118. https://doi.org/10.1207/s15327930pje7402_9

Brunsma, D. L., Embrick, D. G., & Shin, J. H. (2017). Graduate students of color: Race, racism, and mentoring in the white waters of academia. *Sociology of Race and Ethnicity, 3*(1), 1–13. https://doi.org/10.1177/2332649216681565

Carnevale, A. P., Garcia, T. I., & Gulish, A. (2017). Career pathways: Five ways to connect college and careers. *Georgetown University Center on Education and the Workforce.*

Chan, A. W., Yeh, C. J., & Krumboltz, J. D. (2015). Mentoring ethnic minority counseling and clinical psychology students: A multicultural, ecological, and relational model. *Journal of Counseling Psychology, 62*(4), 592–607. https://doi.org/10.1037/cou0000079

Clance, P., & Imes, S. (1978). The impostor phenomenon in high achieving women: Dynamics and therapeutic intervention. *Psychotherapy: Theory, Research, and Practice, 15*(3), 241–247. https://doi.org/10.1037/h0086006

Dancy, T. E., & Brown, M. C. (2011). The mentoring and induction of educators of color: Addressing the imposter syndrome in the academy. *Journal of Social Leadership, 21*(4), 607–634. https://doi.org/10.1177/105268461102100405

Eby, L., McManus, S. E., Simon, S. A., & Russell, J. E. A. (2000). The protégé's perspective regarding negative mentoring experiences: The development of a taxonomy. *Journal of Vocational Behavior, 57*(1), 1–21. https://doi.org/10.1006/jvbe.1999.1726

Grant, C., & Ghee, S. (2015). Mentoring 101: Advancing African American women faculty and doctoral student success in predominately White institutions. *International Journal of Qualitative Studies in Education, 28*(7), 759–785. https://doi.org/10.1080/09518398.2015.1036951

Greenblatt, S. (2005). International students and diversity in American higher education. *International Journal of Diversity in Organizations, Communities and Nations, 5*(2), 163–171. https://doi.org/10.18848/1447-9532/CGP/v05i02/38894

Gusa, D. L. (2010). White institutional presence: The impact of Whiteness on campus climate. *Harvard Educational Review, 80*(4), 464–489. https://doi.org/10.17763/haer.80.4.p5j483825u110002

Harris, T. M., & Lee, C. (2019). Advocate mentoring: A communicative response to diversity in higher education. *Communication Education, 68*(1), 103–113. https://doi.org/10.1080/03634523.2018.1536272

Institute of International Education. (2018). *Open doors 2018.* https://www.iie.org/Research-and-Insights/Publications/Open-Doors-2018

Jones, T. B., Wilder, J., & Lampkin, L. O. (2013). Employing a Black feminist approach to doctoral advising: Preparing Black women for the professoriate. *The Journal of Negro Education, 82*(3), 326–338. https://doi.org/10.7709/jnegroeducation.82.3.0326

Kim, S., & Kim, R. H. (2010). Microaggressions experienced by international students attending U.S. institutions of higher education. In D. W. Sue (Ed.), *Microaggressions and marginality: Manifestations, dynamics, and impact* (pp. 171–191). Wiley.

Kim, Y. (2007). Difficulties in quality doctoral academic advising: Experiences of Korean students. *Journal of Research in International Education, 6*(2), 171–193. https://doi.org/10.1177/1475240907078613

Knox, S., Sokol, J. T., Inman, A. G., Schlosser, L. Z., Nilsson, J., & Wang, Y. (2013). International advisees' perspectives on the advising relationship in counseling psychology doctoral programs. *International Perspectives in Psychology: Research, Practice, Consultation, 2*(1), 45–61. https://doi.org/10.1037/ipp0000001

Kochan, F. (2015). Analyzing the relationships between culture and mentoring. *Mentoring and Tutoring: Partnerships in Learning, 21*(4), 412–430. https://doi.org/10.1080/13611267.2013.855862

Kolman, J. S., Roegman, R., & Goodwin, A. L. (2017). Learner-centered mentoring: Building from student teachers' individual needs and experiences as novice practitioners. *Teacher Education Quarterly, 44*(3), 93–117.

Lewis, A. (2016). Making meaning of race and racialization in the lives of five international graduate students. In K. Bista & C. Foster (Eds.), *Exploring the social and academic experiences of international students in higher education institutions* (pp. 59–78). IGI Global. https://doi.org/10.4018/978-1-4666-9749-2.ch004

Luedke, C. L. (2017). Person first, student second: Staff and Administrators of Color supporting Students of Color authentically in higher education. *Journal of College Student Development, 58*(1), 37–52. https://doi.org/10.1353/csd.2017.0002

Lunsford, L. (2012). Doctoral advising or mentoring? Effects on student outcomes. *Mentoring & Tutoring: Partnership in Learning, 20*(2), 251–270. https://doi.org/10.1080/13611267.2012.678974

Mackey, H., & Shannon, K. (2014). Comparing alternative voices in the academy: Navigating the complexity of mentoring relationships from divergent ethnic backgrounds. *Mentoring and Tutoring: Partnerships in Learning, 22*(4), 338–353. https://doi.org/10.1080/13611267.2014.945738

Manathunga, C. (2007). Supervision as mentoring: The role of power and boundary crossing. *Studies in Continuing Education, 29*(2), 207–221. https://doi.org/10.1080/01580370701424650

McCoy D., Winkle-Wagner R., & Luedke, C. L. (2015). Colorblind mentoring? Exploring White faculty mentoring of Students of Color. *Journal of Diversity in Higher Education, 8*(4), 225–242. https://doi.org/10.1037/a0038676

McIntyre, A., & Lykes, M. B. (1998). Who's the boss? Confronting Whiteness and power differences within a feminist mentoring relationship in participatory action research. *Feminism & Psychology, 8*(4), 427–444. https://doi.org/10.1177/0959353598084003

Montgomery, B. L., Dodson, J. E., & Johnson, S. M. (2014). Guiding the way: Mentoring graduate students and junior faculty for sustainable academic careers. *Sage Open, 4*(4), 1–11. https://journals.sagepub.com/doi/pdf/10.1177/2158244014558043

NAFSA. (2017). *International student economic value tool.* http://www.nafsa.org/ Economicvalue

Nguyen, D. J., & Larson, J. B. (2017). Exploring the influence of student affairs on adjustment and adaptation for Indonesian graduate students. *Journal of International Students, 7*(4), 1010–1029. https://doi.org/10.5281/zenodo.1035955

Okahana, H., Allum, J., Felder, P. P., & Tull, G. (2016). *Implications for practice and research from doctoral initiative on minority attrition and completion.* Council of Graduate Schools. https://www.cgsnet.org/sites/default/files/ 2016.03%2316-01%20Discussion%20on%20DIMAC.pdf

Okahana, H., & West, C. P. L. (2019, October). *Select insights from NAGAP/CGS survey of graduate enrollment management professionals.* https://nagap.org/sites/ default/files/cgs_researchbrief_nagap_oct19_v4.pdf

Okahana, H., & Zhou, E. (2019). *International graduate applications and enrollment: Fall 2018.* Council of Graduate Schools.

Park, Y. S., & Kim, B. S. K. (2008). Asian and European American cultural values and communication styles among Asian American and European American college students. *Cultural Diversity and Ethnic Minority Psychology, 14*(1), 47–56. https://doi.org/10.1037/1099-9809.14.1.47

Park-Saltzman, J., Wada, K., & Mogami, T. (2012). Culturally sensitive mentoring for Asian international students in counseling psychology. *The Counseling Psychologist, 40*(6), 895–915. https://doi.org/10.1177/0011000011429831

Pope, E., & Edwards, K. T. (2016). Curriculum homeplacing as complicated conversation: (Re)narrating the mentoring of Black women doctoral students. *Gender and Education, 28*(6), 769–785. https://doi.org/10.1080/09540253 .2016.1221898

Posselt, J. R. (2018). Rigor and support in racialized learning environments: The case of graduate education. *New Directions for Higher Education, 181*, 59–70. https://doi.org/10.1002/he.20271

Powell, J. A. (2000). Whites will be Whites: The failure to interrogate racial privilege. *University of San Francisco Law Review, 34*(3), 419–464. https://repository.usfca .edu/usflawreview/vol34/iss3/3

Ramaswami, A., Huang, J., & Dreher, G. (2014). Interaction of gender, mentoring, and power distance on career attainment: A cross-cultural comparison. *Human Relations, 67*(2), 153–173. https://doi.org/10.1177/0018726713490000

Tillman, L. C. (2018). Achieving racial equity in higher education: The case for mentoring Faculty of Color. *Teachers College Record, 120*(14), 1–18.

Triandis, H. C., (2018). *Individualism and collectivism.* Routledge.

Turner, C. & Gonzalez, J. (2014). *Modeling mentoring across race/ethnicity and gender: Practices to cultivate the next generation of diverse faculty.* Stylus.

U.S. Bureau of Labor Statistics. (2019). *Table 5.2 Employment, wages, and projected change in employment by typical entry-level education (employment in thousands).* https://www.bls.gov/emp/tables/education-summary.htm

Welton, A. D., Mansfield, K. C., & Lee, P. L. (2015). Mentoring educational leadership doctoral students: Using methodological diversification to examine gender and identity intersections. *NCPEA International Journal of Educa-*

tional Leadership Preparation, 10(2), 53–81. https://files.eric.ed.gov/fulltext/EJ1083100.pdf

Welton, A. D., Owens, D. R., & Zamani-Gallaher, E. M. (2018). Anti-racist change: A conceptual framework for educational institutions to take systemic action. *Teachers College Record, 120*(14), 1–22.

Williams, M. S., Brown Burnett, T. J., Carroll, T. K., & Harris, C. J. (2018). Mentoring, managing, and helping: A critical race analysis of socialization in doctoral education. *Journal of College Student Retention: Research, Theory & Practice, 20*(2), 253–278. https://doi.org/10.1177/1521025116657834

Yeo, H. T., McKee, M., & Trent, W. (2018). EYES theory: A proposed racialization and developmental identity model for understanding concepts of race for international Students of Color studying in US higher education institutions. In J. Hoffman, P. Blessinger, & M. Makhanya (Eds.), *Perspectives on Diverse Student Identities in Higher Education: International Perspectives on Equity and Inclusion* (pp. 95–112). Emerald Publishing Limited.

Yeo, H., Mendenhall, R., Harwood, S. A., & Huntt, M. B. (2019). Asian international student and Asian American student: Mistaken identity and racial microaggressions. *Journal of International Students, 9*(1), 39–65. https://doi.org/10.32674/jis.v9i1.278

Yosso, T. J. (2005). Whole culture has capital? A critical race theory discussion of community cultural wealth. *Race and Ethnicity in Education, 8*(1), 69–91. https://doi.org/10.4324/9781003005995-8

Zamani-Gallaher, E. M., Leon, R. A., & Lang, J. (2016). Study abroad as self-authorship: Globalization and reconceptualizing college and career readiness. In R. Latiner Raby & E. J. Valeau (Eds.), *International education at community colleges* (pp. 111–125). Palgrave Macmillan.

Zhang, Y. L. (2016). International students in transition: Voices of Chinese doctoral students in a U.S. research university. *Journal of International Students, 6*(1), 175–194. https://files.eric.ed.gov/fulltext/EJ1083276.pdf

4

FIRST-GENERATION GRADUATE STUDENTS

Reducing Barriers With Support Mechanisms

Sonja Ardoin and Maria Dykema Erb

When a person encounters something for the first time or enters a new environment, there will be a learning curve. Consider the first time someone attempts to swim, drive a car, find something in a new grocery store, or travel to a country where a language differs from one's primary language. Then, when this newness of environment and experience is layered with structural barriers—obstacles that inhibit access or success for particular individuals because of identities or resources, one's ability to traverse the newness may be overwhelming. This is particularly true if, and when, the person feels as if they are the only one who might be challenged by the newness and barriers.

When first-generation graduate students embark on their master's, doctoral, and/or professional degree experiences, they are reminiscent of Heinlein's (1961) "stranger in a strange land," because first-generation graduate students often feel like they are in a new world where people speak a different language and interact through a new, distinct rulebook. First-generation graduate students may feel separated from their families and home communities, isolated by their continuing-generation peers, and tasked with navigating an academic environment riddled with explicit and implicit expectations that may be in tension with their backgrounds or values (Leyva, 2011). Additionally, the number of first-generation graduate students has been decreasing over the past 30 years; for example, the National Science Foundation (NSF; 2009) Survey of Earned Doctorates highlighted how

51% of doctoral students were first generation in 1987 while this population only accounted for 31% of doctoral students in 2017 (NSF, 2018).

This chapter highlights the structural barriers that first-generation college students face when they enter graduate or professional education programs and offers suggestions on how first-generation graduate students can be supported to and through their graduate or professional school experiences. If the goal is to increase diversity of graduate student populations and prepare a diverse workforce across fields (Holley & Gardner, 2012), which it should be, then attention must be given to not only how to define first-generation graduate students, but also how to support them to degree attainment and job acquisition.

Defining First-Generation Graduate Students

From scholars studying first-generation college students (Ardoin, 2018; Jehangir, 2010; Martin, 2015) to the creation of practice and policy-based centers, such as the Center for First-Generation Student Success, there is increasing attention on the first-Generation college student population in the United States. However, contention around the definition of a first-generation college student at the undergraduate level continues (Peralta & Klonowski, 2017; Toutkoushian et al., 2019) and, to add further complexity, there is both a lack of conversation, generally, and definitional clarity, specifically, around first-generation graduate students (Holley & Gardner, 2012). At this point, higher education is at the beginning stages of pondering who are, or should be, considered first-generation graduate students.

The multitude of definitions that are utilized for first-generation undergraduate students are primarily founded on the following themes: (a) the student is the first in their family to pursue higher education (Cataldi et al., 2018), and/or (b) the student's caretakers or guardians do not hold 4-year, baccalaureate degrees from a college or university (U.S. Department of Education, 2010). Ambiguous aspects of these definitions include what *first generation* means—particularly if a student has a sibling or caretaker who is concurrently enrolled; who is included as parents, guardians, or family; and how international students might be excluded if their caretakers have degrees from countries other than the United States (Ardoin, in press). If educators follow these "clear as mud" standards set by first-generation undergraduate student definitions, first-generation graduate students could, and likely would, be defined as students who are the first in their families to pursue graduate school or students whose caretakers or guardians did not earn a graduate degree. This is where attempts at clarity become even more convoluted because some might believe the only valid definition of a first-generation graduate student would be a first-generation undergraduate student who has continued on into graduate or professional school. In fact, there are individuals who would vehemently oppose the thought of a continuing-generation undergraduate student being deemed a first-generation graduate student because their caretakers or guardians do not hold graduate or professional degrees. While there may not be a right answer about who should be "counted" as first-generation graduate students, there is a choice to be made about how student groups, institutions, and disciplines define first-generation graduate students and, subsequently, serve and support them.

Recognizing the Barriers First-Generation Graduate Students Face

Regardless of which definition is selected to frame the first-generation graduate student population, it is important to recognize and reduce the systemic barriers these students face as they pursue postbaccalaureate education. Unsurprisingly, similarities exist between the barriers first-generation undergraduate students face and the ones first-generation graduate students encounter (Holley & Gardner, 2012; O'Bryant & Schaffzin, 2017; Tomer, 2019). Structural barriers such as sense of belonging challenges (e.g., imposter syndrome and traitor syndrome) and identity dynamics of being a first-generation graduate student in addition to holding other minoritized identities (e.g., Student of Color, student with a poor or working-class origin, student with disabilities, etc.) can influence how first-generation graduate students experience their programs and institutions and whether they complete their degrees.

Dual Alienation

When first-generation graduate students feel divided between their families and home communities and their graduate programs and institutions, such that they partially belong in both environments but not wholly in either, they are likely experiencing dual alienation (Johnson, 2009). Dual alienation can be a result of the combination of imposter syndrome and traitor syndrome. In short, imposter syndrome is when someone questions whether they should be in a space or having an opportunity, while traitor syndrome is when someone harbors guilt or shame around departing from their family or home community—and perhaps their original ways of thinking and being—in order to pursue a new avenue. These syndromes often show up individually or collectively for many first-generation graduate students in graduate school.

Additionally, first-generation graduate students may experience dual alienation when their field of choice calls for them to present differently than their cultural upbringing. In Leyva's (2011) study on first-generation Latina graduate students, participants spoke to the "fundamental dualities" they faced in negotiating their culture and first-generation status with their educational expectations and professional values and in finding a fit, which they likened to "wearing different masks" and "living between two worlds" (pp. 26–27, 29). Feeling bifurcated is a barrier for first-generation graduate students because it influences their sense of belonging in every space or community where they find themselves, which can impact motivation, retention, and completion. However, despite dual alienation challenges, it is critical to emphasize that many first-generation students—undergraduate and graduate—believe their first-generation status is the foundation for their work ethic, persistence, and resilience; an asset they possess; and a point of pride (Holley & Gardner, 2012).

Layering of Identity Dimensions and Experiencing -isms

First-generation graduate students are a heterogenous population; they "have complex identities, making them hard to pigeonhole" (Jehangir, 2010, p. 2). This means there are first-generation graduate students from every racial and ethnic group, age group, gender identification, sexuality, social class, religion or spiritual practice (or not), nationality, and citizenship status who may experience various mental, emotional, or physical disabilities. Tomer (2019) points out that many first-generation law students are also Students of Color, from the poor or working classes, older, and part-time attendees. Holding additional minoritized identities often amplifies the barriers first-generation graduate and doctoral students face, including encountering -isms and discrimination which compound effects on degree attainment (Holley & Gardner, 2012; Willison & Gibson, 2011). This is why it is important to understand that first-generation graduate students are not one population, but a varied group of individuals who may face unique barriers yet share the impactful connection of being the first to forge an educational path and serve as possibility models for their families and communities. Therefore, college and university administrators and faculty members need to recognize that support mechanisms cannot be a one-size-fits-all approach; rather, how might graduate students be supported in both their first-generation status while also honoring students' distinctive combination of identities and how those identities layer with their first-generation status in ways that may create more barriers (e.g., marginalization and discrimination) in their progress to degree?

Supporting First-Generation Graduate Students

Similar to other minoritized and underserved populations, first-generation graduate students often recognize the structural barriers that exist for them before institutions do. As such, many of the supports created for first-generation graduate students are driven by the students themselves. While first-generation graduate students should not have to carry this burden, they often do; they are the ones who notice gaps, ask questions, create initiatives, organize in-person and online communities, and fight for institutionalizing efforts to create more equity in higher education. In this section on supports, both peer-to-peer and institutionalized supports are offered and the originators of these efforts, who are (or were) first-generation graduate students, are honored for paving better pathways for themselves and those who will follow.

Peer-to-Peer Supports

Peer-to-peer support for first-generation graduate students can come in many forms: one-on-one, group-based, in-person, and virtual. Sometimes the students are enrolled in the same program at the same institution, but other times the students are across fields and across the country. In an effort to provide two varying examples that could be scaled, one support that is in-person through a professional school and another that is virtual and across disciplines are highlighted.

The first example of a peer-to-peer support is the First Generation Professionals (FGP) organization at Boston University (BU)'s law school. The group was founded in 2017 by then 1st-year law student Miosotti Tenecora with a goal of creating a community where first-generation professionals could share their struggles and successes (Woolhouse, 2019). FGP defines *first generation professional* as "a law student who has attained or is pursuing a level of education beyond that of their families" (Boston University School of Law, 2020), and over the past 2 years, FGP has offered "mentoring, support, and the occasional class on the [law] profession's sometimes arcane rules of decorum" (Woolhouse, 2019, para. 3). Law students engaged in the group believe it has been invaluable in alleviating some of their imposter syndrome and informing them of the "esoteric customs" (Woolhouse, 2019, para. 8) expected in both law school and the profession at large. Administrators at BU Law note that FGP has been a great support for the increasing number of first-generation college students enrolled at the school, from 39 in 2018 to 55 in 2019, roughly 14–16% of each admitted class (Woolhouse, 2019). The FGP organization is not unique to BU; in fact, similar FGP groups can be found at law schools such as New England College, New York University, Stanford University, University of California Berkeley, University of Georgia, University of Southern California, Yale University (Tomer, 2019), and the University of Pennsylvania (Hachenburg, 2019).

The second example of a peer-to-peer support is the Twitter handle #FirstGenDocs, a virtual space to create community for first-generation doctoral students across disciplines. This initiative was founded in 2017 by Lamesha C. Andrews, Raven K. Cokley, and Jason Wallace, all first-generation doctoral students at the University of Georgia. Acknowledging that graduate school can often be challenging and isolating, the founders wanted to create an intentional space especially for first-generation students who might feel like they were "going it alone" without the traditional support that continuing-education students may hold. The founders shared the following about their mission and purpose:

> Since its inception, #FirstGenDocs has centered on affirming experiences, amplifying voices, and celebrating the brilliance of first generation doctoral students. The community gives aspiring, current, and past #FirstGenDocs a space to make meaning of our first gen identity, find community, and share experiences. We have dedicated ourselves to offering communal support, accountability, and uplift to first generation doctoral students across the globe. Through the processes of sharing our struggles and successes, we have garnered support and new resources for ourselves and our #FirstGenDocs community members. (L. Andrews, R. Cokley, J. Wallace, personal communication, May 2019)

Equally important, the founders have made it a priority to recognize the intersectionality of their members' various social identities, including race, ethnicity, class, gender, place of origin, caregiver status, and ability. Through the Twitter platform, the founders have created a community through monthly chats, virtual writing retreats, and a blog with a regular community member spotlight series. Their followers are nearing 4,000 members in the United States and across the world.

Institutionalized Supports

As evidenced by the previous two examples, graduate students are often encouraged by academic and student affairs administrators to fill any gaps they see by starting their own group to help find peer support and build community. With these student-led organizations, members typically find their own meeting space, coordinate meetings and activities, and frequently find their own funding to support programming, all while trying to balance the demands of a rigorous degree program. This begs the question: At what point is it time for an institution to take on the responsibility of building community if the students asking for support are from a marginalized group, such as first-generation graduate students? A viable solution to alleviate an already stressful graduate education experience is to formalize initiatives that would include oversight by professional staff, faculty, and/or an institutionally supported budget.

An example of what this can look like is the Carolina Grad Student F1RSTS (CGSF) at The University of North Carolina at Chapel Hill (UNC). In 2015, a group of students led by Leslie Adams, now a David E. Bell Postdoctoral Fellow at Harvard University, and Yesenia Merino, a recent PhD graduate from the UNC Gillings School of Global Public Health, formed the first-generation graduate student group to bring people together to build both their social and cultural capital within the world of academia; they shared:

> We listened and responded to the needs of graduate students who wanted a peer network built for them to continue succeeding, share advice, and create a tangible skill set to navigate their master's or doctoral education. Fundamental to the success of the program has been a continual connection to current students and the gaps in training for first generation graduate students because of the implicit assumptions about the homogeneity of students within the academic institution. (Y. Merino & L. Adams, personal communication, May 2019)

After receiving a leadership grant to pilot the first-generation graduate student initiative, Adams and Merino approached the graduate school's associate dean of student affairs to take on the leadership of their group in spring 2016. They strongly believed that an initiative such as this could benefit graduate students across the entire university. At the time, the Diversity and Student Success (DSS) program in the graduate school was creating other initiatives to support Students of Color, international students, LGBTIQA+ students, and military-affiliated students, so it was only natural to also include first-generation graduate students.

Since then, with full-time staff devoted to the DSS umbrella of initiatives, the coordination of CGSF is largely done by the director, program coordinator, and a graduate assistant. The student-centered recruitment and completion plan for CGSF is accomplished through: (a) professional and personal development workshops, (b) community building events,

(c) summer boot camps (e.g., statistics and dissertation writing), and (d) funding awards to support degree advancement, including dissertation completion and conference travel. CGSF, along with the undergraduate first-generation program, Carolina F1RSTS, became one of the inaugural First-Forward Advisory Institutions through the Center for First-Generation Student Success in 2019 because of the university-wide commitment to the success of first-generation students. By lifting the burden of the workload off the first-generation graduate students, they are able to engage with the CGSF offerings, acquire the knowledge that they need, and live out their graduate experience more confidently.

Some other universities that are committing institutional resources for programming and staff support include the First-Gen Grad Initiative in the graduate school at the University of Washington in Seattle, the "I'm First" program in the Brown School at Washington University in St. Louis, and First Generation Support Services at the University of California San Francisco. As research on the first-generation graduate student expands, it is highly likely that the number of institutions providing formal programmatic support will do the same. And, in turn, this will contribute to better retention and degree completion for first-generation graduate students.

Suggestions for Practice

Recognizing that every program, department, and institution has some work to do in increasing support for first-generation graduate and professional students, this section offers some actionable suggestions for practice in beginning or furthering these efforts: (a) recognize and define the first-generation identity on campus, (b) educate graduate school faculty and administrators, (c) institutionalize campus support structures, and (d) collaborate with campus partners.

Recognizing and Defining the First-Generation Identity on Campus

Because institutions are at the beginning stages of recognizing and defining the first-generation identity on campus, there is a rationale for including those students whose caretakers or guardians might have completed an undergraduate degree. Two examples come from CGSF and #FirstGenDocs. CGSF defines *first-generation graduate students* as those whose parents(s)/guardian(s) have not earned a master's or doctoral degree to recognize that graduate students come from a broad range of diverse educational experiences, with many first-generation graduate students also having been first-generation college students. Working from this definitional framework, programming is framed by the assumption that everyone is coming from a first-generation undergraduate background. Students are identified as first-generation graduate students based on the information that they (optionally) provide on the graduate admissions application about their parents'/guardians' highest level of education completed. UNC has been collecting this information since fall 2018 to begin getting an accurate representation of the number of students who are first-generation graduate students.

When CGSF was being formalized, it was imperative to the members that the initiative was inclusive of those who were the first to pursue a graduate degree, even if their caretakers or guardians had a bachelor's degree. Samuel Baxter, a doctoral student and CGSF leader, shared his own personal story as to why this was important. Coming from a southern Black family, Samuel frequently received the message of the importance of getting an education. His mother was a first-generation college student who attended a historically Black college or university (HBCU) and his father earned his bachelor's degree while Samuel was in college. Although Samuel was not the first in his family to go to college, he was the first to attend a predominantly/historically White institution (PWI/HWI) and live hours away from home. Samuel offered the following description of his experience:

> During my master's and doctoral training, I became keenly aware of my first generation graduate student identity. The tips, tricks, and tools I acquired in college were obsolete in graduate school. Generalized first generation student programming was not equipped to meet my unique graduate school needs. Graduate students are expected to know how to find and secure funding, learn to say "no" to safeguard productivity, maintain mental and physical wellness, and grow their professional network. The pace of graduate school made all of this uncharted terrain my source of internalized imposter syndrome; there was so much I didn't know that I didn't know. Furthermore, being surrounded by institutional and symbolic mores of isolation, competition, and whiteness made it difficult to push through. (S. Baxter, personal communication, May 2019)

The founders of #FirstGenDocs also chose to define first-generation status as doctoral students who are in the first generation of their immediate families to pursue a doctoral degree. They recognized that while there is some capital that comes with having parents/guardians who have received bachelor's or master's degrees, doctoral experiences are different and compounded. The founders also acknowledged that institution type (e.g., HBCU, HWI, HSI [Hispanic serving institution]) may drastically influence doctoral experiences (L. Andrews, R. Cokley, & J. Wallace, personal communication, May 2019). Other initiatives like Duke Firsts at Duke University and the Brown School at Washington University at St. Louis also identity their first-generation graduate students in the same manner as CGSF and #FirstGenDocs.

Educating Graduate School Faculty and Administrators About First-Generation Student Needs

Gardner and Holley (2011) emphasized the need for faculty and higher education administrators to be educated about first-generation students' needs. One way to deliver this is through a First Generation Graduate Student Training, similar to Safe Zone training events on college campuses where faculty, staff, and graduate students can become more knowledgeable about the LGBTIQA+ community, the challenges they face, and how to be an ally. By offering this type of training, faculty and administrators can become more aware of the systemic barriers that first-generation graduate students face and learn how to provide support through mentorship. This has already been implemented successfully with UNC's Carolina Firsts program (for undergraduates) under the leadership of Dr. Carmen Huerta-Bapat and can be replicated at the graduate level.

Identifying faculty, administrators, and staff who may have been first-generation graduate students can also provide role models for students because "if they can see it, they can be it." The University of California system has created a First-Generation Faculty Initiative on some of their campuses, most prominently at UCLA, where faculty can self-identify and serve as resources and mentors to first-generation graduate and undergraduate students. Additionally, some first-generation graduate alumni who become faculty or staff members are also invested in raising the visibility of first-generation graduate student initiatives to "pay it forward." Jennifer Harker, an assistant professor at West Virginia University, shared:

> The fellowship and camaraderie among students and mentors involved with the graduate first gen initiative made the whole experience feel much less isolating for me. Hearing the challenges and successes of other first gen graduate students was both empowering and encouraging. Now that I have transitioned into a faculty role, I can take my experiences and those I have learned about, and I can work toward easing the path for my own students—both at the undergraduate and graduate levels. (J. Harker, personal communication, May 2019)

Paul Maurizio, a postdoctoral fellow at The University of Chicago, who also benefited from a formal first-generation graduate student program, noted:

> Now in a postdoctoral fellowship, I have been able to "give back" by mentoring a first generation college student and serving as the keynote speaker at my institution's first generation undergraduate symposium. Being part of a formal first gen graduate initiative left a strong impression, helped

me become more confident in my abilities, develop my voice, and grow my dedication to mentorship of students in situations similar to my own. (P. Maurizio, personal communication, May 2019)

These two examples highlight how institutions can benefit from listening to and learning from their faculty and staff members who are first-generation graduates, utilizing them in training other campus community members, and leveraging their calls for more formalized support systems for those entering graduate school for the first time.

Institutionalizing Campus Support Structures

Once first-generation graduate students are identified at institutions, the most direct way that administrators and faculty can find out what first-generation graduate students need is to simply ask, then listen. While quantitative data and degree completion numbers are important, sometimes the actual voices of the students get lost in the statistics. Joanna Ramirez, a former participant in a first-generation graduate student initiative, emphasized the importance of first-generation graduate student programming:

> Authentic programming for first generation students is responsive and iterative to the direct needs of the students, especially the institutionalized support that we aren't aware we need. As first generation students, we struggle navigating spaces while feeling like everyone else was handed a roadmap that wasn't available to us. Programming should deliver professional development content in a safe space where students feel comfortable asking clarifying questions and building supportive networks with peers, as well as faculty and staff. (J. Ramirez, personal communication, May 2019)

A student advisory board made up of first-generation graduate students that meets at least twice throughout an academic year is a formal means to solicit ideas and feedback. In addition to considering students' needs, it is key to have staff in place who understand the first-generation graduate student experience, someone who is well-versed in this area and can identify and respond to what the students might not know.

With increasing emphasis and research on the first-generation undergraduate experience, it is the right time to begin examining the transition period into graduate school. Research by Winkle-Wagner and McCoy (2016) suggests that incoming graduate students benefit greatly from summer institutes that are offered prior to their first graduate semester. As seen with summer bridge programs for diverse students between high school and college, so too can a cohort model be effective for individuals start-ing a graduate program. Transition programs are opportunities for students "to acquire both the cultural and social capital that could help them to succeed in doctoral programs . . . [and] to create a space for themselves in the academy . . . to make the field fit them" (Winkle-Wagner & McCoy, 2016, p. 199).

Collaborating With Campus Partners

Supporting marginalized groups on campuses is never the sole responsibility of one person or department. For a well-executed support system to suc-ceed, it is important to seek out the champions of first-generation graduate students across the institution. Initial questions include:

- How can various faculty and administrators collectively develop infra-structures to support first-generation graduate students?
- Is there a graduate school/college/division where the initiative can be centralized? If so, who is the best contact or ally?
- Are there other appropriate offices where a first-generation graduate student initiative might reside within a division of student affairs, diversity and inclusion, or elsewhere?

Once an initiative is established, or if it is already established, offering first-generation graduate student-specific workshops in partnership with the graduate school's professional development office or program (if one exists), career services, postdoctoral affairs office, student wellness, and/or counseling and psychological services goes a long way in validating students' backgrounds and experiences. Some workshop examples include but are not limited to the following: how to identify and mitigate imposter syndrome; how to develop strategies to reduce stress and build resilience; how to navi-gate graduate school conversations with family and friends at home; and financial literacy/expectations for self and family. Engaging various offices in programming leads to an investment in first-generation graduate students, especially for offices that might traditionally serve (or are perceived that they only serve) undergraduate students.

Campus collaboration can also take the form of first-generation graduate students mentoring first-generation undergraduates. The graduate students can serve as role models and provide insight and advice on what it is like to pursue an advanced degree. Bringing these two groups together for formal events provides a valuable opportunity for all of the students to practice their networking skills and develop professionally.

The whole campus community can support first-generation graduate students by participating in the annual National First-Generation College Celebration on November 8 sponsored by the Center for First-Generation Student Success. Institutions have celebrated not only just the day, but have also created a week of programming surrounding first-generation college student success. Recognizing first-generation graduate students during this celebration is one of the best ways to bring visibility to this population. Formal events like a graduation recognition or pinning ceremony are an opportunity for a campus to come together and celebrate the ultimate goal of attaining a graduate degree.

Conclusion

While the peer-to-peer and institutional supports and suggestions for practice shared in this chapter are useful, scalable efforts to create more educational equity for first-generation graduate students, the challenge offered to us by Holley and Gardner (2012) endures: "higher education institutions are in a significant position to enhance the experiences of this student population through deliberate programs and actions" (p. 120). It is the responsibility of all of us who serve as educators—administrators and faculty alike—to heed this call and design graduate and professional school environments and experiences that not only recruit more first-generation graduate students to enroll but also support them to and through degree completion as they champion a new pathway for themselves and their families and add new perspectives and contributions to their fields.

References

Ardoin, S. (2018). *College aspirations and access in working-class, rural communities: The mixed signals, challenges, and new language first-generation students encounter.* Lexington Books.

Ardoin, S. (in press). The nuances of first generation college students' social class identity. In R. Longwell-Grice & H. Longwell-Grice (Eds.), *At the intersection: Exploring the intricacies of first generation college students today.* Stylus.

Boston University School of Law. (2022). *Law student affinity groups.* https://www.bu.edu/law/about/diversity/affinity-groups/

Cataldi, E. F., Bennett, C. T., & Chen, X. (2018). First-generation students: College access, persistence, and postbachelor's outcomes. *Stats in Brief.* NCES 2018-421. National Center for Education Statistics.

Gardner, S. K., & Holley, K. A. (2011). "Those invisible barriers are real": The progression of first-generation students through doctoral education. *Equity &*

Excellence in Education, 44(1), 77–92. https://doi.org/10.1080/10665684.2011.529791

Hachenburg, C. (2019, March 25). Penn Law initiative to provide mentorship for first-generation law students. *The Daily Pennsylvanian.* https://www.thedp.com/article/2019/03/penn-law-first-generation-fellows-fgli-upenn-program

Heinlein, R. (1961). *Stranger in a strange land.* G.P. Putnam's Sons.

Holley, K. A., & Gardner, S. (2012). Navigating the pipeline: How socio-cultural influences impact first-generation doctoral students. *Journal of Diversity in Higher Education, 5*(2), 112–121. https://doi.org/10.1037/a0026840

Jehangir, R. R. (2010). *Higher education and first-generation students: Cultivating community, voice, and place for the new majority.* Palgrave Macmillan.

Johnson, C. (2009). The nine needs of lower-income, first-generation college students. In T. H. Housel & V. L. Harvey (Eds.), *The invisibility factor: Administrators and faculty reach out to first-generation college students* (pp. 125–140). BrownWalker Press.

Leyva, V. L. (2011). First-generation Latina graduate students: Balancing professional identity development with traditional family roles. In V. L. Harvey & T. H. Housel (Eds.), *Faculty and first-generation college students: Bridging the classroom gap together* (New Directions for Teaching and Learning, no. 127, pp. 21–31). Wiley.

Martin, G. L. (2015). "Tightly wound rubber bands": Exploring the college experiences of low-income, first-generation White students. *Journal of Student Affairs Research and Practice, 52*(3), 275–286. https://doi.org/10.1080/19496591.2015.1035384

National Science Foundation. (2009). *Doctorate recipients from US universities: Summary Report 2007–08.* Division of Science Resources Statistics, Directorate for Social, Behavioral, and Economic Sciences, National Science Foundation. https://files.eric.ed.gov/fulltext/ED507640.pdf

National Science Foundation. (2018). *Doctorate recipients from U.S. universities: 2017.* Special Report NSF 19-301.

O'Bryant, J. M., & Schaffzin, K. T. (2017). First-generation students in law school: A proven success model. *Arkansas Law Review, 70*(4), 913–958.

Peralta, K. J., & Klonowski, M. (2017). Examining conceptual and operational definitions of "first generation college student" in research and retention. *Journal of College Student Development, 58*(4), 630–636. https://doi.org/10.1353/csd.2017.0048

Tomer, J. (2019, March 22). First-generation law students: Struggles, solutions, and schools that care. *The National Jurist.* http://www.nationaljurist.com/national-jurist-magazine/first-generation-law-students-struggles-solutions-and-schools-care

Toutkoushian, R. K., May-Trifiletti, J. A., & Clayton, A. B. (2019). From "first in the family" to "first to finish": Does college graduation vary by how first-generation college status is defined? *Educational Policy,* 1–41. https://doi.org/10.1177/0895904818823753

U.S. Department of Education, Office of Postsecondary Education. (2010). Federal TRIO programs. http://www.ed.gov/about/offices/list/opc/trio/index.html.

Willison, S., & Gibson, E. (2011). Graduate school learning curves: McNair scholars' postbaccalaureate transitions. *Equity & Excellence in Education*, *44*(2), 153–168. https://doi.org/10.1080/10665684.2011.558416

Winkle-Wagner, R., & McCoy, D. (2016). Entering the (postgraduate) field: Under-represented students' acquisition of cultural and social capital in graduate school preparation programs. *The Journal of Higher Education*, *87*(2), 178–205. https://doi.org/10.1353/jhe.2016.0011

Woolhouse, M. (2019, April 23). First generation law students bond through shared backgrounds. *BU Today.* https://www.bu.edu/today/2019/first-generation-law-students-bond-through-shared-backgrounds/

5

HOW UNIQUE WAYS OF KNOWING, BEING, AND LEARNING CONTRIBUTE TO PERSISTENCE FACTORS AMONG INDIGENOUS GRADUATE STUDENTS

Colin Ben and Jessica Solyom

Few studies or books have considered how developing supportive practices and policies inside and outside the classroom for historically underrepresented graduate students can benefit their increasingly complex needs. What we do know is that literature on the experiences of Graduate Students of Color is limited, focusing mostly on African American students, and that when it comes to persistence for Students of Color, mentors and culturally responsive pedagogy matter. Within the literature on Students of Color, the "data are unevenly distributed . . . with the most research available on African Americans, and the least on Native Americans" (Gay, 2004, p. 266). While research on African American students has been illuminating and continues to be valuable, in order to understand the intersectional experiences of additional diverse student groups more research is needed focusing on the experiences of Latinx, Native American, Native Hawaiian, Pacific Islander, and other historically underrepresented groups. Gay (2004) and MacLachlan (2006) call for additional research exploring Graduate Students of Color's retention experiences with a focus on how they navigate the marginal environments in the academy in pursuit of joining the professoriate and, furthermore, the challenges of being a Professor of Color.

Graduate education must be community-oriented, community-embedded, and research must be use-inspired to ensure it has both purpose and impact. When students are able to connect their education to address existing social, environmental, educational, and health community challenges they report higher rates of education satisfaction and persistence (Gay, 2018). While there are numerous historically underrepresented graduate students, in this chapter we shine a light on American Indian and Alaska Native tribal communities, as graduate student populations not often considered within the context of postbaccalaureate education. Indeed, considering the unique histories and complex social challenges and political structures of the hundreds of American Indian and Alaska Native tribal communities in the United States, incorporating knowledge of a student's individual tribal culture, needs, challenges, and desires is important for persistence. To be culturally responsive, education and educators need to be more than just culturally respectful; they may need to be tribally specific in their curriculum, pedagogy, and mentorship (Brayboy et al., 2014). Involvement in culture-related extracurricular activities, relations with faculty that have an understanding of diverse cultures, tribes, and histories, and financial support from either personal or institutional sources are important. More recent literature on culturally responsive education has also found a relationship between this type of learning pedagogy, curriculum, and practice with enhanced education outcomes and persistence. Although our chapter seeks to add to the literature on graduate student persistence, more research is needed to understand how graduate students' cultural ways of knowing, being, and learning can contribute to persistence and enhanced learning outcomes.

State of American Indian and Alaska Natives in Graduate School

Although research on American Indian and Alaska Native graduate students is small but growing, challenges to enrollment and persistence are generally consistent across the literature (Brayboy et al., 2012; Shotton et al., 2013). Challenges of access, financial aid, and different cultural norms have been found to affect the decision to enroll or remain enrolled in graduate education. Table 5.1 shows the total graduate student enrollment by race/ethnicity in fall 2017.

From Table 5.1, we can see that American Indian and Alaska Native (AI/AN) and Native Hawaiian/Pacific Islander students are among the least represented in graduate student programs which may lead to additional unique experiences and challenges. Prior to enrolling in graduate programs, AI/AN students may lack information about graduate programs available in their

TABLE 5.1

Graduate Student Enrollment by Race/Ethnicity in Fall 2017

Race	Total Graduate Enrollment	Total Percentage
White	908,121	60.8%
Black/African American	188,838	12.6%
Hispanic/Latino	155,936	10.4%
Asian	98,483	6.6%
American Indian/Alaska Native	7,372	0.5%
Native Hawaiian/Other Pacific Islander	2,929	0.2%
Two or More Races	41,307	2.8%
Race/Ethnicity Unknown	91,149	6.1%
Total number enrolled	**1,494,135**	**100%**

Note. From Council of Graduate Schools (2022). *Data and Insights* (Table B20). https://cgsnet.org/graduate-enrollment-and-degrees/. Because not all institutions responded to all items, details may not sum to totals. Percentages are based on total of known race/ethnicity.

geographic area and/or in their field of interest, may lack information regarding requirements to apply for graduate school, and may not know about opportunities for scholarship and grant funding that help offset the cost of participation in graduate education (Nelson, 2015; Patterson et al., 2009; Secatero, 2009). Because AI/AN students may reside in rural communities with limited professional capacity to serve the needs of their community, and sometimes hold leadership positions within their communities, they may prioritize programs that allow them to remain close to home, their families, community, and field of work (Guillory & Wolverton, 2008).

As previously stated, AI/AN graduate student experiences remain understudied in comparison to other racial and ethnic graduate students. This may be, in part, due to their underrepresentation in graduate education. However, as AI/ANs matriculate through graduate school we are becoming increasingly aware of the ways they are uniquely positioned within higher education.

On average, AI/AN students may enroll in graduate education later than their non-Native peers which may present additional economic and family/social responsibilities for students who may have to balance academic obligations with responsibilities associated with being primary caregivers for their children, grandchildren, and/or elders in the family (Brayboy et al., 2012; Shotton et al., 2013). Table 5.2 shows the average age of doctoral students in 2016 by race.

TABLE 5.2
Average Age of Doctoral Students by Race, 2016

Race	Average Age of Doctoral Student
American Indian and/or Alaska Native	39
Black or African American	36
Hispanic or Latino	33
White	32
Asian	31

Note. From National Science Foundation. (2018). Science and Engineering Doctorates: Data Tables. (Table 27). https://ncses.nsf.gov/pubs/nsf19301/data. To our knowledge, a comprehensive data set does not exist for the average age of master's students, so we have chosen to present the average age of doctoral learners here.

When AI/AN graduate students are accepted into graduate programs, they are on average older than their non-AI/AN peers, which requires them to arrange for an increased level of caretaking responsibilities of children and extended family members (Brayboy et al., 2015; Okagaki et al., 2009). It is important to note that AI/AN graduate students may have difficulty accessing resources necessary to fulfill family care and academic needs such as paying for childcare for one or more children, transportation expenses to campus, and other costs associated with attending graduate school. Consequently, AI/AN students may hold full-time jobs and/or multiple jobs while pursuing graduate degrees and may rely on their family for support as they navigate graduate education (Ben, 2018; Hunt & Harrington, 2010).

Once successfully enrolled, AI/AN students may face some similar or shared challenges with other Students of Color. For instance, success of underrepresented students depends largely on overcoming challenges related to culturally inappropriate or inadequate advising, limited finances, student under preparation resulting from poor advising and mentorship, loneliness, lack of shared felt community, improper socialization to the norms and expectations associated with professional degree programs and fields of study, and hostile or unwelcoming campus climate (Ben et al., 2019; Brayboy et al., 2012). These factors can lengthen time-to-degree completion or may serve as reasons why students leave their programs altogether (Brayboy et al., 2014; Flores Carmona, 2017; Gay, 2004; Shotton et al., 2013). American Indian and Alaska Native students have additionally reported challenges with unwelcoming, hostile, racist, and/or anti-AI/AN education spaces, lack of tribally relevant advising, lack of culturally and tribally responsive and relevant curriculum, and lack of culturally or tribally respectful research methodologies (Ben, 2018; Brayboy et al., 2012; Kirkness & Barnhart, 1991; Solorazano &

Yosso, 2002; Solyom, 2014). In order to address many of these challenges and increase persistence, Scholars of Color and their allies have argued for culturally responsive curriculum, practices, advising, and mentorship. For AI/AN students understanding and incorporating Indigenous ways of knowing, being, and learning can help. Such practices must be informed by an understanding of the needs and desires of AI/AN students and their communities, as well as the specific cultural and academic challenges they face in graduate school.

Challenges Faced by Navajo Graduate Students

In 2018, Colin Ben conducted a study that explored the experiences of Navajo graduate students enrolled at a predominantly White 4-year public university in the southwest. This research also explored resources students identified as important for their persistence. Findings from this study suggest that Indigenous epistemologies (ways of thinking) and ontologies (ways of being and learning) are instrumental for persistence. Using the experiences shared by participants in Ben's (2018) study we offer recommendations to increase AI/AN graduate student persistence in the next section.

To date, Ben's study is the only study that has examined the experiences of Navajo graduate students. While we concede it is important to have research examine the experiences of AI/AN students as a whole, with 573 federally recognized AI/AN Nations in the United States, epistemological variation exists due to cultural and environmental diversity, varied histories with colonization and local bordering communities, as well as linguistic and spiritual variation. It is, therefore, important to also undertake tribally focused research as ways of knowing, being, and learning can differ between AI/AN tribes. For this reason, we focus our discussion on graduate education for Navajo students. To preserve the anonymity of the students and faculty in this study, we utilize pseudonyms when sharing their experiences. The recommendations presented at the end of the chapter have been broadened because they are important for addressing and recognizing the needs of all graduate students, particularly those from underrepresented and underserved populations.

Ben's (2018) study highlighted internal factors affecting retention such as difficulty adjusting to graduate education and isolation as well as external factors of unsupportive faculty and financial challenges. In the classroom, participants expressed challenges with adjusting to expectations of classroom work, feelings of isolation, and difficulty with their time management. Some students confided their frustration and hurt with peers and/or professors who demonstrated not just a lack of knowledge of

AI/AN community-focused issues, but lack of interest in issues related to AI/AN sovereignty, self-determination, nation-building, and capacity-building goals. Beyond the classroom, students reported discouraging interactions with advisors and industry mentors who became hostile and threatened to withdraw their support upon learning Navajo students may be interested in returning to their tribal community to work rather than pursue an academic career teaching in another predominantly White institution (PWI). Other challenges included maintaining full-time work responsibilities, financial hardship, and work-related stressors. Multiple internal and external challenging experiences may compound to enhance the overall threat to persistence.

In the Classroom

Richard described how adjusting to the academic demands of coursework in graduate school was difficult during his 1st year as he was the only American Indian in his program. "I didn't know these things would affect me, but it all did. I was stressed out all the time. Not sleeping well. So, after that year, I said, 'How can I succeed as a student in this program?' I had to readjust everything. At the end of the year, I did a self-evaluation." He conducted a self-assessment and revised his academic and personal routine to reduce his overall stress level. To counter feelings of isolation, Richard intentionally studied at the on-campus Native American Center which provided an environment full of American Indian students and staff. This cultural community was missing from his program. On a personal level, Richard scheduled time to exercise and spend quality time with his family. Now in his 4th year, he explained that his self-assessment and well-rounded routine created an opportunity for him to excel academically and personally.

Other students also discussed being the only Student of Color in their classes. For Joe, the negative effects of isolation added to the complexities of adjusting to graduate school. Determined to successfully complete the program coursework, he secluded himself in the first 2 years of his program. After he passed his oral comprehensive exams, he enrolled in elective classes that had "Native students and a Native professor," and made friends with other AI/AN students who asked him to join their Native graduate student organization. In the elective class, and with other Native students in the Native organization, he was able to be his authentic self.

As students began to learn to navigate graduate school, they experienced difficulty adjusting and sought solutions or strategies to ameliorate their feelings of discomfort and not belonging. One student, Cheryl, described how she questioned whether she belonged in the graduate program because she did not initially understand the theoretical frameworks discussed nor how she could articulate how they related to her research interests. After meeting with her peers and mentor, she was able to grasp which framework best applied to her study. Graduate students learned how to effectively navigate student expectations and implemented creative and culturally sustaining strategies to counter isolation and loneliness that enhanced their sense of well-being.

Beyond the Classroom

Participants identified difficult experiences with incongruent faculty and cultural academic expectations, interacting with others, and financial challenges which in combination formed external threats to their persistence. To address their financial hardships, the majority of the participants worked full-time in addition to full-time enrollment in graduate school. Participants had to learn how to balance their time to successfully complete class assignments and work projects.

More than half of Ben's (2018) participants worked in AI/AN-serving positions that required their cultural and professional expertise. The time dedicated to fulfilling their work responsibilities was time not spent on their academic assignments. Cheryl described how the difficulty of working full-time and being a full-time graduate student led her to question whether she should resign from her position and become a full-time student. However, in Cheryl's case, remembering monthly expenses such as car payments, rent, and other bills prevented her from resigning. As Cheryl faced the financial challenges, she turned to her family's teachings to continue to strive for balance and to "walk in beauty." This meant bringing cultural values and pieces from home (i.e., the Navajo Nation) as well as family heritage items to her office which served as a daily reminder of why it is important to persist.

Another student, Shannon, shared a similar struggle. Shannon worked full-time and enrolled in graduate school full-time. She worked approximately 12-hour days and studied 4 hours a night; this schedule, which included only a few hours for sleep, drained her. As a result, she explained, "I [had to take] a sabbatical for a year [from working for my tribal community] to just concentrate on my research, because I knew that working, having a family, and trying to do this was nearly impossible." Although all study participants faced numerous difficulties and threats to persistence, their ability to identify resources to overcome those challenges showcases their problem-solving prowess and ingenuity. Important to note, because the Navajo Nation has the need to fill leadership positions that require advanced skill sets, these graduate students view their graduate matriculation and degree attainment as an opportunity to further meet the needs of their Nation.

Indigenous Ways of Knowing, Being, Learning Can Help Improve Education Outcomes

Indigenous ways of knowing allow students to tap into their cultural foundation and identify important strategies for building relationships and skill sets to successfully navigating graduate education. AI/AN graduate students highlighted examples that illustrate how Indigenous ways of *knowing, being,* and *learning* occur in the academy and the teachings that allowed them to overcome unexpected challenges.

Knowing

Navajo epistemology acknowledges the interrelatedness among their people and the environments as shared through stories and songs. The idea of beauty and balance drives many decision-making practices and behaviors. For Navajo students, this can have implications for research practices as relationship protocols may need to be observed and respected before undertaking research. Two foundational philosophical concepts of Navajo epistemology are *Hozho* and *Sa'ah Naagai Bik'eh Hozhoon* (SNBH), which offer cultural guidance to Navajo people (Aronilth, 1980). The traditional meaning of *Hozho* is to live a harmonious life while balancing one's self with their environment (Lee, 2006). In essence, Navajo epistemology forms a set of actions, knowledge base, and behaviors that guide individuals' engagement with others and their environment.

To better understand how to align curriculum and research with Navajo and AI/AN ways of thinking, educators should familiarize themselves with literature on Indigenous Knowledge Systems and Critical Indigenous Research Methodologies (CIRM; Brayboy et al., 2012). These theoretical approaches provide opportunities for a research process that works with Indigenous communities to identify a concern or need in the community, and together the researcher and community design, collect, analyze, and disseminate findings that address the concern in an effort to improve the quality of life for the Indigenous community.

Being

Navajo students have a unique cultural relationship and responsibility to their family, community, and Nation. Their cultural identity is connected to their Navajo clan relations and can be relied on when overcoming challenging experiences. Navajo students' communal relationship is rooted in traditional teachings. When creating the cultural relationship and responsibility within an educational environment, Aronilth (1992) states four elements for satisfactory achievement, "[c]reating spiritual motivation and having comprehension, [b]uilding a firm structure to make correct decisions in life, [w]orking for a good pattern of life and accomplishment, [and] ability to plan, implement, and think correctly" (p. 48). Traditional concepts of educational elements, cultural identity, and Navajo epistemology provide a unique worldview that students bring to graduate education.

As AI/AN graduate students matriculate through their graduate programs, they may rely on traditional teachings of giving back to their native community as a cultural strategy to increase their persistence (Brayboy et al., 2012, 2014; Lopez, 2018). The traditional value of giving back is a unifying theme in American Indian graduate education literature. Their ability to gain the advanced skill sets in a graduate program provides Navajo students with an opportunity to make positive contributions to their community and Nation and supports motivation and resilience to overcome individual challenges and sacrifices. When Cheryl felt the effects of imposter syndrome and felt distanced from her home community and its teachings, her father lovingly reminded her that she holds cultural knowledge, understands her tribal history and language, and will always have a kinship connection to her community. His encouraging words empowered her to overcome difficult and discouraging experiences throughout her educational journey. Parental advice that reinforces their cultural identity and validates their Indigenous ways of knowing, being, and learning is a nurturing form of family support and love and can remind students of why they are enrolled in graduate programs in the first place.

Learning

American Indian and Alaska Native graduate students are cautious and wary when they enter PWIs (both in and out of the classrooms) and as they learn how to become researchers. AI/AN students must contend with the knowledge of the history of non-AI/AN scholars entering Indigenous communities to conduct deficit-oriented or "damage-centered research" (Tuck, 2009, p. 413). Often non-AI/AN researchers entered AI/AN communities, unannounced and/or uninvited, engaged in culturally disrespectful practices, and failed to provide an end product that was useful to the tribal communities. These scholars trained in Western research methodologies discredited or failed to understand the epistemologies, ontologies, values, and desires of AI/AN peoples and all too often described tribal communities using deficit-oriented language (Pewewardy, 2002).

CIRM is "rooted in [I]ndigenous knowledge systems, is anticolonial, and is distinctly focused on the needs of communities . . . [and] recognizes the self-determination and inherent sovereignty of [I]ndigenous peoples"

(Brayboy et al., 2012, p. 423). Indigenous knowledge systems are grounded in Indigenous epistemologies and honor reciprocity. Indigenous scholars argue that a culturally respectful relationship must be built and maintained between researchers and study participants. The importance of culturally and tribally responsive learning was illustrated in Amber's experience when she met with her professor who encouraged her to apply Navajo theoretical frameworks to her research and provided guidance by offering constructive feedback on how to use CIRM to ensure her study was comprehensive, methodologically sound, and tribally appropriate.

Resources Used to Address Student Challenges

To address the challenges presented by students in ways that align with the elements related to Navajo epistemologies and ontologies, this section describes academic resources used by Ben's (2018) participants to increase their persistence. Students reported effectively working with professors and advisors, encouragement from family members, and establishing a Native campus community.

Encouraging Professors

It is vital for American Indian graduate students to build a respectful rapport with their professors and advisors. Professors who wish to mentor AI/AN students need to understand local history for AI/AN communities and the tribal needs, contexts, and desires of their students' communities. Professors who can do this are more likely to support student development and guide students to design relevant use-inspired, tribally appropriate, and culturally responsive research, writing, and projects. Moreover, having a sense of the history, sovereignty, and self-determination struggles of AI/AN students can help identify appropriate resources and support mechanisms to enhance student success and address any challenges or limitations that may arise. Participants in Ben's (2018) study described encouraging professors as always available to answer their questions, offer constructive feedback on papers, and refer to their American Indian ways of knowing and being as an asset that guides the development of research, knowledge, and solutions.

Encouraging professors assisted students with strategies on how to best transition to graduate studies. For example, Jered shared that he regularly attended his professor's office hours, where they would discuss course materials he did not understand. Once he grasped the materials, he would also clarify assignment expectations. He would then leave the meeting assured that the professor knew he was committed to his course which was important as he was not inclined to ask these questions during class time. Moreover, students sought out Indigenous or culturally diverse professors for mentorship and believed they would share cultural ways of being and knowing. Cheryl intentionally met with Professor Cruz, a Latina professor, because she had an ability to describe complex theories and help her strategically relate the theories in meaningful ways to her research topic. Dr. Cruz acknowledged Cheryl's lived experiences, commitment to serve her Navajo community, and how her Navajo theoretical frameworks lay the foundation for her research. She provided guidance to Cheryl by offering her constructive feedback on how to enhance her outline to ensure her study was comprehensive, in-depth and methodologically sound, and tribally appropriate. Lastly, Navajo student participants met with AI/AN professors to discuss feelings of isolation and their desire to interact with other Native students and faculty. AI/AN professors referred students to cultural resources on campus and helped them find a Native campus community. These opportunities allowed students to receive support from Native and Indigenous faculty about the complex issues of navigating a predominantly White institution.

Supportive Family

In addition to Native faculty and Indigenous faculty offering critical cultural guidance, participants relied on their family and tribal culture's support. Families supported their students by encouraging them to complete their coursework to the best of their ability and to rely on their cultural teachings to help overcome difficult situations. Their family support, prayers, stories, lessons, and teachings strengthened students' persistence by helping them align their graduate degree purpose and experience with their cultural goals, needs, and values. Richard described another form of family encouragement, in which his family knew he needed to remain focused on his academic coursework and not get distracted with minor family matters back home on the Navajo Nation. He appreciated that simple level of understanding and his family's recognition of the time commitment required to complete his studies. Richard's story demonstrates his family's investment in him succeeding.

Family members also offered supportive and loving words of encouragement to their graduate students. When describing how his parents offered their support Richard said, "whether it's [in person], a phone call or a text. They're the ones saying, "*Shiyázhí* [my child] don't give up, *Yéego ánít'í. Áłtso tinilago "hxéh hxéh" didíiniił* [try hard, when you're finished, be thankful and give back]." The traditional concept of giving back to one's family and the larger Navajo community is a value that illustrates Navajo epistemology while the language used to convey this message (Navajo) is an important ontological method of delivery.

Identifying a Native Campus Community

Based on participants' feelings of isolation in their academic departments and colleges, they intentionally sought out other AI/AN graduate students and the Native American Center on campus; both contributed to their persistence. The Native American Center (NAC) staff showed genuine interest in their educational pursuits and provided them with academic resources and fellowship information. Joe benefited from NAC services and said, "I made friends with the [assistant] director. And she was very supportive like a mentor. She's always encouraging and inviting me to speak at events to [other undergraduate AI/AN students]." This finding aligns with research on African American students who report experiencing achievement gaps in online graduate programs, yet sense of belonging, and persistence, is enhanced by mentorship from African American professors (Rovai & Ponton, 2005; Williams et al., 2005). For Native American students, mentorship is multidirectional. Serving as role models and peer mentors to younger students provided a sense of purpose and fulfilled part of their desire to give back to Native communities and peoples while in school.

Navajo students explained that navigating PWI spaces was exhausting and they took refuge within their Native community. Joe felt he could combat the exhausting effects of isolation and microaggressions by visiting and increasing his interaction with AI/AN students and staff at the NAC. He felt like he needed a safe haven, where he could feel like he was back in his hometown. In order to fill this void, he added activities from the Native American Center, with plans to become more involved in those activities in the coming year. He associated the NAC activities with his continued persistence. The NAC was the meeting place for many Native student clubs and organizations. Wallace accepted an invitation to join the Native American graduate student club, increased the number of Native friends in graduate school, and participated in cultural activities with his new friends. The NAC was not only a safe space to network with other Indigenous students and staff, but the staff encouraged students to utilize their resources and apply for graduate fellowships, research projects, and internship opportunities.

Conclusion: How Can Institutions Support Students

Although important for their success, the diverse ways of knowing, being, and learning for Students of Color are not well understood by institutions of higher education (Barnhardt & Kawagley, 2005). We argue that if institutions better understand the various epistemological and ontological commitments, experiences, and goals of their diverse students and their communities, they will be better positioned to support them and enhance their learning outcomes. In this section we offer recommendations for resources and strategies to address current challenges. Strategies such as enhancing opportunities for peer support, enhancing culturally responsive and respectful professor and advisor mentorship, improved professional development opportunities, support of family members, and fostering a welcoming and inclusive campus environment that highlights the presence, contributions, and success of diverse students—specifically American Indians and Alaska Natives (AI/AN)—are discussed. Ultimately, we believe that if institutions of higher education are to increase persistence and success for historically underrepresented graduate students, faculty, advisors, and administrators must be aware of their multiple ways of knowing, being, and learning.

In the classroom, pedagogically and andragogically, it is important to understand education needs to be connected to community persistence and development. We recommend, whenever possible, to use culturally responsive education, curriculum, and practices that are respectful of diverse communities. For AI/AN students, this means having an overt recognition of the sovereign rights and self-determination of Indigenous peoples and understanding the unique cultural and political context of AI/AN communities. Incorporating culturally responsive education and/or place-based curriculum and learning and being aware of diverse epistemologies, ontologies, and research methodologies such as culturally specific knowledge systems, research methodologies, and community-specific research concerns can allow for successful learning experiences and partnerships between professor/mentor and their student. Academically, we believe culturally respectful and supportive education should also include industry mentoring and advising for students who wish to return to work with and for tribal communities.

Beyond the classroom, financially, it is important that education institutions and their various departments provide funding opportunities beyond tuition support. It is important to note that some students may need additional monies beyond the total cost of attendance to include funding to attend conference presentations, pay for childcare subsidies, and meet healthcare needs. To address feelings of isolation and not belonging related to cultural incongruity, it is important to provide peer networking opportunities with other diverse students. To address feelings of invisibility, academic institutions should establish relationships with local diverse and particularly Indigenous peoples, to recognize local history and context of Communities of Color, and to recognize the visibility of AI/AN people with both verbal and institutional recognition of the original inhabitants of the area. For AI/AN peoples, land acknowledgements are important but they must go beyond simply saying the name(s) of tribal nations or original inhabitants of the area.

The institution must establish a commitment to actively support the achievement of Indigenous students and to prepare graduates to meet the needs of their surrounding diverse communities.

To address feelings of under-preparation of insecurity with the research process as well as lack of professional support, we recommend providing opportunities for students to work with other students who are further along in their research program to promote peer mentoring opportunities. Professionally it is important to send diverse students to conferences to share their findings with each other and with diverse audiences (including community leaders, tribal leaders, community members, and federal agency representatives who serve diverse communities). It is also important to provide students with research opportunities that improve cultural congruity between diverse peoples' ways of knowing, being, and learning and how research is conducted and disseminated.

This chapter brought to light the challenging experiences and factors that threaten the persistence of diverse graduate students, particularly AI/AN students, such as internal factors of adjusting to graduate education, isolation, and depression and external factors related to unhealthy relationships with their advisors, mentors, and work-related stressors. Factors that are threats to persistence are in alignment with the few studies about Students of Color in graduate education. However, the most important finding from this research is that institutions can support the persistence of diverse students by working to establish programs, policies, and partnerships with supportive peers, incentivizing professors and mentors to offer culturally responsive and appropriate support, and establishing respectful collaborative relationships with surrounding diverse communities.

References

Aronilth, W., Jr. (1980). *Dine' Bi Bee O'hoo'aah Ba' Sila: An introduction to Navajo philosophy.* Navajo Community College.

Aronilth, W., Jr. (1992). *Foundations of Navajo culture.* Navajo Community College.

Barnhardt, R., & Oscar Kawagley, A. (2005). Indigenous knowledge systems and Alaska Native ways of knowing. *Anthropology & Education Quarterly, 36*(1), 8–23. https://doi.org/10.1525/aeq.2005.36.1.008

Ben, C. (2018). *Navajo students' decision-making factors that influence access and persistence in doctoral education* [Doctoral dissertation, University of Utah].

Ben, C., Poleviyuma, A., Chin, J., Richmond, A., Tom, M., & Abuwandi, S. (2019). The self-contained scholar: The racialized burdens of being nice in higher education. In A. E. Castagno (Ed.), *The price of nice: How good intentions maintain educational inequity.* University of Minnesota Press. https://doi.org/10.5749/j.ctvpwhdfv.12

Brayboy, B. M. J., Fann, A. J., Castagno, A. E., & Solyom, J. A. (2012). *Postsecondary education for American Indian and Alaska Natives: Higher education for nation building and self-determination.* Wiley Periodicals.

Brayboy, B. M. J., Gough, H. R., Leonard, B., Roehl, R. F., & Solyom, J. A. (2012). Reclaiming scholarship: Critical Indigenous research methodologies. In S. D. Lapan, M. T. Quartoli, & F. J. Riemer (Eds.), *Qualitative research: An introduction to methods and designs* (pp. 423–450). Jossey-Bass.

Brayboy, B. M. J., Solyom, J. A., & Castagno, A. E. (2014). Looking into the hearts of Native peoples: Nation building as an institutional orientation for graduate education. *American Journal of Education, 120*(4), 575–596. https://doi .org/10.1086/676908

Brayboy, B. M. J., Solyom, J. A., & Castagno, A. E. (2015). Indigenous peoples in higher education. *Journal of American Indian Education, 54*(1), 154–186. https:// www.jstor.org/stable/10.5749/jamerindieduc.54.1.0154

Council of Graduate Schools (2022). *Data and insights.* https://cgsnet.org/graduate-enrollment-and-degrees/

Flores Carmona, J. (2017). Pedagogical border crossing: Testimonio y reflexiones de una Mexicana Academia. *Journal of Latinos and Education, 17*(1), 92–97. https:// doi.org/10.1080/15348431.2017.1282364

Gay, G. (2004). Navigating marginality en route to the professoriate: Graduate Students of Color learning and living in academia. *International Journal of Qualitative Studies in Education, 17*(2), 265–288. https://doi.org/10.1080/0951839031 0001653907

Gay, G. (2018). *Culturally responsive teaching: Theory, research, and practice.* Teachers College Press.

Guillory, R. M., & Wolverton, M. (2008). It's about family: Native American student persistence in higher education. *The Journal of Higher Education, 79*(1), 58–87. https://doi.org/10.1080/00221546.2008.11772086

Hunt, B., & Harrington, C. F. (2010). The impending educational crisis for American Indians: Higher education at the crossroads. *Indigenous Policy Journal, 21*(3).

Kirkness, V., & Barnhardt, R. (1991). First Nations and higher education: The four Rs—respect, relevance, reciprocity, responsibility. *Journal of American Indian Education, 30*(3), 1–10. https://www.jstor.org/stable/24397980

Lee, L. (2006). Navajo cultural identity: What can the Navajo Nation bring to the Native American identity discussion table? *Wicazo Sa Review, 21*(2), 79–103. https://doi.org/10.1353/wic.2006.0020

Lopez, J. D. (2018). Factors influencing American Indian and Alaska Native postsecondary persistence: AI/AN millennium falcon persistence model. *Research in Higher Education, 59*(6), 792–811. https://doi.org/10.1007/s11162-017-9487-6

MacLachlan, A. J. (2006). *Developing Graduate Students of Color for the professoriate in science, technology, engineering, and mathematics (STEM)* (Research and Occasional paper series: CSHE.6.06, 1–14). University of California, Berkeley.

Nelson, C. (2015). *American Indian college students as native nation builders: Tribal financial aid as a lens for understanding college-going paradoxes* [Doctoral dissertation, University of Arizona].

Okagaki, L., Helling, M. K., & Bingham, G. E. (2009). American Indian college students' ethnic identity and beliefs about education. *Journal of College Student Development, 50*(2), 157–176. https://doi.org/10.1353/csd.0.0060

Patterson, D. G., Baldwin, L. M., & Olsen, P. M. (2009). Supports and obstacles in the medical school application process for American Indians and Alaska Natives. *Journal of Health Care for the Poor and Underserved, 20*(2), 308–329. https://doi.org/10.1353/hpu.0.0150

Pewewardy, C. (2002). Learning styles of American Indian/Alaska Native students: A review of the literature and implications for practice. *Journal of American Indian Education, 41*(3), 22–56. https://www.jstor.org/stable/24398583

Rovai, A. P., & Ponton, M. K. (2005). An examination of sense of classroom community and learning among African American and Caucasian graduate students. *Journal of Asynchronous Learning Networks, 9*(3), 77–92. https://doi.org/10.24059/olj.v9i3.1786

Secatero, S. L. (2009). *Beneath our sacred minds, hands, and hearts: Stories of persistence and success among American Indian graduate and professional students* (Order No. 3368075) [Doctoral dissertation, University of New Mexico]. ProQuest Dissertations and Theses Global.

Shotton, H., Lowe, S., & Waterman, S. (2013). *Beyond the asterisk: Understanding Native students in higher education.* Stylus.

Solorazano, D. G., & Yosso, T. J. (2002). Critical race methodology: Counter-storytelling as an analytical framework for education research. *Qualitative Inquiry, 8*(1), 23–44. https://doi.org/10.1177/107780040200800103

Solyom, J. A. (2014). *The (in)visibility paradox: A case study of American Indian iconography and student resistance in higher education* [Doctoral dissertation, Arizona State University].

Tuck, E. (2009). Suspending damage: A letter to communities. *Harvard Educational Review, 79*(3), 409–428. https://doi.org/10.17763/haer.79.3.n0016675661t3n15

Williams, M. R., Brewley, D. N., Reed, R. J., White, D. Y., & Davis-Haley, R. T. (2005). Learning to read each other: Black female graduate students share their experiences at a White research I institution. *The Urban Review, 37*(3), 181–199. https://doi.org/10.1007/s11256-005-0008-0

6

UNVEILING THE HIDDEN CURRICULUM WITHIN GRADUATE EDUCATION

Chelsea H. Lyles, Natali Huggins, and Claire K. Robbins

As an international student I encounter a wide range of unexplained experiences while navigating a foreign educational culture and interacting with faculty. There seem to be a lot of expectations from me that are not written in course syllabi, and my PhD program seems to have unwritten expectations about academic language and writing, research interests, funding dynamics, conference attendance, and networking. These experiences can be simultaneously amazing, confusing, challenging, and frustrating, and frequently change depending on the context, professor, course, and stage of the doctoral program. I believed these experiences were personal struggles from my own limitations as an international student. I did not know these challenges were part of the hidden curriculum.

—Natali Huggins

Natali's words powerfully convey how it feels to encounter the "hidden" expectations of graduate education. Students enroll in graduate degree programs to obtain training, earn credentials, and develop expertise in their academic disciplines and professional fields (Perez, 2016). To fulfill these objectives, one of the key tasks facing those who educate graduate students is to develop and refine a "curriculum" that acts as an organizing framework for students' coursework and relevant field experiences. Beyond the formal academic curriculum, students also encounter an informal curriculum where individuals are held responsible for learning tacit knowledge about everything from securing an assistantship to writing academic papers in a particular style. Like a game with unspoken rules, Natali's graduate school experience led her to attribute her struggles to her identity as an international student. In reality, she was encountering a *hidden curriculum* for graduate education.

There is no singular set of unwritten expectations for graduate education since graduate programs vary widely across disciplines, degree types, and institutions. However, some expectations of graduate students are consistent across settings, as evidenced by Calarco's (2018) claim that there is "a hidden curriculum at every level of schooling" (para. 2). With this in mind, this chapter discusses the hidden curriculum of graduate school. We begin by reviewing the various, and at times competing, culture(s) of graduate education. Next, we define and describe how graduate students make meaning of these unstated expectations and provide illustrations of how the hidden curriculum appears for graduate students inside and outside the classroom. Finally, we offer strategies to expose the hidden curriculum by highlighting actions administrators, faculty, and graduate students can take to promote student success in graduate education.

Culture(s) of Graduate Education

For many students, one of the most challenging cognitive requirements of graduate education involves making sense of multiple cultures, often with competing norms (Gardner, 2008; Perez, 2016). During graduate training, students may simultaneously encounter the sociocultural conventions of their institution, department, program, academic discipline, professional field, and one or more subspecialty in their discipline and/or field (Mendoza & Gardner, 2010; Perez, 2016; Perez et al., 2019). Meanwhile, students must navigate cultural dimensions of other settings, including the geographic community/region where they reside, which may or may not be the same as the institution they attend. In fact, students attending wholly or partially online institutions, or online programs within brick-and-mortar institutions, encounter yet another complexity—navigating all of the previous cultural dynamics within the context of online education. Online students have additional challenges in building community among peers and faculty, finding answers to questions, and identifying resources (see Yao & Garcia, ch. 2 of this volume; Yao et al., 2017). Finally, students must make sense of complex cultural norms operating in the United States—a task that may be taken for granted by many domestic students, but an all-encompassing part of life for international students, particularly those living in the United States for the first time (Curtin et al., 2013).

Adding to the already complex task of navigating multiple cultural dimensions, students may be newcomers to some cultural dimensions of graduate school but highly familiar with others (Holley & Gardner, 2012). For example, some students may move to a new region to attend graduate school, but have family members who hold graduate degrees, perhaps even in the same field. Others may be the first in their family to attend college and/ or graduate school but be familiar with the surrounding community and/ or geographic region. Still others may be familiar with professional norms but new to the norms of the academic discipline associated with their degree program. Thus, students may have a strong sense of community or belonging in some cultural dimensions of graduate school while feeling like an outsider in others.

Graduate students also encounter sociocultural norms and group dynamics associated with their social identities, including but not limited to race, ethnicity, class, gender identity and expression, sexual orientation, disability status, nationality, and worldview (i.e., their political, social, and/ or religious beliefs). These norms and dynamics may shift significantly across contexts; for example, graduate students may recognize differences in identity group dynamics on campus versus at the grocery store down the road. Furthermore, at historically and/or predominantly White institutions (which house most graduate programs in the United States), Graduate Students of Color are often more likely to recognize these dynamics, leading them to question the extent to which they belong in particular contexts (Gay, 2004; Harris & Linder, 2018; Perez et al., 2019). Meanwhile, White graduate students often have the privilege of not having to notice their racial identity or question whether they belong (Robbins, 2016). Chelsea has experienced this privilege firsthand:

> Coming from a business and athletics background, I was aware of gender bias, but I did not realize that as a cisgender, White, heterosexual woman from a middle-class family with college-educated parents, I held mostly majority identities. I was unaware of the privilege I carried due to them. An unexpected, but very necessary and difficult, benefit of my graduate school experience has been learning about race. (Chelsea H. Lyles)

For students, making sense of multiple dimensions of culture can be one of the most challenging aspects of graduate education. How students resolve tensions between and within different cultural dimensions may influence whether they persist in their degree programs and the extent to which they achieve desired post-graduation outcomes, including professional identity formation, relevant knowledge and skill development, and employment (Gardner, 2008; Haley et al., 2014; Perez, 2016). The complexity of this task may be even greater for students whose social identities are minoritized in their institution, program, discipline, and/or field (Harris & Linder, 2018;

Perez, 2016; Perez et al., 2019). Making sense of the culture(s) of graduate school is essential not only for students' individual well-being and success, but also for advancing equity, diversity, and inclusion in the institutions they attend and the disciplines and fields they aspire to enter (Perez, 2016; Perez et al., 2019). Supporting graduate students in navigating the cultural complexity of graduate school is essential to their success, but doing so requires unveiling a part of the graduate school curriculum that is too frequently hidden from both students and educators.

The Hidden Curriculum Within Graduate Education

Experts have talked about different ways to organize graduate education (e.g., Cassuto, 2015). While these frameworks are helpful, the curriculum of graduate education is much broader than many acknowledge. The hidden curriculum encompasses a set of implied and hidden messages, assumptions, beliefs, values, and attitudes situated within academia (Calarco, 2020). These messages are imparted to students formally and informally, at times unintentionally and without recognition from either faculty members or students (Villanueva et al., 2018). The hidden curriculum is contextual and situational. It affects students differently depending on how they process information given their values, beliefs, and circumstances (Martin, 1994). Even when unrecognized by the faculty member and student, the hidden curriculum operates a prominent role in graduate education, as illustrated through the examples in the following sections.

Graduate Student Experiences Encountering the Hidden Curriculum

In a blog post, Calarco (2018) compiled and reflected on several tweets from a thread on Twitter related to the hidden curriculum in graduate school. These examples and many others under the Twitter hashtag #hiddencurriculum offer a brief glimpse into the wide spectrum of hidden curriculum manifestations in graduate education. For example, a tweet in this thread by Lauren Schudde illustrates one common source of confusion for graduate students, authorship order for various stages of a research project (see Figure 6.1).

The hidden curriculum appears in and out of the classroom and may be associated with required academic processes or nonacademic expectations. Additionally, each academic discipline has its own terminology (Gardner, 2007) and many graduate students struggle with the hidden curriculum when encountering these unfamiliar terms (Calarco, 2018). Students may

Figure 6.1. Lauren Schudde tweet about hidden curriculum.

Lauren Schudde
@LaurenSchudde

Replying to @JessicaCalarco

As a 1st-yr doc student, I assisted on a project and pulled together results for a conference poster. Since I did all the work for this step, I put my name first - not knowing the implications of author order. I realized later and really wished it had been explicitly discussed.

11:15 PM · Jul 22, 2018 · Twitter for Android

feel embarrassed and not want to admit that they don't know the meaning of a word. Over time, faculty, administrators, and advanced graduate students forget that the language they use daily is not accessible to students new to the discipline.

> Neither my bachelor's nor master's degrees were in the same field as to my doctoral program. I worked at six universities before taking a class in the higher education program at the same institution where I was employed full time. Even with 13 years of work experience in higher education, doctoral studies at a research university were still a shock. My MBA was designed for working professionals and did not include a thesis component. I learned about student development theory, student affairs and student life curricula, and research for the first time in my doctoral program. At times I felt unprepared and inexperienced, and was judged to be a "practitioner" rather than a "scholar" (as if that was a bad thing and I couldn't be both). (Chelsea H. Lyles)

Chelsea's reflection illustrates graduate students entering a new field of study are not just encountering new terminology, disciplinary content, and values of a profession, but they are also learning how to conduct research or to write in a style not used in their prior schooling, such as American Psychological Association (APA) style.

Furthermore, students may be navigating a new campus or encountering the U.S. higher education system, which introduces additional sources of confusion before a student even enters the classroom. Students may not be familiar with U.S. grading approaches, add-drop period processes, or assignments emphasizing critical thinking more than rote memorization

(Hariharan, 2019). Enrolling in classes and accessing course materials online were new processes and contained unfamiliar language for Natali:

> In my country you fill out a form and you go to a specific office for registrations. I got here and I did not know there was a special system and you can do everything online. After registration, I started receiving emails from professors about Canvas [an online course management system] and the syllabus. I did not know what Canvas or a syllabus were, and I did not know any peers in my program to ask basic questions. After starting courses, I engaged with peers and oftentimes I was just lost in the middle of the conversation. I did not understand terms related to expectations and beliefs about graduate education. I did not find the answer written anywhere. I always thought I was lost in the conversation just for being an ESL student, but now I understand that these casual conversations are part of thriving in graduate education in the U.S.

Unfamiliar campuses that differ from a student's undergraduate institution may contain offices, procedures, or services with which students are not accustomed. One student may have attended the institution as an undergraduate, but may struggle with new academic and social experiences, even while remaining on the same campus. Students unfamiliar with the institution may encounter classmates who are familiar with the campus or work there and have "insider" knowledge. Students may have been academically socialized in a very competitive environment. They may not realize the value of developing relationships with graduate student peers. They may not disclose which opportunities or jobs they are applying for or topics they are researching out of fear of "being scooped" by a classmate. Even if they do find a support network within their peers, then they may still experience jealousy or feelings of being less than when classmates are chosen over them for research or teaching opportunities, award nominations, or committee roles.

Students also experience the hidden curriculum in ways not associated with academic requirements. It appears through interactions between faculty members and students, transitions between employee and student, conference attendance, everyday life activities, and when applying and interviewing for jobs. Doctoral students may face additional challenges with the advisor relationship and expectations for engagement in the intellectual life of the department or field (Barnes & Austin, 2009).

Though some institutions do not require faculty members to have office hours written on their course syllabi, not all students understand the purpose or benefits of office hours during graduate education. Office hours may have been considered a place where undergraduate students who were earning poor grades or struggling in the class went to get help. Students may not want to appear as if they are struggling in front of the person they need to serve as a future reference. They may be anxious about how they would start a conversation with faculty or wondering why they would even have one. They may be afraid of damaging relationships with their classmates by developing too close of a relationship with an advisor (Cassuto, 2015). Students may consider developing a close relationship with faculty a risk, or even inappropriate, due to the power difference in their positions (Hagenauer & Volet, 2014). They may fear being perceived as encouraging or initiating an inappropriate relationship with a professor by meeting eoutside of an office in a casual setting, or even meeting in a professor's office if the door is closed.

Part-time students especially must balance academic requirements and work expectations, which may overlap or conflict (Gardner & Gopaul, 2012). They may be expected to (or feel as if they are expected to) compartmentalize their identities and transition back and forth between a dichotomous student/learner to expert/professional depending on if they are in class or in a workplace. Part-time students (Gardner & Gopaul, 2012) may feel they are lacking a "traditional" graduate school experience, and like part-time students, online students (Garcia & Yao, 2019) may struggle with additional feelings of disconnection from their program.

Full-time graduate students with funding may have some of these same concerns when developing a relationship with their assistantship supervisor, if it is a person different from their dissertation advisor. They may be experiencing their first job or having a difficult conversation with a supervisor for the first time, or they may have more work experience than their supervisor. Students may encounter colleagues at their assistantship who have different views of the contributions of graduate assistants, not knowing or regardless of any prior professional experience the student brings to their positions. Alternatively or additionally, students may have other sources of funding or may be worrying about how they will fund their education. They may have another part-time or full-time job to cover their living expenses, or they may be required to complete an additional practicum or unpaid internship in addition to courses.

Conference attendance brings additional confusion for students, including expected attire, attendance at social events, networking (Hariharan, 2019), and standards for presenting at research paper or poster sessions (Calarco, 2018). Many first-time conference attendees overschedule themselves for educational sessions and avoid leaving free time to network and build relationships in the hallways between or during sessions or at social events. A lack of clarity on what is expected of students extends to similar "extra" developmental activities that take place both on and off campus:

> In my first semester as a PhD student, all my energy was focused on becoming a student again after working for over 12 years, it was a challenging transition and I focused just on coursework. On several occasions I was encouraged to engage in networking, conferences, publications, Twitter, and student socials. I was confused. How was I going to fulfill all these expectations in addition to my coursework and my personal life? Are these activities as valuable as earning good grades? With time I learned that these activities are essential components of graduate education. (Natali Huggins)

Even everyday life activities such as parking and meals can be another source of frustration for graduate students. Graduate students may be living in a rural community for the first time, without access to public transportation. They may be new or unused to driving a personal vehicle, learning how to read road signs in an unfamiliar language, trying to remember where they are allowed to park without receiving a ticket, or not understanding why parking rules are different for football or basketball games. Meals also bring together different cultures and expectations. Some, but not all, faculty permit eating in their classes, including those that cover the noon and evening hours. The culture of a student's workplace or assistantship may have another set of expectations, which may vary based on time, place, and audience. Different classrooms and buildings may have their own policies on food and beverages, and signs may be posted and enforced or posted and ignored. These mixed messages, differing cultures, and conflicting expectations add layers of confusion to the student.

Doctoral students encounter many cultural—academic and community—barriers. For example, Hariharan (2019) learned while taking a prerequisite class for her master's degree that she was permitted, and expected, to disagree with a faculty member and classmates during class discussions. This pedagogical approach countered her prior training where she assumed the role of passive recipient of knowledge. Not until the later stages of her PhD program did she learn that she could also disagree with mentors outside of the classroom. This seemingly simple example is but one example of a foundational experience that students learn from observation during graduate education.

Doctoral students may also be expected (without a clear invitation) to participate in "the intellectual life of the department beyond the classroom" (Sullivan, 1991, p. 410) to develop as a researcher. What makes this complicated and hidden for students is that these activities are not explicitly required to earn the doctoral degree. These optional activities may include research assistantships or apprenticeships, faculty colloquia where faculty share results of research or research-in-progress, faculty candidate presentations, teaching development workshops, study groups, software training sessions, and professional association involvement at the national, regional, or local level.

The hidden curriculum extends through completion of academic requirements to the job application and interview processes (Calarco, 2018). Job market advice may be shared by a peer, an advisor, a program, a graduate school, or a career placement service office, or even no one at all. The decentralized structure of graduate education produces a result that some students receive this information, some students seek it out, and some students never learn it. The hidden curriculum advantages students who know how to work the system over others, through no fault of their own. Instead, this information should be made available to all students.

Findings from Gardner's (2007) qualitative study of doctoral education in history and chemistry offer a poignant illustration of the consequences of the hidden curriculum. In this study, doctoral students' experiences involved "contradictions and balance, constantly trying to understand and meet the implicit and explicit guidelines and expectations that were demanded of them, both externally and internally" (p. 730). Students encountered ambiguity and uncertainty, relying on "the graduate student grapevine" (p. 736) for information that was essential to their success. They depended on the grapevine while struggling to balance multiple responsibilities (for example, teaching, research, and their own coursework), and experienced differing degrees of independence that did not always match what they needed in each phase of the doctoral process. Students also noted the central role of peer and faculty supports and described the doctoral process as developmental in unanticipated ways. To reveal and successfully navigate the hidden curriculum, the next section offers recommendations for institutional administrators, faculty, and graduate students.

Recommendations

While not considered an exhaustive list, we offer recommendations to make aspects of the hidden curriculum explicit and help students more equitably navigate the hidden curriculum. These strategies are organized into recommendations for three categories of stakeholders: (a) institutional administrators, (b) faculty, and (c) graduate students.

Institutional Administrators

Institutional administrators (i.e., department head, graduate school director) possess the positional authority to make systemic changes through enactment of policies, practices, training sessions, or events. Administrators can reveal the hidden curriculum through institutional funding, campus climate, and social activities. Administrators might fund graduate student support offices to help students identify and navigate the hidden curriculum. Institutions can provide funding to support students' participation in academic conference and networking events. These research funds should be tailored for different academic programs and student populations, such as racially minoritized students (Orón Semper & Blasco, 2018). Doing so would allow institutions and departments to more equitably distribute financial resources, while also making information available to all students that may rely on funding for participation in these socialization activities.

Exploring the hidden curriculum from an organizational lens may also uncover issues imposed by institutional climate (Villanueva et al., 2018). Administrators might focus on fostering an inclusive institutional climate and a place where the hidden curriculum is recognized. In practice, faculty would be encouraged and incentivized to find ways to support students in their process of recognizing and overcoming struggles linked to the hidden curriculum. Climate surveys may be reviewed for evidence of existing hidden curriculum, as well as altered to be a tool for institutional researchers to better understand students' and faculty members' perceptions of and experiences with the hidden curriculum. Administrators should respond accordingly to the results of climate surveys by keeping, improving, or creating institutional approaches related to making the hidden curriculum transparent for graduate students.

Administrators can bring in experts to offer trainings for faculty members to help them identify the ways hidden curriculum affects their students' personal and educational pursuits (Neve & Collett, 2018). Administrators can also bring in experts to offer sessions for students to help them recognize, internally process, and navigate the hidden curriculum. University librarians may be incentivized to collaborate with faculty to develop discipline-specific tutorials and resources, which may be of special interest to 1st-year online graduate students (Yao et al., 2017). Finally, university counseling services can be promoted to students to discuss academic and personal development, and administrators can facilitate peer mentoring initiatives among both faculty and students (Orón Semper & Blasco, 2018).

Orón Semper and Blasco (2018) offer several additional strategies to uncover the hidden curriculum through institutional structures, the curriculum, and relationships. For example, they encourage administrators to consider which behaviors are incentivized or sanctioned, how students respond to these incentives or sanctions, and how students make meaning of these implicit messages. They also advocate for considering "What routines, rituals, and practices exist in the institution (e.g., competitions, ceremonies, induction courses, meetings, clubs and associations)?" and "What kind of messages and values do the students take away from these?" (p. 492).

Finally, administrators might focus on the dual purposes that may be served by university social activities. They can encourage social activities where students can develop support groups, mentoring relationships, and friendships among peers (Neve & Collett, 2018). Research universities could learn from other institutional types on how these institutions build community. Additionally, each institution needs to understand its own values, beliefs, climate, and culture while exploring how other institutional types are handling the hidden curriculum, because what works at one institution may or may not work at another.

Faculty

In addition to administrator engagement in unveiling the hidden curriculum, faculty play an important interfacing role with graduate students. Faculty can make the hidden curriculum explicit by acknowledging "the interpersonal dimension of learning, both as it pertains to themselves and to their students" (Orón Semper & Blasco, 2018, p. 482) by recognizing students' unique characteristics, experiences, and learning contexts. Faculty members may influence the outcomes of the hidden curriculum by recognizing that "learning is not only a product of teachers' and students' doing but also of their being" (Orón Semper & Blasco, 2018, p. 483). Orón Semper and Blasco (2018) describe this phenomenon as a move from "student centered" education to "interpersonal relation-centered" education. For example, attending joint meetings where faculty and students discuss policies that affect both groups or engaging in professional development opportunities together are two examples of ways faculty and students can develop interpersonal relationships in environments that lessen the power difference between faculty and students (Orón Semper & Blasco, 2018).

Faculty members can also address the hidden curriculum in the classroom or through online modules. For example, seminars where students learn skills expected of graduate degree holders, such as using software programs, presenting a research paper, submitting to various journals, creating a curriculum vitae, reviewing a journal article, interviewing for a job, or writing a grant application are one way to make explicit the hidden curriculum (Larson et al., 2019; Sullivan, 1991). Garcia and Yao (2019) found that a 1st-year doctoral seminar for online doctoral students helped them overcome doubt in their academic abilities through peer interaction, community building, and validation from faculty and an advanced doctoral student serving as a course assistant. In cases where some of these activities are not part of the formal curriculum, faculty and students could cover these topics through built-in professional development that could be recorded and distributed to students not able to participate directly. Faculty whose programs do not offer a credit-bearing seminar might seek out seminars in other programs to see if their students could be invited to relevant sessions or take the course as an elective:

> We have affiliate faculty from engineering education, and they opened up their seminar to higher education students. In one class, I learned about authorship order and how to initiate and regularly revisit that conversation. It came in handy when I was invited to be a "contributor" to this very book chapter. That seminar gave me the confidence and language to ask for clarification about chapter authorship. (Chelsea H. Lyles)

Chelsea was able to exercise agency, in part due to what she learned in a seminar, but also because she felt comfortable with Claire, having established an advisor–advisee relationship through office hours and conversations outside of class. Office hours offer a venue through which students can gain confidence in speaking with and developing relationships with faculty. Students may use this time to ask faculty not just about class or program requirements, but also about the hidden curricular elements (e.g., conference attendance, job market) and navigation strategies. Office hours also may be a space for students to discuss, examine, and develop their own academic identity. For office hours to be effective, students need to attend. One way to dispel preconceived or previously held notions about office hours is for faculty to require or strongly encourage student participation in office hours in their first semester to allow them to become familiar with the location, office layout, and see the faculty member as a regular person. Faculty teaching in online programs or just simply using technology as a way to connect with students can use office hours as a way to develop relationships and rapport building with students. Additionally, they can remove a language barrier and explain that office hours are simply a "time to meet with faculty" (Ardoin & martinez, 2019, p. 182).

Graduate Students

The hidden curriculum is "not something one just finds; one must go hunting for it" (Martin, 1994, p. 158). Graduate students can draw from their own lived experience and support each other while navigating the hidden curriculum in a multitude of ways. While faculty members can and should encourage students to ask for help and reach out to peers, especially those further along in the program, students can also initiate these relationships. Students can also be a source of breaking down the hidden curriculum by identifying elements unfamiliar to advanced students and using it as a way to pave pathways for earlier career doctoral students. For example, Larson et al. (2019) created a professional development group at Michigan State that was used as a mechanism for addressing aspects of doctoral education not formally addressed in the doctoral curriculum. This example takes the form of a student-led and initiated peer professional development group that exposed students to conference presentations, how-to workshops on scholarly tools, and job market preparation events. Calarco (2018) offers several tips on how to choose a support network that includes faculty and peers to navigate the hidden curriculum. Peer interactions are a critical factor for student success, and it is important for graduate students to experience regular socialization and peer-to-peer mentoring to create awareness about the hidden curriculum's existence, share their own experiences, and support each other while internally processing the hidden curriculum and developing coping mechanisms (Neve & Collett, 2018). However, peers and program faculty are not the only source of support. Part-time students may be more likely to find support from their family members, partners, and work colleagues (Gardner & Gopaul, 2012).

Students experience positive or negative outcomes from the hidden curriculum dependent on their ability to recognize and respond to these unspoken hints (Villanueva et al., 2018). It is part of the student's academic identity development and a crucial factor for thriving in higher education. Graduate students bring prior experience and skills connected to their social identities that help them navigate the hidden curriculum. For example, Dylan recognized "skills such as resilience and complex critical thinking that came, in part, from seeing siblings commit crimes to feed their substance use and learning to love them anyway" (Ardoin & martinez, 2019, p. 55) as talents to be utilized to earn a master's degree. Discovering and harnessing the hidden curriculum may empower students, if they are able to explore, articulate, and make sense of the hidden curriculum by themselves while reflecting on and evaluating their own experiences (Neve & Collett, 2018).

Conclusion

Based on the literature available on this topic, and the active discussion on social media, the hidden curriculum is a topic in need of further exploration and research for graduate education. The hidden curriculum may be an important piece in better understanding why nearly half of graduate students fail to complete their degrees. Students cannot be expected to meet markers of success if those markers are not clearly articulated for them. Administrators, faculty, and students all have a part to play in unveiling the hidden curriculum, which is necessary to create equitable opportunities for graduate student success and completion.

References

Ardoin, S., & martinez, b. (2019). *Straddling class in the academy: 26 stories of students, administrators, and faculty from poor and working-class backgrounds and their compelling lessons for higher education policy and practice.* Stylus.

Barnes, B. J., & Austin, A. E. (2009). The role of doctoral advisors: A look at advising from the advisor's perspective. *Innovative Higher Education, 33*(5), 297–315.

Calarco, J. (2018, July 28). Guest post: Grad school's hidden curriculum. *Scatterplot: The unruly darlings of public sociology.* https://scatter.wordpress.com/2018/07/24/guest-post-grad-schools-hidden-curriculum/

Calarco, J. M. (2020). *A field guide to grad school: Uncovering the hidden curriculum.* Princeton University Press.

Cassuto, L. (2015). *The graduate school mess: What caused it and how we can fix it.* Harvard University Press.

Curtin, N., Stewart, A. J., & Ostrove, J. M. (2013). Fostering academic self-concept: Advisor support and sense of belonging among international and domestic graduate students. *American Educational Research Journal, 50*(1), 108–137. https://doi.org/10.3102/0002831212446662

Garcia, C. E., & Yao, C. W. (2019). The role of an online first-year seminar in higher education doctoral students' scholarly development. *The Internet and Higher Education, 42*, 44–52. https://doi.org/10.1016/j.iheduc.2019.04.002

Gardner, S. K. (2008). Fitting the mold of graduate school: A qualitative study of socialization in doctoral education. *Innovative Higher Education, 33*(2), 125–138.

Gardner, S. K. (2007). "I heard it through the grapevine": Doctoral student socialization in chemistry and history. *Higher Education, 32*, 383–408. https://doi.org/10.1007/s10734-006-9020-x

Gardner, S. K., & Gopaul, B. (2012). The part-time doctoral student experience. *International Journal of Doctoral Studies, 7*(12), 63–78. https://doi.org/10.28945/1561

Gay, G. (2004). Navigating marginality en route to the professoriate: Graduate Students of Color learning and living in academia. *International Journal of Qualitative Studies in Education, 17*(2), 265–288. https://doi.org/10.1080/09518390310001653907

Hagenauer, G., & Volet, S. E. (2014). Teacher–student relationship at university: An important yet under-researched field. *Oxford Review of Education, 40*(3), 370–388. https://doi.org/ 10.1080/03054985.2014.921613

Haley, K. J., Jaeger, A. J., & Levin, J. S. (2014). The influence of cultural social identity on graduate student career choice. *Journal of College Student Development, 55*(2), 101–119. https://doi.org/10.1353/csd.2014.0017

Hariharan, J. (2019). Uncovering the hidden curriculum. *Science, 364*(6441), 702. https://doi.org/10.1126/science.364.6441.702

Harris, J. C., & Linder, C. (2018). The racialized experiences of Students of Color in higher education and student affairs graduate preparation programs. *Journal of College Student Development, 59*(2), 141–158. https://doi.org/10.1353/csd.2018.0014

Holley, K. A., & Gardner, S. (2012). Navigating the pipeline: How socio-cultural influences impact first-generation doctoral students. *Journal of Diversity in Higher Education, 5*(2), 112–121. https://doi.org/10.1037/a0026840

Larson, J. B., Nguyen, D. J., Opoczynski, R., & Vizvary, G. (2019). Designing a professional development group for leader learners enrolled in graduate education. *Journal of Leadership Studies, 13*(2), 73–76. https://doi.org/10.1002/jls.21644

LaurenSchudde [@LaurenSchudde]. (2018, July 22). *As a 1st-yr doc student, I assisted on a project and pulled together results for a conference poster. Since I did all the work for this step, I put my name first - not knowing the implications of author order. I realized later and really wished it had been explicitly discussed* [Tweet]. Twitter. https://twitter.com/LaurenSchudde/status/1021232332144021505

Martin, J. R. (1994). What should we do with a hidden curriculum when we find one? In J. R. Martin (Ed.), *Changing the educational landscape: Philosophy, women, and curriculum* (pp. 154–169). Routledge. https://doi.org/10.2307/1179759

Mendoza, P., & Gardner, S. K. (2010). The PhD in the United States. *On becoming a scholar: Socialization and development in doctoral education.* Stylus.

Neve, H., & Collett, T. (2018). Empowering students with the hidden curriculum. *The Clinical Teacher, 15*(6), 494–499. https://doi.org/10.1111/tct.12736

Orón Semper, J. V., & Blasco, M. (2018). Revealing the hidden curriculum in higher education. *Studies in Philosophy and Education, 37(5)*, 481–498. https://doi.org/10.1007/s11217-018-9608-5

Perez, R. J. (2016). A conceptual model of professional socialization within student affairs graduate preparation programs. *Journal for the Study of Postsecondary and Tertiary Education, 1*, 35–52. https://doi.org/10.28945/2344

Perez, R. J., Robbins, C. K., Harris, L. W., Jr., & Montgomery, C. (2019). Exploring graduate students' socialization to equity, diversity, and inclusion. *Journal of Diversity in Higher Education.* Advance online publication. https://doi.org/10.1037/dhe0000115

Robbins, C. K. (2016). White women, racial identity, and learning about racism in graduate preparation programs. *Journal of Student Affairs Research and Practice, 53*(3), 256–268. https://doi.org/10.1080/19496591.2016.1143834

Sullivan, T. A. (1991). Making the graduate curriculum explicit. *Teaching Sociology, 19*(3), 408–413. https://doi.org/10.2307/1318208

Villanueva, I., Carothers, T., Di Stefano, M., & Khan, M. (2018). "There is never a break": The hidden curriculum of professionalization for engineering faculty. *Education Sciences, 8*(4), 157. https://doi.org/10.3390/educsci8040157

Yao, C., Wilson, B., Garcia, C., DeFrain, E., & Cano, A. (2017). Helping graduate students join an online learning community. *EDUCAUSE Review.*

PART TWO

ADDRESSING ACADEMIC AND PROFESSIONAL SKILL DEVELOPMENT

7

TEACHING PROFESSIONAL DEVELOPMENT FOR GRADUATE STUDENTS

Lucas B. Hill

There is considerable interest in the holistic development of graduate students (both master's and doctoral) for an array of careers in academia, government, and industry. This focus was, in part, driven by large-scale research studies that indicated incongruities between graduate students' goals, the training provided, and the careers they envision (Bieber & Workley, 2006; Golde & Dore, 2001; Terosky & Gonzales, 2016). In addition, there remain significant concerns about doctoral and master's student attrition (Council of Graduate Schools, 2013; Lovitts, 2001) and the ability to produce high quality graduates who can fill local and national job market needs such as in science, technology, engineering, and mathematics disciplines (National Academies of Sciences, Engineering, & Medicine, 2018). Given these factors, scholars and practitioners have argued for more expansive professional development for graduate students that prepares them for multifaceted roles and responsibilities.

Teaching, in particular, has been a major focus of graduate student professional development due to graduate students' interest in faculty careers (Connolly et al., 2016; Golde & Dore, 2001) and current graduate student teaching responsibilities, regardless of interest in faculty careers. It is also due to the rich potential application of pedagogical skills to nonfaculty career paths, as evidenced by core professional competencies advocated by graduate schools (e.g., University of California, Berkeley, 2019; University of Virginia, 2019) and professional organizations (e.g., Hobin et al., 2012; National Postdoctoral Association, n.d.). Advances in professional development focused on teaching have also been highly motivated by the lack of training that graduate students receive for future teaching responsibilities (Heflinger & Doykos, 2016; Lattuca et al., 2014), both for faculty work contexts and other career paths that can draw on transferable instructional skills such as organizing and communicating complex information to various audiences and developing employee trainings (Austin & McDaniels, 2006). Such lack of preparation has prompted the development of large-scale initiatives such as the Preparing Future Faculty (PFF) initiative (Gaff et al., 2003) and the Center for the Integration of Research, Teaching, and Learning (CIRTL; Center for the Integration of Research, Teaching, and Learning, 2017) to encourage, through professional development, the adoption of evidence-based teaching strategies (e.g., Brewer & Smith, 2011; National Research Council, 2012). Teaching professional development opportunities provides easier transitions to faculty careers, provides valuable skills for those without faculty aspirations, and exposes graduate students to careers within multiple institution types (e.g., research universities, liberal arts colleges, community colleges). Thus, teaching professional development can enrich the career preparation for all graduate students.

In addition to career preparation, there has been a related, though distinct, body of literature that has focused on graduate students' current teaching roles as teaching assistants (TAs), which is also a means of socialization to faculty roles (Mena et al., 2011). Many graduate students with and without faculty career aspirations become TAs to fund their programs and are a major teaching force, though many are not the instructors of record and instead teach lab sections, occasionally give lectures, or otherwise assist faculty members (Dunn-Haley & Zanzuchhi, 2012; Gallardo & Petrovich, 2017; Gilmore et al., 2014). According to the 2017 Survey of Earned Doctorates, 20.6% of all doctoral recipients funded their program through a teaching assistantship, with some disciplines reporting much higher percentages (e.g., math and computer science, 36.6%; humanities and arts, 37.4%; National Science Foundation, National Center for Science and Engineering Statistics, 2018). Similar to the previously described challenges, TAs receive limited training for their classroom or lab responsibilities, which may breed stress, limit their potential pedagogical impact, and could even dissuade them from pursuing careers with teaching responsibilities (Cho et al., 2011; Gardner & Jones, 2011). Such stressors are more apparent with international students as they have to navigate limited support with the added challenge of language barriers (Luo et al., 2001; Tyler, 1992). Graduate student TA experiences are also quite parallel to the experiences of new K–12 educators who, despite receiving structured teacher training, often feel ill-equipped for their teaching roles (Onafowora, 2005), which can result in attrition from the K–12 system

(Clandinin et al., 2015). In light of these challenges, many have argued for teaching professional development that goes beyond the typical orientation sessions and imbues graduate students with real pedagogical knowledge for their current roles.

In summary, extant literature demonstrates the need to support graduate students in their current and future teaching roles. Diverse stakeholders are responsible for providing graduate students with mentorship, training, and teaching experiences to empower, address role stress, build pedagogical skills, and provide exposure to diverse career paths that involve teaching. These supports will be broadly referred to as *teaching professional development* (TPD) for the rest of the chapter.

Graduate Student Teaching Professional Development Framework

In this section, the graduate student teaching professional development framework (see Figure 7.1) is presented, which frames the major elements involved in teaching development for graduate students. Elements include: key stakeholders, TPD topics, TPD opportunities, TPD program success

Figure 7.1. Graduate student teaching professional development framework.

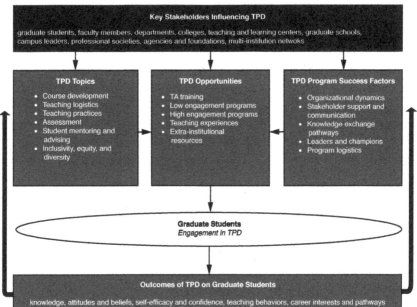

factors, and the outcomes and benefits that result from TPD participation. The framework was developed from a review of the literature and from the author's experience in CIRTL, a large, multi-institutional network focused on teaching professional development. Using the framework, the chapter concludes with key recommendations for those who implement, support, and benefit from TPD programs.

Key Stakeholders

The graduate student teaching professional development framework includes key stakeholders, who are responsible for and/or are able to influence TPD for graduate students. These parties include graduate students, faculty members, departments, colleges, teaching and learning centers, graduate schools, campus leaders, professional societies, agencies and foundations, and multi-institutional initiatives. These individuals, campus units, and external organizations can affect and help prioritize what topics are included in TPD and what TPD opportunities are available that meet the needs and interests of graduate students and the labor market. These same stakeholders can help shape organizational dynamics and support structures (e.g., providing resources) to build and sustain TPD programs, thus influencing program success factors (see as follows). Those who offer TPD are some of the most important stakeholders because they most directly influence topics, opportunities, and programmatic success.

Formal teaching professional development programs for graduate students can be offered by several campus units. Most commonly this includes academic departments, colleges, teaching and learning centers, and graduate schools. It is quite common, given the decentralized nature of most higher education institutions, that multiple campus units offer services without knowing about each other's offerings (Connolly et al., 2016). To increase success, regular and meaningful communication must be established between stakeholders to coordinate goals, activities, and resource allocation. Graduate students should also be included in this communicative cycle among all responsible stakeholders who are able to influence TPD programs and topics.

TPD Topics

TPD covers a wide range of topics (see Table 7.1), ranging from course preparation and development; course/institutional logistics; classroom teaching practices; assessment and evaluation of student learning, which includes the application of the scholarship of teaching and learning (SoTL; Cruz et al.,

2019); teaching roles outside of the classroom such as student mentoring and advising; and the holistic incorporation of inclusivity, equity, and diversity into all teaching activities (Gillian-Daniel & Kraemer, 2015). Topics of TPD programs are also often formulated to meet specific disciplinary contexts, usually in connection to disciplinary-based education research efforts.

It is important to note that typically, programs do not address multiple topical categories in a single offering, but instead offer a suite of offerings at various levels of depth, further complemented by opportunities at other institutions or networks, and web-based resources. This approach allows graduate students to engage at a level that matches their interests and time availability and operates under a hope that they will continue their teaching development over time versus picking up a few "tips and tricks" on an ad hoc basis. However, while there is no basic ideal introductory training for graduate students with and without faculty aspirations, literature indicates the need for all teachers to understand the needs of their students (Weimer, 2002),

TABLE 7.1
Teaching Professional Development Topics

Category	Examples
Comprehensive Overviews	• Introduction to college teaching • Teaching in biology
Course Preparation	• Developing a syllabus • Building a curriculum and teaching plan • Crafting a teaching philosophy statement
Course/Institutional Logistics	• Academic dishonesty • Grading policies
Teaching Practices	• Active learning • Classroom management • Teaching with technology • Creating community
Assessment and Evaluation	• Designing assessment instruments • Data-driven teaching improvement
Mentoring and Advising	• Undergraduate research mentor training • Graduate student mentoring • Undergraduate advising
Diversity, Equity, Inclusion	• Inclusive teaching strategies • Classroom climate • Social identities in learning environments

which will prompt future development and the selection of pedagogical strategies that address those needs.

TPD Opportunities

There are many types of TPD programs available to graduate students. While there are programmatic archetypes, there is considerable autonomy in how they are structured and implemented within unique institutional contexts. For instance, in a recent study of high engagement programs in the CIRTL Network, Schein et al. (2018) found that even though programs held thematic consistency to match the vision and values of the Network, how local CIRTL programs were organized and run varied greatly across member institutions. Thus, even if two campuses run a TA training program, the content, scope, duration, and activities may vary greatly between the two institutions. Regardless of this variety, it is extremely useful to describe the major types. These include: TA training, low and high engagement programs, teaching experiences, and extra-institutional resources.

TA Training

One of the most common types, TA trainings provide incoming graduate students with a foundation of logistical-oriented and pedagogically minded activities to prepare them for their teaching responsibilities (Border, 2011). They can range from a few hours to multiple days and can be administered locally by departments or at a university level via centralized units like the graduate school (Gilmore et al., 2014). Because TA trainings were originally conceived to focus more on course and institutional logistics, many TA training programs retain this element and have a small portion dedicated to pedagogy development (e.g., Dragisich et al., 2016) whereas others emphasize the teaching element much more (e.g., Gallardo-Williams & Petrovich, 2017). Furthermore, most TA trainings end once the initial programming is complete, although some programs maintain connection with their TAs for ongoing development, usually coupled with other types of TPD described as follows.

Low Engagement Programs

Often in the form of short presentations or workshops that typically last less than a day, low engagement programs require little from graduate student participants in terms of time commitment or prerequisites. Those that offer TPD realize that graduate students are quite busy and often face pressure from their advisors or principal investigators to not spend time on non-research activities (Baiduc et al., 2016). Low engagement programs provide an easy access point for graduate students to become exposed to effective teaching, with the hopes that such programs will provide a stepping-stone to higher engagement activities.

High Engagement Programs

This type of TPD requires a much more substantial time commitment with most lasting longer than a day and some as long as a few semesters. Examples of these programs include a single, albeit intensive course (O'Loughlin et al., 2017), comprehensive summer institutes (Rivera, 2018), programs involving a sequence of activities such as workshops, courses, and mentored experiences that can lead to a teaching certificate (Medina & Herrig, 2011), and the implementation of evidence-based, often mentored, teaching and learning projects that investigate student learning and how to improve teaching practice (Prevost et al., 2018). In addition, high engagement TPD programs often promote social learning mechanisms with other graduate students, faculty, and other stakeholders through the use of learning communities (Linenberger et al., 2014) and mentoring programs (Gaia et al., 2003). Overall, high engagement programs not only expose graduate students to pedagogical ideas but provide the means for discussion, integration, and application.

Teaching Experiences

While not typically considered a form of TPD, graduate students also advance their teaching abilities through teaching experiences (Connolly et al., 2016). Graduate students, serving as TAs, often carry out some of the teaching load for a particular course, such as running a lab section. Some also become teachers of record and are responsible for the entire course preparation, implementation, and assessment. In addition, there are opportunities to engage in supplemental instruction opportunities such as engagement in study sessions with students in challenging courses to improve retention (Doubleday & Townsend, 2018) and mentored teaching experiences that consist of working with faculty mentors who are more "hands on" to help graduate students gain the most of their teaching experience (Baltrinic et al., 2016; Cascella & Jez, 2018). In short, graduate students develop teaching confidence and competencies through professional development programs and by engaging in the act of teaching. The two are, or at least should be, inseparable.

Extra-Institutional Resources

Beyond local offerings, there are numerous online resources available that graduate students can access independently to advance their learning such as collections of "how to" articles, including centers for teaching and learning resource repositories, YouTube videos, and online programming and courses such as massive open online courses (MOOC). Some professional societies and associations also provide workshops and trainings to their membership, including graduate student attendees, and may host additional web-based content. In short, many different groups and constituencies offer teaching professional development for graduate students. A select resource list is included at the end of this chapter.

TPD Program Success Factors

To build successful TPD programs, it is necessary to consider the people involved, program content, processes, context, and intended short- and long-term outcomes (Hill et al., 2015). Building upon these foundational components, Hill et al. (2019) investigated the characteristics of developing and sustaining local CIRTL TPD programs for graduate students. They found that campus culture, support from stakeholders such as faculty and campus leaders, the organizational placement of the TPD program at the institution, program leadership, program logistics of staffing and funding, and benefits from CIRTL Network membership all played a key role in TPD program success. Gaff et al. (2003), in outlining successful PFF program attributes, indicated several related facets: leadership, identifying partners, appointing a steering committee, paying attention to recruitment strategies, flexibility, and securing support from faculty and those who make funding decisions. Others cited the importance of a faculty champion (Brightman, 2009), user friendly and flexible program offerings rooted in disciplinary needs (Chadha, 2013), and the importance of intrinsic motivators (Parker et al., 2015). In summary, to build a successful TPD program, it is necessary to pay close attention to organizational dynamics, support from and communication with campus stakeholders, knowledge-exchange pathways, program leadership, and program logistics. Each of these factors are dynamic and change over time, thus requiring regular monitoring.

Leaders of TPD programs play a particularly key role in programmatic success. These individuals often directly interface with graduate students and other key stakeholders to define what topics will meet the needs of their graduate students and align with effective pedagogical practices. TPD leaders can also examine how their program is addressing factors that promote TPD program success as defined previously. For example, how will their campus TPD program, with the help of local program staff, make connections with different campus units, faculty, and graduate students? How will the program stay apprised of new knowledge and information, locally or national derived, that could inform their TPD efforts? Thus, TPD program leaders need to simultaneously look upstream and downstream to examine program development, the needs of graduate students, and the resultant impacts that result from program participation.

Outcomes of TPD on Graduate Students

Most research and evaluation studies about the outcomes of TPD for graduate students focus on specific programs. Connolly et al. (2016), one of the few large-scale studies of the effect of teaching development, found that a large sample of STEM doctoral students (n = 3060) who later transitioned to early career faculty positions reported no changes to time-to-degree, an increased interest in teaching undergraduates, and an expanded confidence in their teaching abilities as a result of engagement in TPD, especially with 20 hours or more of participation (Connolly et al., 2018). Program-specific studies, across disciplines, have found positive outcomes related to teaching knowledge, teaching skills and abilities, beliefs and attitudes about teaching, expanded self-efficacy/confidence, teaching behaviors, and career interests and trajectories (e.g., Baiduc et al., 2016; Bosman, 2013; Dragisich et al., 2016; Flaherty et al., 2017; Gilmore et al., 2014; Lattuca et al., 2014; Prevost et al., 2018). While there is a need for more cross-program research to determine the pervasiveness of TPD outcomes, there is considerable evidence to suggest that participation in such programs helps graduate students feel more confident in their abilities as teachers, thus lessening the role stress discussed previously and increasing the likelihood for positive contributions to their current and future teaching contexts. In addition, graduate students without faculty career aspirations can benefit from participation in TPD because it can alleviate current TA role stressors and help develop skills not common in research-centric preparation. For instance, those trained in effective teaching can develop general employment skills related to public speaking, active listening, observation of human behavior, and practical strategies they can apply to future training scenarios in noneducation sectors.

Regardless of faculty or nonfaculty aspirations, the outcomes that result from TPD opportunities need to be tracked and measured to engage feedback loops as shown in the framework figure as black arrows to the various stakeholders who influence and shape aspects of TPD. Evaluation efforts should not be limited to immediate assessment just after TPD opportunities have ended. Instead, improved, expanded, and even longitudinal metrics are needed to measure the pervasiveness of TPD impact within and across institutions to better inform TPD efforts, solicit support from additional stakeholders who support and who do not yet support TPD, and distribute limited resources in efficient ways.

Recommendations

The graduate student teaching professional development framework demonstrates that key stakeholders should carefully consider how they influence topics, programs, and program success factors and how they collectively work to advance outcomes for graduate students. The following are targeted recommendations for three groups: those who implement TPD, those who support TPD, and graduate students.

Those Who Implement TPD

TPD program implementers are responsible for providing graduate students with a variety of opportunities to meet their needs, interests, and demanding schedules. However, TPD offerings are often not coordinated across multiple campus units, leaving graduate students to haphazardly navigate disconnected resources. TPD providers are encouraged to explore their campus to see who is offering TPD, the perceived needs of graduate students with and without faculty aspirations, and how unnecessary redundancies can be removed. In addition, TPD providers can collaborate on strategies to collectively increase support for TPD among different campus stakeholder groups.

   While good intentions are a key catalyst in grassroots movements, those that lead and run TPD programs should find ways to communicate the growing literature on the outcomes and benefits of TPD and develop effective evaluation strategies to show success at their institution that is in line with campus stakeholder goals (e.g., job placement). More specifically, TPD can demonstrate that (a) TPD is worth graduate students' time, (b) TPD does not negatively affect other professional growth and development, and (c) TPD has numerous benefits that match graduate student needs and institutional goals.

Those Who Support (or Could Support) TPD

Based on TPD benefits, stakeholders within or outside higher education institutions can use their positionality to advocate for the growth of TPD and provide sufficient resources. For example, campus leaders can use their influence to direct funding to TPD opportunities, department chairs can encourage a relationship with the teaching and learning center, faculty can speak up for the importance of TPD among their colleagues, and funding agencies can fund initiatives to develop and expand TPD opportunities. In short, supporters of TPD can use their current roles to promote the proliferation of TPD.

TPD supporters can also advocate for an expanded approach to assessing and evaluating the development, implementation, and outcomes of TPD programs. More comprehensive data, especially from a cross-institutional perspective, will help advance and improve TPD, which will help graduate students. As recipients of outcome reporting, TPD supporters and would-be supporters can use their position to motivate TPD providers to expand their assessment and evaluation efforts and encourage cross-institutional collaborations and research to expand potential data collection, while at the same time advocating for the necessary resources to do so.

Graduate Students

The most obvious recommendation for graduate students is to participate in TPD, whether or not they have faculty career aspirations. The benefits are clear and there are many options to match specific interests and time availability that it behooves graduate students to gain important and transferable skills to take to any career path. In addition, career paths can change, so having an additional set of skills can be quite fortuitous in the future.

Lastly, graduate students have great capacity to advocate for TPD among their peers and even faculty advisors and mentors. As the new stock of various career pathways, graduate students possess the ability to shape their field and use their colleague connections to make a case for TPD and demonstrate the lived outcomes of TPD participation.

Conclusion

Numerous stakeholders are responsible for developing useful professional development opportunities that meet the current and future needs of graduate students. Graduate students have been historically ill-equipped to face their teaching responsibilities, at the detriment of their own growth and the proliferation of ineffective teaching strategies in higher education institutions. Graduate students are a sound investment to advance teaching and learning for the benefit of individuals, institutions, and greater society. In addition, the skills gained through TPD are transferable to nonacademic careers, providing an additional incentive for all graduate students to engage in TPD to maximize their employability. It is our job as higher education leaders, practitioners, and scholars to lay the foundation for successful TPD programs and opportunities, communicate results, and continually improve offerings to meet dynamic needs.

Select Resources

- Books:
  - Hanstedt, P. (2018). *Creating wicked students: Designing courses for a complex world.* Stylus.
    - The authors provide compelling advice for designing courses that empower their students to tackle large, messy problems found within the world today.
  - Lang, J. M. (2016). *Small teaching: Everyday lessons from the science of learning.* Jossey-Bass.
    - Drawing on a cognitive theory perspective, Lang outlines several small strategies to improve one's teaching to improve student learning.
  - McGuire, S. Y. (2015). *Teach students how to learn.* Stylus.
    - McGuire discusses multiple teaching strategies to help students be more motivated, study better, and self-reflect on their learning to improve their academic success.
  - McKeachie, W., & Svinicki, M. (2013). *McKeachie's teaching tips.* Wadsworth, Cengage Learning.
    - The authors present comprehensive advice on how to structure courses and implement instruction to aid in the learning of students.
  - Nilson, L. B. (2013). *Creating self-regulated learners.* Stylus.
    - Nilson describes numerous helpful strategies across several subjects for helping students become more self-directed in their learning efforts.
- Teaching and learning center resources:
  - https://cft.vanderbilt.edu/teaching-guides/
  - https://fctl.ucf.edu/teaching-resources/
  - https://ctl.columbia.edu/resources-and-technology/resources/
  - The weblinks provide example collections of helpful teaching resources that can assist postsecondary education teachers with focused and practice-oriented advice to improve their instruction. Numerous other teaching and learning centers at other higher education institutions across the country will likewise have similar collections.
- Online Course: An Introduction to Evidence-Based Undergraduate STEM Teaching, a Massive Open Online Course offered by CIRTL, http://stemteachingcourse.org/
  - Sponsored by the Center for the Integration of Research, Teaching, and Learning (CIRTL), this MOOC walks participants through

the fundamentals of evidence-based instruction. While focused on STEM, the content will be applicable and useful to a wide range of disciplines.

- Online Course: The Inclusive STEM Teaching Project, a National Science Foundation-funded project, https://www.inclusivestemteaching.org/
  - This MOOC helps participants develop fundamental knowledge and skills in inclusive teaching practices. Like the CIRTL MOOC, the content will be applicable to a wide range of disciplines despite its STEM focus.
- Academic journals dedicated to teaching, such as *College Teaching, Teaching in Higher Education*, and *Journal of College Science Teaching.*
  - Readers are encouraged to scan the article titles of these three popular teaching-focused journals, which contain research on teaching and practical advice to improve postsecondary instruction.

References

Austin, A. E., & McDaniels, M. (2006). Preparing the professoriate of the future: Graduate student socialization for faculty roles. *Higher Education: Handbook of Theory and Research, 21*, 397–456. https://doi.org/10.1007/1-4020-4512-3_8

Baiduc, R., Linsenmeier, R., & Ruggeri, N. (2016). Mentored discussions of teaching: An introductory teaching development program for future STEM faculty. *Innovative Higher Education, 41*(3), 237–254. https://doi.org/10.1007/s10755-015-9348-1

Baltrinic, E. R., Jencius, M., & McGlothlin, J. (2016). Coteaching in counselor education: Preparing doctoral students for future teaching. *Counselor Education & Supervision, 55*(1), 31–45. https://doi.org/10.1002/ceas.12031

Bieber, J. P., & Worley, L. K. (2006). Conceptualizing the academic life: Graduate students' perspectives. *The Journal of Higher Education, 77*(6), 1009–1035. https://doi.org/10.1080/00221546.2006.11778954

Border, L. L. B. (2011). *Mapping the range of graduate student professional development: Studies in graduate and professional student development.* New Forums Press.

Bosman, J. S. (2013). Graduate student teaching development: Evaluating the effectiveness of training in relation to graduate student characteristics. *Canadian Journal of Higher Education, 43*(1), 100–114. https://eric.ed.gov/?id=EJ1007032

Brewer, C., & Smith, D. (2011). *Vision and change in undergraduate biology education: A call to action.* American Association for the Advancement of Science.

Brightman, H. J. (2009). The need for teaching doctoral students how to teach. *International Journal of Doctoral Studies, 4*(1), 1–11. https://doi.org/10.28945/42

Cascella, B., & Jez, J. M. (2018). Beyond the teaching assistantship: CURE leadership as a training platform for future faculty. *Journal of Chemical Education, 95*(1), 3–6. https://doi.org/10.1021/acs.jchemed.7b00705

Chadha, D. (2013). Reconceptualising and reframing graduate teaching assistant (GTA) provision for a research-intensive institution. *Teaching in Higher Education, 18*(2), 205–217. https://doi.org/10.1080/13562517.2012.696537

Center for the Integration of Research, Teaching, and Learning. (2017). *Home page.* https://www.cirtl.net/

Cho, Y., Kim, M., Svinicki, M., & Decker, M. (2011). Exploring teaching concerns and characteristics of graduate teaching assistants. *Teaching in Higher Education, 16*(3), 267–279. https://doi.org/10.1080/13562517.2010.524920

Clandinin, D. J., Long, J., Schaefer, L., Downey, C. A., Steeves, P., Pinnegar, E., Robblee, S. M., & Wnuk, S. (2015). Early career teacher attrition: Intentions of teachers beginning. *Teaching Education, 26*(1), 1–16. https://doi.org/10.1080/10476210.2014.996746

Connolly, M. R., Lee, Y. G., & Savoy, J. N. (2018). The effects of doctoral teaching development on early-career STEM scholars' college teaching self-efficacy. *CBE—Life Sciences Education, 17*(ar14), 1–15. https://doi.org/10.1187/cbe.17-02-0039

Connolly, M. R., Savoy, J. N., Lee, Y. G., & Hill, L. B. (2016). *Building a better future STEM faculty: How doctoral teaching programs can improve undergraduate education.* Wisconsin Center for Education Research, University of Wisconsin-Madison.

Council of Graduate Schools. (2013). *Completion and attrition in STEM master's programs: Pilot study findings.* https://cgsnet.org/completion-and-attrition-stem-masters-programs-pilot-study-findings

Cruz, L., Cunningham, K., Smentkowski, B., & Steiner, H. (2019). The SoTL scaffold: Supporting evidence based teaching practice in educational development. *To Improve the Academy, 38*(1), 50–66. https://doi.org/10.3998/tia.17063888.0038.105

Doubleday, K. F., & Townsend, S. A. (2018). Supplemental instruction as a resource for graduate student pedagogical development. *Yearbook of the Association of Pacific Coast Geographers, 80,* 134–156. https://doi.org/10.1353/pcg.2018.0007

Dragisich, V., Keller, V., & Zhao, M. (2016). An intensive training program for effective teaching assistants in chemistry. *Journal of Chemical Education, 93*(7), 1204–1210. https://doi.org/10.1021/acs.jchemed.5b00577

Dunn-Haley, K., & Zanzucchi, A. (2012). Complicity or multiplicity? Defining boundaries for graduate teaching assistant success. In H. L. Schwartz (Ed.), *Interpersonal Boundaries in Teaching and Learning* (New Directions for Teaching & Learning, no. 131, pp. 71–83). Wiley. https://doi.org/10.1002/tl.20028

Flaherty, A., O'Dwyer, A., Mannix-McNamara, P., & Leahy, J. J. (2017). Evaluating the impact of the "Teaching as a Chemistry Laboratory Graduate Teaching Assistant" program on cognitive and psychomotor verbal interactions in the laboratory. *Journal of Chemical Education, 94*(12), 1831–1843. https://doi.org/10.1021/acs.jchemed.7b00370

Gaff, J. G., Pruitt-Logan, A. S., Sims, L. B., & Denecke, D. D. (2003). *Preparing future faculty in the humanities and social sciences.* Council of Graduate Schools.

Gaia, A. C., Corts, D. P., Tatum, H. E., & Allen, J. (2003). The GTA mentoring program. *College Teaching, 51*(2), 61–65. https://doi.org/10.1080/87567550309596413

Gallardo-Williams, M. T., & Petrovich, L. M. (2017). An integrated approach to training graduate teaching assistants. *Journal of College Science Teaching, 47*(1), 43–47. https://doi.org/10.2505/4/jcst17_047_01_43

Gardner, G. E., & Jones, M. G. (2011). Pedagogical preparation of the science graduate teaching assistant: Challenges and implications. *Science Educator, 20*(2), 31–41. https://eric.ed.gov/?id=EJ960634

Gillian-Daniel, D. L., & Kraemer, S. B. (2015). Faculty development to address the achievement gap. *Change, 47*(6), 32–41. https://doi.org/10.1080/00091383.2015.1089757

Gilmore, J., Maher, M. A., Feldon, D. F., & Timmerman, B. (2014). Exploration of factors related to the development of science, technology, engineering, and mathematics graduate teaching assistants' teaching orientations. *Studies in Higher Education, 39*(10), 1910–1928. https://doi.org/10.1080/03075079.2013.806459

Golde, C. M., & Dore, T. M. (2001). *At cross purposes: What the experiences of today's doctoral students reveal about doctoral education.* The Pew Charitable Trusts. www.phd.survey.org

Heflinger, C., & Doykos, B. (2016). Paving the pathway: Exploring student perceptions of professional development preparation in doctoral education. *Innovative Higher Education, 41*(4), 343–358. https://doi.org/10.1007/s10755-016-9356-9

Hill, L. B., Austin, A. E., Bantawa, B., & Savoy, J. N. (2019). Factors of success: Building and sustaining teaching professional development opportunities for doctoral students and postdocs. *Higher Education Research & Development, 38*(6), 1–15. https://doi.org/10.1080/07294360.2019.1616677

Hill, L., Connolly, M. R., Savoy, J. N., & Associates. (2015). *The anatomy of teaching development programs: A taxonomic dissection* (LSFSS Brief Series, No.2). Wisconsin Center for Education Research, University of Wisconsin-Madison.

Hobin, J. A., Fuhrmann, C. N., Lindstaedt, B., & Clifford, P. S. (2012, September). So you think you have skills. *Science Careers.* https://www.sciencemag.org/careers/2012/09/so-you-think-you-have-skills

Lattuca, L. R., Bergom, I., & Knight, D. B. (2014). Professional development, departmental contexts, and use of instructional strategies. *Journal of Engineering Education, 103*(4), 549–572. https://doi.org/10.1002/jee.20055

Linenberger, K., Slade, M. C., Addis, E. A., Elliott, E. R., Mynhardt, G., & Raker, J. R. (2014). Training the foot soldiers of inquiry: Development and evaluation of a graduate teaching assistant learning community. *Journal of College Science Teaching, 44*(1), 97–107. https://www.jstor.org/stable/43631783.

Lovitts, B. E. (2001). *Leaving the ivory tower: The causes and consequences of departure from doctoral study.* Rowman & Littlefield.

Luo, J., Grady, M. L., & Bellows, L. H. (2001). Instructional issues for teaching assistants. *Innovative Higher Education, 25*(3), 209–230. https://doi .org/10.1023/A:1007603816555

Medina, M. S., & Herring, H. R. (2011). An advanced teaching certificate program for postgraduate year 2 residents. *American Journal of Health-System Pharmacy, 68*(23), 2284–2286. https://doi.org/10.2146/ajhp100459

Mena, I., Diefes-Dux, H., & Capobianco, B. (2011). *Doctoral students as course instructors: Three engineering teaching assistants' socialization experiences* (School of Engineering Education Graduate Student Series: Paper 7). Purdue University Libraries. https://doi.org/10.18260/1-2--17790

National Academies of Sciences, Engineering, and Medicine. (2018). *Graduate STEM education for the 21st century.* The National Academies Press.

National Postdoctoral Association. (n.d.). *The NPA postdoctoral core competencies.* https://www.nationalpostdoc.org/page/CoreCompetencies

National Research Council. (2012). *Discipline-based education research: Understanding and improving learning in undergraduate science and engineering.* The National Academies Press.

National Science Foundation, National Center for Science and Engineering Statistics. (2018). *Doctorate recipients from U.S. universities: 2017* (Special Report NSF 19-301). https://ncses.nsf.gov/pubs/nsf19301/

O'Loughlin, V. D., Kearns, K., Sherwood-Laughlin, C., & Robinson, J. M. (2017). How do we train our future faculty to teach? A multidisciplinary comparison of graduate-level pedagogy courses offered at a large midwestern university. *College Teaching, 65*(4), 172–181. https://doi.org/10.1080/87567555.2017.1333081

Onafowora, L. L. (2005). Teacher efficacy issues in the practice of novice teachers. *Educational Research Quarterly, 28*(4), 34-43. https://eric.ed.gov/?id=EJ718120

Parker, M. A., Ashe, D., Boersma, J., Hicks, R., & Bennett, V. (2015). Good teaching starts here: Applied learning at the graduate teaching assistant institute. *Canadian Journal of Higher Education, 45*(3), 84–110. https://eric.ed.gov/?id=EJ1085405

Prevost, L. B., Vergara, C. E., Urban-Lurain, M., & Campa, H. (2018). Evaluation of a high-engagement teaching program for STEM graduate students: Outcomes of the Future Academic Scholars in Teaching (FAST) Fellowship program. *Innovative Higher Education, 43*(1), 41–55. https://doi.org/10.1007/s10755-017-9407-x

Rivera, S. (2018). A summer institute for STEM graduate teaching assistants: Exploring teaching perceptions. *Journal of College Science Teaching, 48*(2), 28–32. https://doi.org/10.2505/4/jcst18_048_02_28

Schein, J., Hill, L. B., Austin, A. E., & Rollert-French, K. (2018). *The variability of high-engagement teaching-as-research programs* (CIRTL Research Brief #3). Center for the Integration of Research, Teaching, and Learning.

Terosky, A. L., & Gonzales, L. D. (2016). Re-envisioned contributions: Experiences of faculty employed at institutional types that differ from their original aspirations. *The Review of Higher Education, 39*(2), 241–268. https://doi.org/10.1353/rhe.2016.0005

Tyler, A. (1992). Discourse structure and the perception of incoherence in international teaching assistants' spoken discourse. *Tesol Quarterly, 26*(4), 713–729. https://doi.org/10.2307/3586870

University of California, Berkeley. (2019). *Graduate professional development guide.* Berkeley Graduate Division. https://grad.berkeley.edu/professional-development/guide/

University of Virginia. (2019). *Assessment of skills and competencies.* https://gradcareer.virginia.edu/assessment-of-skills

Weimer, M. (2002). *Learner-centered teaching: Five key changes to practice.* Jossey-Bass.

8

FOSTERING UNIQUE SCHOLARLY VOICES

Developing Graduate Student Writing Skills

OiYan Poon, Josefina Carmona, Carmen Rivera, and Kim Nehls

The successful completion of a graduate degree requires students to acquire competencies in various styles of scholarly writing. However, there is evidence to suggest that the development of student skills beyond the baccalaureate can suffer from a lack of investment in the teaching of writing in graduate education (Allen, 2019; Boote & Beile, 2005; Cotterall, 2011; Stevens, 2018). Furthermore, few works on graduate writing pedagogy directly address these topics as they affect diverse student populations with minoritized identities, many of whom have faced systemic barriers to educational opportunities for scholarly development (see e.g., Brunsma et al., 2016; Griffin et al., 2010; Larson et al., 2019; McCoy et al., 2015; McCoy & Winkle-Wagner, 2015; Twale et al., 2016).

In this chapter, we begin by briefly exploring some implications of limited investments in graduate student writing development. Although this chapter is particularly relevant for teaching and supporting the scholarly skills of students who have thesis or dissertation requirements as part of their degree, the suggestions presented are also relevant to all graduate students, who must become familiar with, and critique research as applied to their fields of professional leadership, practice, and development. For example, master's students across disciplines should learn about their fields of research inquiry and consider and analyze research from their vantage points as developing scholar-practitioners and professionals. Such research to practice connections can simultaneously help strengthen the development of research-informed leadership and scholarly public engagement to address problems across fields.

We then identify some pedagogical principles for teaching students scholarly writing skills. The chapter ends with a presentation of several teaching tools to support graduate students in cultivating their scholarly voices. Throughout this chapter, we center the scholarly perspectives and reflections of Josie Carmona and Carmen Rivera—respectively a PhD candidate and an alumnx in the Colorado State University Higher Education Leadership Studies program at the time of writing this chapter, who both identify as Latina women—to emphasize the importance of engaging in collective approaches between and among faculty and students in the development of unique scholarly voices. This Colorado State University program, delivered through a hybrid online curriculum, offers students the opportunity to complete their doctoral studies in a program that includes both synchronous online and residential meetings, centering the development of scholar-practitioners.

Lack of Investment in Graduate Student Writing Development

Although the development of writing skills should be a central teaching and learning objective in graduate education, some authors have problematized the state of scholarly writing styles and mechanics (Allen, 2019; Stevens, 2018; Sword, 2012). For example, in the opening to *Stylish Academic Writing*, Helen Sword (2012) explained:

> Pick up a peer-reviewed journal in just about any academic discipline and what will you find? Impersonal, stodgy, jargon-laden, abstract prose that ignores or defies most of the stylistic principles outlined [by guides on effective writing]. There is a massive gap between what most readers consider to be good writing and what academics typically produce and publish. (p. 3)

This passage underscores the need to focus graduate education on writing skills, to improve academic writing quality in general.

Research suggests that the problems with graduate student writing quality are many. Some have identified inadequate writing skills, ineffective writing strategies and revision practices, problems in argumentation and organization, grammar and syntax, as well as writing anxiety and negative self-perceptions, among other problems (Allen, 2019; Can & Walker, 2010; Maher et al., 2014). Specifically addressing graduate student competencies in writing literature reviews in the field of education, Boote and Beile (2005) revealed:

> [The] dirty secret known by those who sit on dissertation committees is that most literature reviews are poorly conceptualized and written. Our

secret is made public by editors and reviewers who openly lament the inadequacy of literature reviews in manuscripts submitted for journal publication. (p. 4)

In short, writing is a problem in graduate education, but the real "dirty secret" may be that graduate programs rarely engage in systemic investments in pedagogies and support for scholarly writing development (Boote & Beile, 2005; Lee & Kamler, 2008). The critical reflections presented by Josie and Carmen emphasize how graduate students and candidates shoulder the implications of limited writing support and development in graduate school. Indeed, the lack of systemic approaches to cultivating graduate student scholarly writing skills affects quality of educational experiences, not just the state of research.

Josie Carmona's Critical Reflection

As much as I hate to admit it, my writing challenges as a doctoral student stemmed from lack of confidence in seeing myself as a scholar, positive writing habits, and meaningful faculty feedback. Expectations set forth to me by my master's level faculty indicated that as long as I was able to meet the paper deadlines, answer their specific writing prompts, and grasp the overarching constructs being discussed, I would achieve a "passing" grade. Another layer of complexity was that my first responsibility was to a job, a full-time job and/or part-time jobs while I was enrolled in graduate studies. This challenge led to a development of a "binge writing" cycle, where I could easily work round the clock across the span of several days, in order to meet writing deadlines. This unsustainable cycle and habit included reading, analyzing supporting references, and developing my framework for responding to the assigned paper projects all in the same short time frame. Further compounding this cycle was a lack of meaningful feedback, other than a few comments in the margin saying "good job," "nice work," or highlighting some grammatical error on my part. Most grades ranged from 88–98 and I was able to maintain a 4.0 in my master's program. Rarely did a professor ever challenge my understanding or arguments of particular subjects (social sciences). Therefore, while I was never happy with my work, I took the grade and moved on, never looking at or thinking about my submissions again. I had no reason to engage in a deeper reflective learning process, and my full-time work status did not allow me to see my graduate work as anything more than a means toward checking a credentials box for that next promotion.

I waited 6 years before beginning my doctorate, and frankly, the 1st year was similar to what I had experienced in my master's degree program.

Initially, I relied heavily on my classmates to critique my work and I was still receiving less than stellar feedback from my professors. It was not until a few new faculty members, bringing new pedagogical practices, joined the program that I began to receive critical feedback, which challenged my entire writing process, from beginning to end. This new form of feedback forced me to evaluate my writing process and recognize that if I didn't adjust, then I would not be successful in completing a high-quality dissertation—one of my goals for this educational experience. And while I knew that this binge writing cycle was not sustainable, it was challenging to change my bad habits, especially given the difficulties in balancing my studies with the very real need for me to work full-time to support my family. It wasn't until my last class, a proposal writing course, that I began to incorporate various tips and suggestions, which are provided in this chapter, from my current advisor, OiYan Poon. I attribute the change in my writing style/cycle and habits to not only these tips, but also more importantly to the thoughtful and constructive feedback she provided. The consistent message from my dissertation committee members communicated to me that they believed in me and, in turn, reinscribed confidence in my ability as a scholar.

Carmen Rivera's Critical Reflection

It seemed as though I was not able to hit my writing stride until the end of my doctoral coursework. While I didn't struggle in terms of writing fundamentals or completing assignments consistent with expectations, I did not fully understand how collaborative writing was as an activity or how important meaningful feedback is to developing as a writer. Thinking back to my first major assignment requiring research as a final component, I was stressed and overwhelmed. Stress occurred because I was out of practice with reading and writing scholarly works. It took more time and effort than I had imagined. Fast-forward to the middle of this doctoral program, and I had developed muscle memory for reading, writing, and revising. However, much of my scholarly work was focused on meeting the faculty's expectations and rubrics rather than also intentionally focusing on how these assignments were helping me develop my scholarly writing skills and habits. I waited for critical feedback from my faculty, often not getting anything substantial depending on the faculty member. When I did get extensive feedback and solid critique, I was thrilled and felt both challenged and affirmed.

I then began to review drafts of my peers' papers more regularly. I had not even considered asking peers to look at my work, not out of competition, but out of my own socialization around how I was supposed to do "school work" in isolation. From early on in higher education, it was drilled into my head to "do my own work." This messaging translated into a performative approach rooted in perfectionism and failed to consider the benefits of community in the writing process to help me develop and strengthen my skills. By the time we got to writing our dissertation proposals, the student community had established a regular practice of peer review. It made me a better, more confident writer. Additionally, I was being pushed by my faculty advisor, Susana Muñoz, to center my voice in my writing in ways I hadn't been before. It was both empowering and challenging. I was becoming a better writer and scholar in large part not only because of my coursework but how I engaged in my academic community. I began to see myself differently in an academic sense and it was reflected both in my written products and in my attitude toward my scholarship.

Principles for Developing Graduate Student Writing Skills

The specifics of Josie and Carmen's stories may feel familiar to some readers while unfamiliar to others. Nonetheless, both authors' experiences and reflections highlight key challenges and strategies for graduate student writing development found in relevant published research. Research on graduate student writing development generally calls for systemic attention and approaches to cultivating writing skills (Allen, 2019; Boote & Beille, 2005). Some specifically called on faculty mentors and supervisors to provide adequate support, feedback, and guidance for students to engage in peer-review publication processes (Cotterall, 2011; Lee & Kamler, 2008). Other research suggested pedagogical tools and techniques to help students work on their writing skills and habits, such as collective writing groups, feedback loops, and participation in critical review processes (Can & Walker, 2010; Lee & Kambler, 2008; Maher et al., 2014; Olson & Clark, 2009; Stevens, 2018; Swadener et al., 2015). These suggestions underscore the need to help students recognize and engage in a reflective and continual process of writing development.

Drawing from the literature and our experiential knowledge, in this section, we highlight three interconnected principles of writing to guide efforts, activities, and pedagogies for graduate student writing development. First, writing as a developmental process, especially in gaining familiarity with a field of research and articulating a unique voice for analyzing and commenting on existing research. Second, writing as an iterative process. Third, feedback loops are necessary and important practices to build into writing processes.

Developmental Process

Becoming a scholarly writer is a developmental process that should help students cultivate their unique scholarly voices. This developmental process should foundationally begin with practicing the construction of literature reviews, which involves a time-intensive practice of assessing the state of research literature relevant to one's topic of interest, reflecting on one's point of view, and how it shapes the articulation of critiques and identification of future areas of inquiry that would advance the area of research. This process demands that students read numerous texts, understand the various discourses related to their chosen dissertation topic, and synthesize these texts into a well-argued literature review, which serves as the foundation for their research process (Boote & Beile, 2005; McAlpine, 2012; Onwuegbuzie et al., 2011). By critically engaging in reviewing their field of research, graduate students begin to develop their scholarly identity and carve out a space for their research interests in the world of academia. While the literature review process is messy and not always focused upon in the thesis or dissertation process, it is the stage at which emerging scholars establish the scope of the research study and establish their unique or new perspective on the subject (Boote & Beile, 2005). Through this process, students begin to articulate a scholarly, or scholar-practitioner, identity in relation to their academic and professional field (Nguyen et al., 2019).

Graduate students who have developed certain writing habits, such as binge writing, often find themselves reading and writing at the same time (see Josie's account), not allowing enough time to digest, analyze, and thoughtfully consider how their newly acquired information contributes to their scholar identity and research (Luedke et al., 2019). Suggested pedagogies to support graduate students in scholar identity development include the centering of reading as crucial, encouraging reading outside of their chosen genre in an effort to understand shared academic literacy practices, and exploration of different writing genres (Cotterall, 2011; McAlpine, 2012). Reading poetry, fiction, scholarly books and articles, grant proposals, and other texts can challenge writers to consider different styles of writing and to take risks in their own work. In explicitly centering reading as crucial, graduate students can also begin to deconstruct texts and understand the time required in writing, and plan accordingly. For students like Josie and Carmen juggling full-time work, personal responsibilities, and studies, the time to read may be challenging but as discussed later in this chapter, there are tools and tips which can help to mitigate the time factor. These strategies allow for a recognition that in the long run, time invested in continuous and iterative reading and writing leads to more sustainable and stronger writing skills and habits.

Writing as Iterative Requiring Feedback Loops

Related to understanding graduate school writing as a developmental process is the need to center and incorporate feedback loops into practice. Writing is an iterative process, requiring time, various systems for feedback, commitment to evaluating feedback, and incorporating changes that are meant to enhance and strengthen a student's research. It is not a linear, singular, or solitary process. Similar to research conducted utilizing a grounded theory approach (i.e., constant feedback loops throughout each stage of development), promoting writing as iterative also requires a level of organization on the part of the student to prepare and reserve, and hold sacred, sufficient time to write, review/edit, submit for feedback, and incorporate suggested changes (Odena & Burgess, 2017). Binge writing, procrastinating, and being underprepared are all examples of how students, and other writers, may be responding to the conditions of their experiences. Engaging in forward thinking planning practices that embrace the iterative and evolving nature of the writing process can offer new possibilities for sustainable, collective, and enjoyable writing habits. These habits include feedback loops.

Often, graduate students are under the impression that first drafts must be "perfect" and do not seek feedback from faculty and/or peers. In contrast to perfectionist feelings and fear of feedback, scholarly growth and development require a comfort with vulnerability to allow others to review their work. Successful feedback loops involve certain conditions, including the development of a trusting and positive relationship between advisor and student, student openness to requesting and receiving feedback from faculty and peer reviewers, and student reflection and incorporation of feedback into their scholarly and writing habits and approaches (Can & Walker, 2010; Lee & Kamler, 2008; Maher et al., 2014; Stevens, 2018). Equally important to students' willingness to engage in feedback loops for reflective learning is how reviewers frame the delivery of feedback (Can & Walker, 2010). Reviewers should provide feedback in substantive and constructive ways to help students grow as scholarly writers with honing their skills in writing research and research-informed works for various audiences (e.g., preliminary exams, dissertation, peer-reviewed article, research briefs or reports, op-ed essay, etc.) and incorporating feedback (Lee & Kamler, 2008).

Teaching Tools

Bringing together the highlighted principles for writing development from the research, we now turn our attention to offering tangible tools faculty and students can use to nurture scholarly writing skills. We start by emphasizing the importance of writing accountability communities. We then describe three tools for familiarizing students with writing literature reviews. These three writing activities can help teachers scaffold learning and cultivate unique scholarly perspectives in the context of selected areas of research. Finally, we end this section by offering readers guidance and encouragement to plan out their semesters, quarters, or summers. As the National Center for Faculty Development and Diversity (NCFDD, https://www.facultydiversity.org/), an organization that works with faculty and students to cultivate healthy writing and research habits, explains, "every semester/summer needs a plan" for success.

Accountability Community: The Case for "The Crew"

An essential component for both Josie and Carmen's writing success came as a result of an informal peer group, affectionately self-named "The Crew." With some of their classmates in their program cohort, they developed The Crew after the 1st year of their doctoral program, which uses a cohort model approach. Members of the group, who were predominantly Students of Color, showed up for each other in meaningful ways to support each other toward degree completion (e.g., checking in via texting groups, Marco Polo video chats, Snapchat, regularly scheduled Zoom meetings, and phone calls to simply ask "what can we do to support you?"). Commitment to each other in The Crew materialized in several ways that focused on accountability and support, which evolved in practice over time and stage during their progress toward degree completion. It echoed research suggesting that community building can significantly impact how students develop their scholarly identities, expand upon their writing skills and abilities, and increase the likelihood of degree completion and publishing their work beyond the dissertation (Aitchison, 2009; Olson & Clark, 2009; Stevens, 2018; Swadener et al., 2015).

As both Josie and Carmen mentioned in their narratives, the peer review aspect was a critical component of how this student-initiated and student-led group supported each other. There were collaborative writing projects via class assignments. There was voluntary sharing of work to solicit feedback from each other beyond editing, including content feedback, critical feedback, and affirming feedback. There were often lively discussions about group members' dissertation topics where the group would engage in informal presentations of sorts having to explain their research questions, theoretical perspectives, methodology, and other issues. The standard was multimodal, iterative, and dynamic but also served to create hope among those who were feeling inadequate and/or struggling with the writing process (Allen, 2019; Swadener et al., 2015).

The focus on accountability and support continued to grow throughout the program. The Crew had developed several modes of communication that addressed the cross-country nature of the group. Group texts, shared documents, and video calls were all methods used to remain in communication. The Crew began their supportive practices well before coursework was completed, but their community became critical once members were in the more solitary dissertation stage. At this point, support and accountability nearly became synonymous. The Crew checked in with each other about goals and deadlines. Others would respond with direct questions about what support looked like. Most members read most, if not all, of each other's proposals and dissertations, demonstrating the level of commitment the group had to collective and individual development and success. It was not only a cheering squad for when a member succeeded. It was a motivating group to push each member to accomplish what they set out to do, especially when the challenges seemed unending. In this case, the group, in search of a "homeplace" and belonging, actually achieved much more, developing an awareness of their competencies and capabilities, emphasizing self-actualization and the formation of a healthy self-esteem as a way to exercise or experience freedom (hooks, 1990, 2003). As demonstrated by relevant research and personal experiential knowledge, a collective community of writing support is vital to graduate student writing progress, and to help diverse students make meaning of various writing development tasks and activities, as highlighted next.

Entering the Scholarly Conversation: Teaching Literature Review

> A substantive, thorough, sophisticated literature review is a condition for doing substantive, thorough, sophisticated research. "Good" research is good because it advances our collective understanding. To advance our collective understanding, a researcher or scholar needs to understand what has been done before, strengths and weaknesses of existing studies, and what they might mean. A researcher cannot perform significant research without first understanding the literature in the field. Not understanding the prior research clearly puts a researcher at a disadvantage. (Boote & Beile, 2005, p. 3)

The craft of writing a literature review is foundational to the development and growth of any research scholar. Although few graduate programs provide formal courses on learning how to write literature reviews (Boote & Beile, 2005), students should learn the mechanics of constructing a literature review at some point through their coursework, during participation in research apprenticeships, or other graduate writing support opportunities. In learning how to write a literature review, students should first develop an assessment of the state of research related to their topic of interest. The task here is to gain a sense of how an academic field has developed, and how a topic has been studied—what paradigms and methods have been applied.

In reading and reviewing available research, ideally with the support of a skilled librarian, they should be learning to draw from their own bases of experiential and theoretical knowledge to consider how future inquiry might bring innovative insights to the study of a topic area.

For some students, being asked to question the state of research can be an intimidating task that may counter years of social conditioning in schooling, where didactic forms of teaching are common (Poon et al., 2017). As Paulo Freire (2000) explained, banking education (i.e., where the teacher possesses all knowledge, and students are presumed to have no knowledge) can diminish students' self-efficacy to problematize the state of the world, leading them to be passive receivers of information. However, if a scholar does not actively question the state of published research and engage in a speculation of what could be possible, then they will always find it difficult to produce a successful literature review.

Literature reviews allow researchers the basis to articulate a unique scholarly perspective in relation to the broader context of a chosen academic field. When there are already ongoing scholarly conversations in the form of published texts on any given topic, why does a proposed scholarly project matter? How does one propose to enter ongoing conversations in specific research areas? In a social situation, you likely would not interrupt an ongoing conversation, and would probably start by listening to and gauging the state of the conversation before offering your own questions and insights. The etiquette for entering social conversations as a newcomer is generally the same for developing a literature review to inform scholarly inquiry design.

We offer two teaching and learning tools for emerging scholars to strengthen their self-efficacy to construct thoughtfully written literature reviews. A well-written literature review is the foundational building block for any well-designed study. The first activity is a literature review matrix, which is a tool for scholars to begin organizing information about relevant scholarly publications. The second is a mind map that can help writers plot out how various research connects to each other and especially to concepts underlying a research question. The most engaging literature reviews are written in a way that tells a story about a body of relevant existing research, identifying its strengths, key points, limitations, and future research opportunities to offer a scholarly intervention. These tools for synthesizing literature can help a writer learn how to get started with explaining the story of the ongoing scholarly conversation and set up the story for their own research agenda.

Literature Review Matrix
By completing a literature review matrix, an author can begin synthesizing research. The matrix activity is an approach to organizing and summarizing

TABLE 8.1
Sample Matrix Format

Text Citation	Research Question	Central Argument(s)	Theoretical Lens	Methods	Study Findings	Implications for Research and Practice	Questions Raised

key points of each relevant publication. Table 8.1 provides an example format for what a matrix can look like.

Other examples of matrices can be found on websites for university libraries (http://guides.library.jhu.edu/lit-review/synthesize) and writing centers (https://academicguides.waldenu.edu/writingcenter/assignments/literaturereview/matrix).

As you read, jot down notes in your matrix document. You may want to include columns unique to the topic of research, such as country of study for international projects. Researchers should design the matrix in a way that is most useful where the individual can begin seeing patterns and themes in the literature. Keep a document of notes about these patterns you observe about the body of literature you're reviewing. These themes will be the key points, or story plot points, presented in your literature review.

Mind Mapping
Once the matrix is completed, begin mapping out how the information in various reviewed texts relates to each other, and most importantly, to your central research question. Figure 8.1 demonstrates how to create a mind map. Think of the mind map as an illustration and storyboard, or outline, for your literature review.

Starting with the central research question, reflect on how each word or conceptual phrase relates to each other, and what each concept presented in the question really means. What does the reviewed research say about each of the concepts in the research question? Never assume that readers understand exactly how you are defining each term, and the body of research literature you are drawing on. For example, in our field of higher education, it should not be assumed that readers will generally understand the theoretical concept of "student success." There is a robust body of research defining the notion of "student success" and how it is supported or hindered. By deconstructing the research question, you may begin to notice which ongoing scholarly conversations you are most hoping to enter with your research, writing, and point of view.

Figure 8.1. Mind map activity (Rowland, as cited by https://twitter.com/WriteThatPhD/status/958275037827620864).

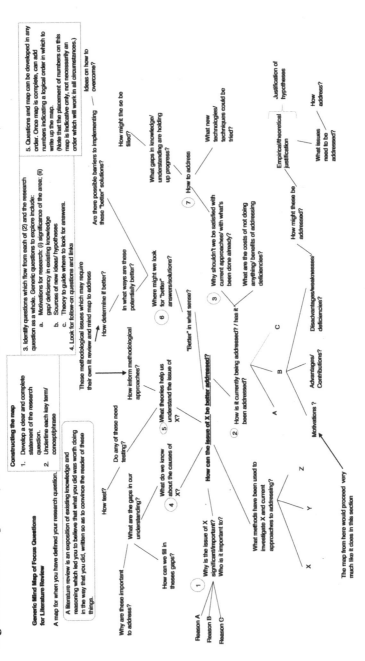

"Every Semester Needs a Plan"

Finally, we turn to the writing process itself. Many novice and advanced scholarly writers face the challenge of setting specific, realistic, and tangible goals that can be obtainable within a specific amount of time. As the National Center for Faculty Development & Diversity teaches its members, "Every semester, or summer, needs a plan" to set participating writers up for success (https://www.facultydiversity.org/webinars/semesterplan18). Figure 8.2 provides an example format of a semester plan that writers can use to plan for the completion of multiple projects and address various life demands over a specific amount of time.

Writers will often say they will complete a specific project by a certain time without recognizing that time is finite and fleeting, and that there are multiple demands on one's time. Creating a semester or summer plan for writing and other responsibilities can be a clear aid for realistic planning. A plan like this can also help in determining whether to take on additional responsibilities and tasks. Laying out realistic plans and goals can set up a writer for successfully meeting goals, and developing self-efficacy in writing.

Conclusion

The development of strong scholarly writing skills and voice requires thoughtful pedagogy, communities of accountability, and habits for effective project management. Assuming that new students arrive in graduate school with scholarly writing skills and knowledge of how to write a literature review does a disservice to students and our academic fields. We may presume that graduate students possess some raw writing talents when they arrive in our classrooms, but they will require guidance, mentorship, and support. Additionally, as graduate student demographics continue to diversify by race, economic class, and other identities, it is important to also recognize that some talented students with marginalized identities may have faced barriers to accessing writing development support and mentorship (McCoy et al., 2015), thus emphasizing the need for graduate educators to be thoughtful in supporting holistic writing pedagogies.

In this chapter, we discussed the need to intentionally cultivate graduate student writing skills, voice, and good habits, by centering the leadership, insights, and perspectives of recent graduate students who identify as Latina students who worked full-time in professional positions while enrolled in a hybrid-online PhD program. In order to effectively support students to meaningfully engage in an iterative and developmental writing process, we

Figure 8.2. Sample semester plan—created by OiYan Poon.

WEEK	TRAVEL/CONF	PERSONAL	RER R&R	Op-Ed	Critical Leadership Ch
W0: 09/01–09/05		3x workout; 4x 10k steps	Outline matrix and delegate tasks for R&R; begin revising theoretical section		
W1: 09/8–09/12		3x workout; 4x 10k steps; dim sum w/Aurora, Connie, and Mei	Finish revising theoretical framework section; address reviewer 2's comments re: critiques		
W2: 09/15–09/19	NACAC (Indy)	3x workout; 4x 10k steps	Expand on how invoking MMM can reinforce (see Paul Willis' work) intro and throughout; be explicit about CRT in Introduction		Identify objectives (Dian)
W3: 09/22–09/26	Advancing justice (DC)	3x workout; 4x 10k steps	Improve middleman minority definition	Outline key arguments; identify outlet	Outline chapter (Dian)
W4: 09/29–10/03	Lisa's wedding	3x workout; 4x 10k steps	Revise conclusion, better integrate Lakoff's concepts into manuscript	1st draft to ARC	

(Continued)

Figure 8.2. (*Continued*)

WEEK	TRAVEL/CONF	PERSONAL	RER R&R	Op-Ed	Critical Leadership Ch
W5: 10/06–10/10		3x workout; 4x 10k steps	Review/edit full manuscript		1st draft of chapter
W6: 10/13–10/17		3x workout; 4x 10k steps	Check for "one voice"	Send to editor	Review/revise chapter
W7: 10/20–10/24		3x workout; 4x 10k steps			
W8: 10/27–10/31		3x workout; 4x 10k steps			
W9: 11/03–11/07	NASPA IV-E (Columbus)	3x workout; 4x 10k steps			Finalize draft and send to John/Natasha
W10: 11/10–11/14		3x workout; 4x 10k steps	Finalize and resubmit		
W11: 11/17–11/21	ASHE (DC)	3x workout; 4x 10k steps			

presented several introductory tools for teaching and learning writing skills and habits in graduate education. The primary takeaway from this chapter is to encourage more investment of time and energy into developing skills and habits to foster the formation of a scholarly identity.

References

Aitchison, C. (2009). Writing groups for doctoral education. *Studies in Higher Education, 34*(8), 905–916. https://doi.org/10.1080/03075070902785580

Allen, J. E. (2019). *The productive graduate student writer: How to manage your time, process, and energy to write your research proposal, thesis, and dissertation and get published.* Stylus.

Boote, D. N., & Beile, P. (2005). Scholars before researchers: On the centrality of the dissertation literature review in research preparation. *Educational Researcher, 34*(6), 3–15. https://doi.org/10.3102/0013189x034006003

Brunsma, D. L., Embrick, D. G., & Shin, J. H. (2016). Graduate Students of Color: Race, racism, and mentoring in the White waters of academia. *Sociology of Race and Ethnicity, 3*(1), 1–13. https://doi.org/10.1177/2332649216681565

Can, G., & Walker, A. (2010). A model for doctoral students' perceptions and attitudes toward written feedback for academic writing. *Research in Higher Education, 52*(5), 508–536. https://doi.org/10.1007/s11162-010-9204-1

Cotterall, S. (2011). Doctoral students writing: Where's the pedagogy? *Teaching in Higher Education, 16*(4), 413–425. https://doi.org/10.1080/13562517.2011.560381

Freire, P. (2000). *Pedagogy of the oppressed.* Continuum.

Griffin, K. A., Pérez, D., II, Holmes, A. P. E., & Mayo, C. E. P. (2010). Investing in the future: The importance of faculty mentoring in the development of students of color in STEM. *New Directions for Institutional Research, 148*, 95–103. https://doi.org/10.1002/ir.365

hooks, b. (1990). *Yearning: Race, gender, and cultural politics.* Routledge.

hooks, b. (2003). *Teaching community: A pedagogy of hope.* Routledge.

Larson, J. B., Nguyen, D. J., Opoczynski, R., & Vizvary, G. (2019). Designing a professional development group for leader-learners enrolled in graduate education. *Journal of Leadership Studies, 13*(2), 73–76. https://doi.org/10.1002/jls.21644

Lee, A., & Kamler, B. (2008). Bringing pedagogy to doctoral publishing. *Teaching in Higher Education, 13*(5), 511–523. https://doi.org/10.1080/13562510802334723

Luedke, C. L., Collom, G. D., McCoy, D. L., Lee-Johnson, J., & Winkle-Wagner, R. (2019). Connecting identity with research: Socializing Students of Color towards seeing themselves as scholars. *The Review of Higher Education, 42*(4), 1527–1547. https://doi.org/10.1353/rhe.2019.0074

Maher, M. A., Feldon, D. F., Timmerman, B. E., & Chao, J. (2014). Faculty perceptions of common challenges encountered by novice doctoral writers. *Higher*

Education Research and Development, 33(4), 699–711. https://doi.org/10.1080/07294360.2013.863850

McAlpine, L. (2012). Shining a light on doctoral reading: Implications for doctoral identities and pedagogies. *Innovations in Education and Teaching International, 49*(4), 351–361. https://doi.org/10.1080/14703297.2012.728875

McCoy, D. L., & Winkle-Wagner, R. (2015). Bridging the divide: Developing a scholarly habitus for aspiring graduate students through summer bridge programs participation. *Journal of College Student Development, 56*(5), 423–439. https://doi.org/10.1353/csd.2015.0054

McCoy, D. L., Winkle-Wagner, R., & Luedke, C. L. (2015). Colorblind mentoring? Exploring White faculty mentoring of Students of Color. *Journal of Diversity in Higher Education, 8*(4), 225–242. https://doi.org/10.1037/a0038676

Nguyen, D. J., Mathuews, K., Herron, A., Troyer, R., Graman, Z., Goode, W. A., Schultz, A., Tackett, K., & Moss, M. (2019). Learning to become a scholar-practitioner through research experiences. *Journal of Student Affairs Research and Practice, 56*(4), 365–378. https://doi.org/10.1080/19496591.2019.1611591

Odena, O., & Burgess, H. (2017). How doctoral students and graduates describe facilitating experiences and strategies for their thesis writing learning process: A qualitative approach. *Studies in Higher Education, 42*(3), 572–590. https://doi.org/10.1080/03075079.2015.1063598

Olson, K., & Clark, C. M. (2009). A signature pedagogy in doctoral education: The leader–scholar community. *Educational Researcher, 38*(3), 216–221. https://doi.org/10.3102/0013189x09334207

Onwuegbuzie, A. J., Leech, N. L., & Collins, K. M. T. (2011). Innovative qualitative data collection techniques for conducting literature reviews/research syntheses. In M. Williams & W. P. Vogt (Eds.), *The SAGE Handbook of Innovation in Social Research Methods* (pp. 182–204). SAGE Publications. https://doi.org/10.4135/9781446268261.n13

Poon, O., Sihite, E., Turman, N., Griffin, B., & Bishundat, D. (2017). For Women of Color who have considered critical social theories: When the dominant narrative is no longer enough. In K. T. Edwards & M. d. G. Davidson (Eds.), *College curriculum at the crossroads: Women of color reflect and resist*. Routledge. https://doi.org/10.4324/9781315194752-6

Stevens, D. D. (2018). *Write more, publish more, stress less! Five key principles for a creative and sustainable scholarly practice*. Stylus.

Swadener, B. B., Peters, L., & Eversman, K. A. (2015). Enacting feminist alliance principles in a doctoral writing support group. In C. S. Turner (Ed.), *Mentoring as Transformative Practice: Supporting Student and Faculty Diversity* (New Directions for Higher Education, vol. 2015, no. 171, pp. 97–106). Wiley. https://doi.org/10.1002/he.20146

Sword, H. (2012). *Stylish academic writing*. Harvard University Press.

Twale, D. J., Weidman, J. C., & Bethea, K. (2016). Conceptualizing socialization of graduate students of color: Revisiting the Weidman-Twale-Stein framework. *Western Journal of Black Studies, 40*(2), 80–94. https://www.proquest.com/openview/fcf2a3aa2a218ddec8e66eac8714d888/1.pdf/advanced

9

PARTICIPATING IN PROFESSIONAL ASSOCIATIONS

Kim Nehls

For the past decade, I have had the pleasure of serving as executive director of the Association for the Study of Higher Education (ASHE). ASHE is a nonprofit organization that began in 1976 to function as a scholarly society for individuals engaged in research about colleges and universities. The primary mission of ASHE is to foster scholarly inquiry for the purpose of increasing knowledge about higher education. ASHE promotes collaboration among its members and others engaged in the study of higher education through research, conferences, and publications, including its highly regarded academic journal. During my time with ASHE, I grew to appreciate the role that professional associations occupy in higher education. As Bickel (2007) wrote, "Professional societies form a living matrix where minds meet and engage and where trusted colleagues pool their knowledge, helping each other to glimpse and plumb larger forces at work, to see connections among events, and to imagine the future" (p. 91).

Professional associations and societies have deep roots in higher education going back to the 17th century. The Royal Society of London, originating in 1660, claims to be the oldest learned society (Jorgensen, 2017). Although 3 centuries separate the creation of The Royal Society and my association, the missions of both organizations are surprisingly similar: "The Royal Society now has a significant role in supporting and disseminating [research] through policy work, journals, scientific meetings, events, worldwide partnerships, grants and awards" (Jorgensen, 2017, p. S1). Many scholarly societies and professional associations in higher education would tout those same goals regardless of the subject matter or discipline. Professional associations are key sites of socialization for graduate students to learn about important trends and discussions and set future directions within a discipline. Studies examining graduate student attrition and persistence have identified several factors that positively impact retention including better academic integration (e.g., Golde, 2000, 2010; Lovitts, 2001), and getting involved in professional associations is one way to develop increased academic integration into the discipline. With these goals in mind, the purpose of this chapter is to highlight the importance of professional associations for graduate students, the benefits and challenges of participation, and the ways associations support graduate students through grants, fellowships, and other professional opportunities.

Work of Professional Associations

Knoke (1986) defined an association as "a formally organized named group, most of whose members—whether persons or organizations—are not financially recompensed for their participation" (p. 2), and that definition will suffice for the benefit of this chapter. Knoke's definition recognizes the significant participation of association members to be a successful operation. Participation is evident through paid membership dues and conference fees, but also in significant volunteer hours spent writing and reviewing conference proposals, presenting research at conferences, and serving on boards and committees. Associations are only as strong as its members' contributions, and as members of professional associations, graduate students engage in the same activities and contributions as other members. I would argue that graduate students' volunteerism is not only a welcome, but necessary, contribution to the lifeblood of a growing and thriving organization.

Noordegraaf (2011) extensively studied the structures and management of organizations and recommended that "associations have to rely upon certain mechanisms for structuring work, legitimating occupational spaces, and regulating work practices" (p. 439). These mechanisms shape the work of associations. The three mechanisms as defined by Noordegraaf are "*cognitive mechanisms:* education, training, knowledge, skills, conferences, books, journals and magazines; *normative mechanisms:* membership criteria, selection criteria, entry barriers, codes of conduct, sanctions and discipline; and *symbolic mechanisms:* rites of passage, stories, heroes, codes of ethics, service ideals and missions" (p. 470). In doing these three things that are cognitive, normative, and symbolic, professional associations gain legitimacy within their fields, while socializing their members to what the association values.

But what constitutes the "professional" in professional associations? Again, I turn to the literature for reference regarding who or what is a professional: "Being 'professional' is an honorific status which arises out of interaction among specific audiences. Occupational label is no necessary indicator of professional status; the status of people of particular occupational titles can vary markedly in different formal organizations" (Bucher & Stelling, 1969, p. 4). The notion of occupational titles varying in formal organizations is important, especially as it relates to graduate students' involvement. The lack of a "Dr." in front of a name or a "PhD" to follow should not preclude involvement in professional organizations. Bucher and Stelling (1969) asserted that professionals (in the sense of professional associations) make claims to have or are developing competence in an area. I suggest that we are all learning and developing new ideas and research, and thus, are all professionals developing competence in our areas.

Most professional associations develop competence by disseminating research at conferences and in scholarly publications, as well as through policy work, grants, awards, newsletters, and other types of communications. Over the past few years, social media, blogs, and webinars have become popular distribution mediums for research. Individual scholars frequently share their recent publications via Twitter and book publishers are highlighting author videos and blogs on their websites. ASHE started offering conference-themed webinars featuring prominent higher education professionals in the months leading up to an annual conference. Lately, graduate students within ASHE have been communicating via social media, especially Facebook and Twitter, and an ASHE Grads Blog features great content like "Combating burnout after candidacy: How to take care of yourself after a major accomplishment" by University of Georgia's Raven Cokley. This blog post is just one example of how graduate students can engage with other graduate students beyond their own institution when they get involved in a professional association. As technology continues to evolve, I anticipate that we will continue to engage in new ways of disseminating research and building connections throughout the world via our professional associations. To be sure, graduate students will be engaged in and even leading those endeavors.

Benefits for Graduate Students Participating in Organizations

Some of the greatest benefits of joining professional associations as a graduate student include expanding your network, rejuvenation, fostering new skills, and getting engaged in issues that are important to you. Paramount among these is expanding your network. In fact, I was asked to write this chapter thanks to a connection I had with an ASHE graduate student representative. Because we work at institutions that are 3,000 miles away, we likely would not have developed a long-lasting connection without our mutual involvement in ASHE.

Involvement in professional organizations can foster relationships with peers, practitioners, and more senior scholars that may impact your future career whether in academia or beyond. Several graduate students in ASHE expanded their scope of job opportunities by working outside of higher education for other scholarly associations, think tanks, private foundations, research entities in governmental organizations, and in a multitude of practitioner and industry roles. Many association conferences have specific programming and content for graduate students, including sessions on exploring jobs beyond the ivory tower. The new friend you meet at a graduate luncheon might be a future writing collaborator. The faculty member you meet at an evening reception might write your external letter for tenure one day or invite you to serve on a panel at a future event. A peer who laughs at the same joke in a conference session might one day send you a job opening for the perfect practitioner role. Therefore, while the networking you are doing at conferences today may not benefit you today or tomorrow, it could benefit you in the long run. As a result, it is important not to overlook future opportunities with an emerging connection. Claire Kamp Dush (2016), a professor at Ohio State University, also extols networking at professional organization conferences as a place to meet future employers: "When you are on the job market, you can set up meetings at the conference with search committee members. This can often tell you a lot about the position" (p. 1). Whether the position is for a role in student affairs or fundraising, a postdoc, faculty line, adjunct teaching, or even for a job outside of the academy, the advice for meeting search committee members at an association conference is a great one. Do not underestimate the benefits of meeting people face-to-face and gauging potential future colleagues. Additionally, ideas, values, skills, and latest trends are communicated at conferences. As part of socialization, professional associations signal what can be important or provide a guiding light for shaping practice or methodological expertise.

Professional associations' conferences and events are also a good opportunity for rejuvenation. It is easy to get bogged down with the daily tasks of being a graduate student—classes, writing, research projects, and expectations for teaching all while juggling work, family, and typically low pay; however, going to conferences and participating in association events are important socialization events (Duran & Allen, 2020; Gardner & Barnes, 2007; Larson et al., 2019; Nguyen & Rowe, 2021) . Even if meetings are online, these events can provide a feeling of connectedness, togetherness, and encouragement. It is almost a relief when you hear that someone else is struggling with the same methodological issue or is frustrated with an absent committee member. It is an instant connection when you chat about your graduate assistantship being just as demanding as the one at another institution or program. The feeling of solidarity and an extra push to continue is worthwhile. Do not underestimate the value of also seeing people like you at professional conferences who have already attained graduate degrees and goals. It shows you what is possible. Particularly noteworthy, "within professional societies, a generative and upbeat mood usually predominates. Individuals come for and find new sources of energy, ideas, motivation" (Bickel, 2007, p. 91). After a few years of attending conferences and meetings, professional associations can honestly feel like a happy reunion of old friends.

Professional associations can also provide opportunities to foster new skills in ways that other aspects of graduate work cannot. For example, one of the graduate student members of ASHE, Candace Hall of Washington University of St. Louis, was asked to use her graphic design skills to create some marketing materials for two recent ASHE conferences. Her work was timely, relevant, colorful, and earned her a free membership and conference registration. But she was also engaging with scholars in a creative way that built upon her skill set in unique ways outside of traditional scholarly pursuits. Candace's talents have created "super fans" in the ASHE leadership. Even if you do not have graphic design skills like the newly minted Dr. Hall, you can still learn new skills that are beneficial to organizations such as how to manage a webinar, how to set up a conference app, and how to introduce and manage timing of a conference symposium. Other growth opportunities include strategic planning, communication, project management, and adaptability (Pearson, 2019). The possibilities of involvement are endless, and fostering new skills like these can both build networks and be applicable to future job opportunities in and out of academia.

Another benefit of professional associations for graduate students is getting involved with issues that are important to you. Several constituency groups and special interest groups exist within subcultures of larger professional associations, and these smaller advocacy groups can be the perfect outlet for graduate student engagement. For example, the American Psychological Association (APA) has 54 divisions, and among a variety of subjects is the Society for Military Psychology (APA Division 19) which focuses on "providing mental health services, teaching, consulting, work with Congressional committees, and advising senior military commands" among other research endeavors (see https://www.apa.org/about/division/div19). Regardless of your interests or advocacy work, you can find outreach examples like these in many associations. In a 2012 article from *Inside Higher Ed*, then-doctoral student Terry Brock wrote about getting involved in discipline-specific activities. Brock wrote, "My professional organization [Society for

Historical Archaeology] has multiple subcommittees that are for and led by students. . . . Similarly, graduate students can be members of regular committees, participate in workshops, host roundtables at conferences, or volunteer as part of the conference organizing committee" (Brock, 2012, p. 1). If it is not obvious how to get involved as a graduate student, then contact committee chairs or the executive director to ask how to foray into the association.

Austin and McDaniels (2006) posited that graduate students' involvement may be viewed as "a dialectical process, through which newcomers bring perspectives, values, and ideas that interact with the expectations within the organization" (p. 401). Graduate students can and do bring new perspectives to an established organization. Students can start learning about professional associations now and look for opportunities for involvement for a lifetime of benefits. So, while assimilating in professional associations, you are also building your network, feeling rejuvenated, fostering new skills, better understanding the values and trends of your field, and getting engaged in issues important to you.

Challenges for Graduate Students Participating in Organizations

When I attended my first ASHE conference in 2005, I knew two people in a sea of a thousand. At the time, I was a graduate student from a small higher education program, and it felt very overwhelming without the big cohorts from other universities that were represented at the conference. Everyone else seemed to know each other and were giving hugs and handshakes aplenty. Not being part of that "in crowd" felt exclusionary and tiresome when trying to make inroads. It is possible that professional associations can seem close-knit and even distrustful of outsiders; often, associations can seem like difficult communities to "really" join even after paying membership dues. My suggestion is to seek out additional graduate students and others doing similar kinds of work and research. Attend sessions that coincide with your personal and professional interests so you can contribute to the conversation. Many associations have dedicated graduate student social events and online networking platforms, like a Facebook group or Twitter hashtag, which can help create contacts. Two of my friends, who are now in their 50s and have coauthored several books together, met while attending a Graduate Student Public Policy Seminar in the early 1990s. You truly never know where grad connections might lead.

However, another challenge of participation in professional associations is the time involved. Most individuals who work for an organization are volunteers; thus, involvement is rarely compensated. It is possible to earn a free membership or conference registration for some contributions, but weigh your volunteer work against other graduate student duties. Perhaps your time may be better spent writing an article for publication or working in a research lab or industry internship for pay. Brock (2012) indicated,

> I consider a number of elements when I weigh the time I dedicate to my society against my graduate work: Am I making a difference in my field and organization? Is my work being valued by my peers? Is my service resulting in building a sizable and valuable network within my profession? Is it resulting in new opportunities to expand my interests? Is it having a noticeable effect on my production as a grad student? If I don't feel as if my involvement is helping both my career and my organization in the amount of time I've allotted for it, then I need to reevaluate my involvement. (p.1)

Another challenging aspect of involvement is the cost. Not only are you rarely paid for your work, but you are usually paying the organization for membership and conference attendance. Graduate students are rarely flush with funds to join several associations and attend all their conferences, especially when conferences require travel across the country or overseas. Although professional associations usually have discounted membership and registration fees for grad students, the cost of conferences is still astronomical with said fees, flights, hotel, meals, and more if you need to print a poster or create handouts. Students should be judicious when joining organizations to determine which ones could have the greatest returns on investment such as finding the greatest networks or having opportunities to earn awards, grants, or scholarships. Find your fit. It is better to be involved in one or two worthwhile organizations than simply a member of a dozen. The following are some examples of support that associations provide to graduate students. Before joining an organization, you should find out if and how your association is building the future of the profession.

Examples of Graduate Student Outreach Through Professional Associations

This list is by no means meant to be exhaustive of organizational opportunities; it simply offers some examples of ways that organizations support graduate students. The approaches for graduate student assistance vary widely within professional associations.

- The American Mathematics Association's website (ams.org) indicates that "meetings are an important part of any young mathematical scientist's professional development. Listening to talks, meeting active researchers, connecting with old friends, learning about professional issues and resources, and making new professional connections are building blocks of the early career" (http://www.ams.org/programs/travel-grants/grad-students/emp-student-JMM). Therefore, AMS offers $250 graduate student travel grants to regional meetings and $500 to its national conference. Graduate students can apply for these travel grants at any time.

- The American Association of Hispanics in Higher Education (AAHHE) honors selective graduate student fellowships following an application process. Graduate student fellows are chosen from a variety of disciplines and institutions to represent the organization. Part of the fellow commitment entails sharing a research project among members of the AAHHE community with the goal of receiving critical and constructive feedback for a work in progress including dissertation work. Earning a prestigious fellowship and garnering useful feedback on research is a win-win situation. Learn more about the AAHHE Graduate Student fellowship at https://www.aahhe.org/Programs/GradFellows.aspx.

- Geological Society of America (GSA) awarded a remarkable $778,594 to 381 graduate students in 2018 for research projects. The average grad research grant amounted to $2,044 with the intention to provide partial support of master's and doctoral thesis research in the geological sciences for graduate students enrolled in universities in the United States, Canada, Mexico, and Central America. (https://www.geosociety.org/GSA/Education_Careers/Grants_Scholarships/Research_Grants/GSA/grants/gradgrants.aspx).

One more recommendation is to get involved in professional associations specifically created for graduate students. At University of Texas at Dallas, Robert Pearson, the director of professional development for the UTD Office of Graduate Education, recommended getting involved in your own campus's graduate student associations. He wrote,

Ever since the Graduate Student Assembly was established at the university one year ago, I have marveled at the impactful work their student leaders have accomplished for their fellow graduate students. I have especially admired the leadership experience that those involved have gained through their participation. These remarkable individuals have begun building a strong sense of community among graduate students, and they have even organized very popular career, professional, academic and social events based on input from their own members. (Pearson, 2012, p. 1)

At the University of Nevada-Las Vegas (UNLV), we have the Graduate and Professional Student Association (GPSA) and all graduate students at the university are automatically included in the organization as part of their student enrollment and fees regardless of academic discipline. The goal of UNLV's GPSA is to promote and represent the interests of graduate and professional students, and each department or discipline on campus elects a GPSA representative. The representatives' commitments are not significant unless they want them to be. For example, the GPSA selected a representative to serve campus-wide on a presidential search committee. Grad students can seek out additional leadership roles and grant opportunities within GPSA, and your institution may have a similar type of organization for involvement, socializing, and activism on campus.

Speaking of campus, the financial support provided by institutions, departments, and programs varies greatly for graduate students' involvement in professional associations. For example, the marketing department at your institution may cover all the costs of 30 MBA students to participate in American Marketing Association case study competitions at AMA conferences, while another program may only reimburse registration for two doc students at a conference—and only then if they are presenting research. No consistency among institutional support appears to exist. Ask your program coordinators and department chairs for clarification of financial support if not obvious. Pockets of money may be reserved specifically for graduate students or travel funds from faculty could be donated to students. In my former department, the chair rewarded faculty who attended graduation ceremonies with $200 to bestow upon the grad student of their choice to attend a conference or professional development opportunity.

Support can exist in many forms. Of course, financial recompense is always welcome for graduate students—especially in the form of professional association membership and conference fees. However, institutions, departments, and programs would be remiss not to encourage graduate student involvement in professional organizations through a variety of means. Some examples that I have seen include departments organizing brown bag luncheons for grad students to watch professional organization webinars in a classroom together. Programs have also coordinated practice runs of conference presentations by graduate students prior to big association meetings. Institutions may hold poster sessions on campus to highlight the good work that graduate students are doing within their own organizations far and wide from chemistry to engineering to education. Also, I personally have delivered dozens of presentations on campus about how to submit a proposal to a conference. Indeed, this varies from field to field, but this first hurdle of submitting a conference proposal can be a tremendous feat for a graduate student who has never attended a higher education conference. Taking the first step to write and submit a conference proposal may be an initial gateway into a professional organization, and departments and programs can provide examples of past successes to emulate. With institutional, departmental, and/or programmatic support, graduate students can flourish in professional associations and bring prestige and information back to the institution.

Social Capital From Involvement in Professional Associations

As a final note, I want to mention the role of social capital in professional associations. Social capital is sometimes referred to as "who you know" as in "it's not what you know, it is who you know." Think about all the people that you have met or potentially could meet through professional associations; they are now part of your network which increases your social capital. Pierre Bourdieu (1986) conceptualized the theory of social capital, in which he defined the concept as the "aggregate of the actual or potential resources which are linked to the possession of a durable network of more or less institutionalized relationships of mutual acquaintance and recognitions" (p. 248). Bourdieu's approach focused on links between networks and positive individual outcomes, particularly in the context of professional advancement and status for economic benefit. More recently, theorists have moved away from an economic-only benefit to note positive individual advantages more broadly defined thanks to interconnected networks. The network of relationships is what makes for social capital, and by getting involved in professional associations, individuals may increase their social capital. Psychologists Pooley et al. (2005) refer to social capital (SC) as the "glue" in associations. They wrote

> In layman's terms, when we talk about SC, we contend that we are referring to the "glue" that holds groups of individuals together in communities. The "glue" refers to the connections between individuals and groups, which are the relationships, networks and competencies that characterize social capital. Without this "glue," we are merely a collection of individuals unconnected to one another. Therefore, from a psychological viewpoint in order to develop SC, we are trying to optimize the strength of the connections between individuals. (p. 73)

When you are part of a professional organization, you are part of the "glue" and can therefore become "stickier" by increased participation and involvement. Consider how sticky you want to be in an organization.

The interaction of "glue" creates collective assets and characteristics that enhance the effectiveness of associations (Ortega, 2011). When members have social capital and act in concert around shared goals, the result can be a greater social impact.

Conclusion

Here is a secret about involvement in professional associations: Very few people email association leadership to ask for volunteer opportunities. Most graduate students dread new or additional volunteer roles since they are understandably stretched thin. If you feel like you can make a position contribution by emailing the executive director or a conference chair an offer of help, you set yourself apart from other students in your field. If you are interested in joining a committee, or providing insights to a recent issue, or volunteering at the registration desk when a conference is in your hometown or a city you really want to visit, then you will be offering help that is usually very welcomed. The key is to do the work well and ensure your participation is a success. Offering to help and then not following through on the job is worse than not offering at all. Consider all your commitments and then see where you can make the biggest impact for future results.

This chapter highlighted the importance of professional associations for graduate students, the benefits and challenges of participation, and some ways that associations and institutions are supporting graduate students. Professional associations are key sites of socialization for graduate students to learn about important trends and discussions and set future directions for the field. The importance of involvement cannot be overlooked, but it must be tempered against other commitments and grad student responsibilities. Lastly, professional preparation should not stop once the degree is earned. A case for continuing professional education has been made for many years, with a mounting urgency and vigor (Janosik et al., 2006). Even after your degree is earned, you should continue involvement in professional organizations to build a greater network and learn new skills. And consider the possibilities of now creating opportunities for graduate students to follow.

References

Austin, A. E., & McDaniels, M. (2006). Preparing the professoriate of the future: Graduate student socialization for faculty roles. In J. C. Smart (Ed.), *Higher Education: Handbook of theory and research* (21st ed., pp. 397–456). Kluwer Academic Publishers. https://doi.org/10.1007/1-4020-4512-3_8

Bickel, J. (2007). The role of professional societies in career development in academic medicine. *Academic Psychiatry, 31*(2), 91. https://doi.org/10.1176/appi.ap.31.2.91

Bourdieu, P. (1986). The forms of social capital. In J. Richardson (Ed.), *Handbook of theory and research for the sociology of education* (pp. 241–258). Greenwood.

Brock, T. (2012, April 8). Professional service: Getting involved in your discipline. *Inside Higher Ed.* https://www.insidehighered.com/blogs/gradhacker/professional-service-getting-involved-your-discipline

Bucher, R., & Stelling, J. (1969). Characteristics of professional organizations. *Journal of Health and Social Behavior, 10*(1), 3–15. https://doi.org/10.2307/2948501

Duran, A., & Allen, E. (2020). Exploring how professional associations socialize student affairs graduate students and new professionals. *Journal of Student Affairs Research and Practice, 57*(2), 132–147. https://doi.org/10.1080/19496591.2019.1625779

Dush, C. K. (2016, September 7). Professional organizations: Why you should join them, how to get the most out of their meetings, and how to avoid going broke doing so. *The Ohio State University HDFS.* https://u.osu.edu/adventuresinhdfs/2016/09/07/professional-organizations/

Gardner, S. K., & Barnes, B. J. (2007). Graduate student involvement: Socialization for the professional role. *Journal of College Student Development, 48*(4), 369–387. https://doi.org/10.1353/csd.2007.0036

Golde, C. M. (2000). Should I stay or should I go? Student descriptions of the doctoral attrition process. *Review of Higher Education, 23*(2), 199–227. https://doi.org/10.1353/rhe.2000.0004

Golde, C. M. (2010). Entering different worlds: Socialization into disciplinary communities. In S. K. Gardner & P. Mendoza (Eds.), *On becoming a scholar: Socialization and development in doctoral education* (pp. 79–95). Stylus.

Janosik, S. M., Carpenter, S., & Creamer, D. G. (2006). Beyond professional preparation programs: The role of professional associations in ensuring a high quality workforce. *College Student Affairs Journal, 25*(2), 228–237.

Jorgensen, A. (2017). The secret life of a learned society. *Landscape Research, 42*(sup1), S1–S4. https://doi.org/10.1080/01426397.2017.1400266

Knoke, D. (1986). Associations and interest groups. *Annual Review of Sociology, 12*(1), 1–21. https://doi.org/10.1146/annurev.so.12.080186.000245

Larson, J. B., Nguyen, D. J., Opoczynski, R., & Vizvary, G. (2019). Designing a professional development group for leader learners enrolled in graduate education. *Journal of Leadership Studies, 13*(2), 73–76. https://doi.org/10.1002/jls.21644

Lovitts, B. E. (2001). *Leaving the ivory tower. The causes and consequences of departure from doctoral study.* Rowman & Littlefield.

McCoy, D. L., Winkle-Wagner, R., & Luedke, C. L. (2015). Colorblind mentoring? Exploring white faculty mentoring of students of color. *Journal of Diversity in Higher Education, 8*(4), 225–242.

Nguyen, D. J., & Rowe, A. K. C. (2021). Developing class consciousness leadership education in graduate and professional schools. In Ardoin S., & Guthrie, K. L. (Eds.), *Leadership Learning Through the Lens of Social Class* (New Directions for Student Leadership, vol. 2021, no. 169, pp. 111–119). Wiley. https://doi.org/10.1002/yd.20427

Noordegraaf, M. (2011). Remaking professionals? How associations and professional education connect professionalism and organizations. *Current Sociology, 59*(4), 465–488. https://doi.org/10.1177/0011392111402716

Ortega, N. (2011). The role of higher education associations in shaping policy that connects immigration to educational opportunity: A social capital framework. *Journal of Hispanic Higher Education, 10*(1), 41–65. https://doi.org/10.1177/1538192710391803

Pearson, R. (2019, April 22). Join your grad student or postdoc association. *Inside Higher Ed.* https://www.insidehighered.com/advice/2019/04/22/professional-development-benefits-joining-graduate-student-or-postdoc-association.

Pooley, J. A., Cohen, L., & Pike, L. T. (2005). Can sense of community inform social capital? *The Social Science Journal, 42*(1), 71–79. https://doi.org/10.1016/j.socij.2004.11.006

IO

ENGAGING IN INTERNATIONAL EDUCATION OPPORTUNITIES

Meggan Madden and Jennifer Donaghue

This chapter discusses ways in which administrators and faculty can encourage and support graduate students who wish to pursue international experiences as part of their program of study. There are many different ways in which an international experience can be pursued by master's and/or doctoral students, such as participating in a short-term faculty-led study abroad program, studying on a graduate student exchange, engaging in international field research, attending conferences abroad, or volunteering in an international service-learning program. This chapter is written primarily for graduate students in the United States or Canada and applies equally to international graduate students studying in these contexts.

The chapter starts by closely examining the unique challenges and opportunities that graduate students face when engaging with international study and/or research. There are many challenges, such as the time limitations around working full-time while attending graduate school full-time. Many of these challenges can be turned into opportunities for universities to support international experiences at the graduate level, such as using employee benefits (vacation time, sabbaticals, academic leave, or tuition remission, for example) to participate in a short-term study abroad programs.

After presenting a clear idea of the opportunities and challenges, strategies and good practices are highlighted for administrators and faculty to best support graduate students to successfully navigate international experiences. These strategies include outlining how funding works for short-term study abroad programs, offering workshops on how to seek out international opportunities during graduate school, and training academic advisors on how to navigate the institutional processes necessary to study abroad (so that students aren't left on their own to figure it out!).

Lastly, a road map will sketch steps graduate students can take to pursue international opportunities. This road map suggests a timeline for when students should begin planning for an international experience and offers advice on which offices students should contact in order to understand university policy related to international education experiences. Finally, tips will be given for how students can make the most of their experiences while abroad.

Unique Challenges and Opportunities for International Study and/or Research

U.S. graduate schools' enrollment of first-time graduate students remained essentially flat in 2017 according to the Council of Graduate Schools (Okahana & Zhou, 2018). Among first-time U.S. citizens and permanent resident graduate students in the fall of 2017, about 23.9% were underrepresented minorities, including American Indian/Alaska Native (0.5%), Black/African American (11.9%), Native Hawaiian/Other Pacific Islander (0.2%), and Hispanic/Latino (11.3%) (Okahana & Zhou, 2018). As graduate student demographics shift, and campuses adapt to increasingly diverse graduate enrollments, higher education must be nimble in responding to student needs beyond the traditional undergraduate experience.

Study abroad is often thought of as a staple activity of internationalization, especially for the elite during their undergraduate experiences. The benefits of study abroad are numerous and noted in the international education literature. Generally, education abroad participants graduate on time, and acquire useful skills such as foreign language acquisition, intercultural competency, and self-efficacy through the study abroad experience (Cubillos & Ilvento, 2013; Dolby, 2007; Luo & Jamieson-Drake, 2015; Posey, 2003). Further, evidence shows that global learning and experiences enhance career competitiveness and opportunities (Farrugia & Sanger, 2017).

The internationalization of education consists of the practices put into place by institutions to adapt to the global academic environment (Altbach & Knight, 2007). By including graduate education into campus internationalization efforts, graduate students are better prepared for the globally competitive marketplace. International academic experiences benefit emerging scholars, especially when conducting research or presenting research abroad. Yet graduate students enter their programs from varying points in their lives, including diversity of age, life experiences, and career stages. This diffuse starting point for graduate study presents challenges for graduate student global mobility, while also offering opportunities for higher education to respond to this need.

Not only is study abroad perceived to be primarily an undergraduate student experience, a perspective that disregards the potential of graduate student contributions to research through international mobility, it is also a fundamentally different experience for graduate students. Jasinski and Davis (2018) highlight how international experiences for graduate students depart from the traditional study abroad experience for undergraduate students, finding that the graduate experience is inherently more independent in nature to reflect the maturity and focus of participants.

Challenges

Whereas undergraduate students may have the luxury of studying abroad for semesters or years at a time, graduate students are typically at different points in their lives on the learning continuum (Dewey, 1933). Indicative of their decision to pursue further education beyond the undergraduate level, graduate students are likely to seek serious research opportunities (e.g., dissertation fieldwork, language acquisition) that indicate a return on investment for the time and financial resources put toward graduate education. In addition, graduate students may have different financial constraints, and career and familial responsibilities germane to their maturity in their life course that make their experience unique (Nguyen, 2016).

Graduate students and undergraduate students alike struggle with finding funding to study abroad. This need for financial support is apparent in the undergraduate study abroad experience as well, yet it becomes even more acute with graduate students. Students who pursue graduate study may arrive already saddled with debt that makes the study abroad experience appear to be an expensive, and potentially an unnecessary, add-on activity.

The age at which researchers begin and complete doctoral studies varies by country and discipline, as well as chosen career path (Ackers & Gill, 2008). Many graduate students cannot afford the cost of a study abroad experience because their financial aid packages or university fellowships are needed for personal or family funds (Avveduto, 2001). Additionally, parenting and familial responsibilities of young children, partners, and family members can present time constraints and financial effects, which becomes a significant factor in the choice to pursue global mobility (Ackers & Gill, 2008).

Many graduate students work simultaneously while studying. For full-time working professionals it may be unrealistic to take time off, use leave, be unpaid, or remove oneself from the career setting to pursue study abroad for long periods of time. In addition to work obligations, very few participants in study abroad have work authorization while abroad, which further constrains income avenues while they are overseas.

Graduate students have considerable onus for preparation and anticipation of their own needs of participation including their academic agenda, while juggling the demands of coursework, familial, professional, and other obligations. Given these challenges, there are many opportunities that surface for higher education leadership and study abroad offices to expand intentionally beyond the traditional undergraduate student experience and reimagine what is possible on the graduate side.

Opportunities

The unique challenges of the graduate student experience present an opportunity for higher education institutions to stretch to accommodate their needs. This stretching includes tailoring international education programs around time duration and financial and familial needs, with a focus on providing academic research opportunities and opening doorways to career opportunities. Indeed, graduate students provide an interesting opportunity to divert from traditional study abroad semester or annual experiences for undergraduate students, and to instead imagine the possibilities of research opportunities and outcomes for graduate students that ultimately raise the profile of the institution.

Opportunities for graduate students to participate in study abroad are not as widely known or utilized by the students. Knight and Madden (2010) found a dearth of research surrounding graduate student mobility and highlighted the missed opportunity for graduate student study abroad participation to grow areas of research and networking unique to the graduate student experience. They called for institutional and national policies to address graduate student mobility separately from the undergraduate experience, highlighting the need for financial support and the potential for short-term study abroad for this group (Knight & Madden, 2010). Interest in graduate student mobility has continued to expand with literature highlighting the unique experiences of graduate students abroad and the potential of the transformational impact on graduate knowledge and skills (Anderson Sathe & Geisler, 2017; DuVivier & Patitu, 2017).

How Institutions Can Support Students With International Engagement Interests

As articulated in the section on challenges and opportunities for graduate students, institutions need to consider the following five points when committing interest and resources to international opportunities for graduate school. The first point is the departmental and institutional leadership support necessary for internationalization efforts, which include support for international conference participation, researcher exchange, or short-term faculty-led programs. The second point is to reconceptualize international education for graduate students, given their work and family commitments. The third point is that funding structures are needed to support graduate-level international experiences, as well as workshops on how graduate students can access these funds. The fourth point is that faculty and advisors need to understand the bureaucratic steps graduate students need to take (the obstacles that get in their way) to successfully engage in an international experience. Lastly, that international education programming for graduate students needs strong career orientations.

Defining Institutional Commitment and Support for Internationalization

Despite the restrictions to international academic mobility for graduate students, there is great potential. Graduate research abroad offers opportunities for groundbreaking, collaborative research, international acclaim, and bragging rights that can increase enrollment prospects, philanthropic giving, and an institution's bottom line. To tap into the potential for graduate level international education, institutions should define their institutional commitment and support for internationalization and education abroad. Institutions that maintain an appreciation for global mobility allow for an easier expansion of resources beyond undergraduate study abroad activity. Leadership must take into consideration the opportunity graduate students present for the institution's increased global footprint.

Reconceptualizing International Education for Graduate Students

Graduate student mobility must be conceptualized in a way that recognizes graduate student needs that vary greatly from the needs of the undergraduate student. Short-term faculty-led exchanges provide the opportunity for shorter stays abroad focused on specific areas of research relevant to graduate student interests. Conferences abroad allow graduate students to expand their knowledge in their chosen field, potentially present their research, and network with their international counterparts. Further, conferences offer the potential for shorter stays abroad that may work better for the graduate student life schedule. Service-learning opportunities allow for briefer stays abroad and potentially the application of practical skills or research relevant to the graduate student experience. Other graduate study abroad opportunities may also be found through governmental exchanges, such as the Fulbright program, which offer in some cases paid funding for research abroad, or shorter stays for administrators. Despite the shorter length, these brief opportunities still present a possible lasting impact on a graduate student's academic and future career opportunities.

New Funding Models for International Graduate Study

Funding structures for international exchange remain a prime challenge. Financial support mechanisms for education abroad for graduate students pale in comparison to undergraduate funding resources. For institutions committed to graduate student mobility, funding must be earmarked by leadership and/or academic departments toward offsetting the associated costs for graduate student abroad experiences. Inspiring a culture within the university or department reiterates the importance of global mobility for graduate students and for the institution that serves as a call to the entire community to assist.

Understanding the Bureaucracy of International Education

The bureaucratic steps required to implement exchange activities that fit graduate student needs for global exchange need to be made transparent and efficient. Faculty who lead programs abroad for graduate student experiences and research need to know and understand how to navigate the institutional bureaucracy of bringing an exchange program to fruition. On a departmental level this includes expectations regarding revenue generation or outflow, longevity of a program from one year to the next, and courses that fit seamlessly into an academic plan. From a broader, institutional perspective, this means agreements around designated funding and staffing for a program, the expectations of the institution around exchanges, credit transfer, and safety while abroad. Additionally, safety abroad is not only about having health insurance. Graduate students who conduct research abroad may choose field sites in countries that are considered by the United States to be "high-risk." This creates a challenge between the value of research in areas of conflict against the institutional charge to oversee student safety while balancing the limits of institutional accountability. Awareness of these issues upfront helps manage expectations from inception.

An integral piece of research often includes approval to conduct research through the Institutional Research Board (IRB). Research opportunities abroad require additional scrutiny for IRB approval. Due to the time-sensitive nature of research opportunities abroad, IRB offices must carefully consider what is required to streamline the efficiency of their processes and what is required for submission as well. This need to streamline presents an opportunity for institutions to examine IRB processes and refine systems to ensure the institution is supporting research abroad, versus serving as a hindrance. In addition, graduate students need training on how to navigate cultural differences that become apparent in the consent process that is expected of research with human subjects.

Not only is awareness of the bureaucratic needs required for faculty who may arrange a short-term abroad program, it is also required for students and their academic advisors. The shorter nature of master's level programs and the prolonged nature of doctoral programs calls for agility in integrating education abroad into curricular requirements. Academic advisors need to know the opportunities and barriers that exist within the institution and be equipped with the advising and coaching skills to ensure graduate international experiences are feasible for their students.

Supporting Career Development Through International Education Opportunities

Career coaches play an additional role in conceptualizing the magnitude of the education abroad experience on career outcomes. Graduate student researchers should be coached on how to communicate effectively the skills they acquired through their opportunities abroad to prospective employers. Workshops for academic and career advisors as well as administrators who work in providing services to students help in creating advanced planning institutionally to ensure graduate students perform research abroad. In addition, career coaches and advisors should be trained in understanding the various international practices for résumés, cover letters, and the hiring process in international contexts.

The hope is that graduate students arrive at the end of their studies having acquired new skills and experiences that allow them to competitively enter the job market. Skills gained through study abroad have a long-term impact on career progression and promotion (Farrugia & Sanger, 2017). While short-term abroad programs do not instill the same benefits as longer term stays abroad, they do help in developing teamwork skills (Farrugia & Sanger, 2017), which serve as a strong talking point with potential employers. Graduate student study abroad opportunities, for even short amounts of time, allow students to leverage their international experiences in different ways with prospective employers. It allows for the acquisition of social capital which opens doors through networks and even in some cases rapport with prospective employers who have shared experiences. It also allows them to showcase their work on a team, and their own research interests and capabilities.

An International Opportunities Road Map

There are several different opportunities for graduate students to internationally engage during their studies, such as studying on a short-term faculty-led study abroad program, volunteering in an international service-learning program, participating in a graduate student exchange, engaging in international field research, or attending conferences abroad. This section will explain each of these different options.

Participating in a Short-Term Faculty-Led Study Abroad Program

Short-term study abroad programs are becoming more popular as alternatives to longer programs. Opportunities for the graduate population are made more easily accessible through short-term abroad programs versus traditional semester or yearlong experiences. Faculty-led experiences for shorter stays, which typically last 1–6 weeks, are not always recurring opportunities due to acquiring necessary funding and administrative support to run the programs.

Short-term programs, including those with a service-learning component, also present a more feasible opportunity for graduate students, allowing shorter durations of time away from commitments at home, a less expensive experience than longer commitments abroad, and an opportunity to give back to the local community (Lightfoot & Lee, 2015). Dirkx et al. (2010) found that graduate student short term abroad experiences differ from undergraduates regarding interpretation of their experiences, with the sense making process of their experiences reflected in a complex relationship between academic goals they create for the experience and their own career goals. Short term abroad programs are often led by faculty members within an academic program, providing a strong correlation for future academic work for graduate student participants, and practical exposure to the field of international education (Witkowsy & Mendez, 2018).

Volunteering in International Service-Learning Programs

Another way to gain international experience in a short timeframe is to participate in an international service-learning program. These programs are often sponsored outside of study abroad offices within experiential learning or service-learning program offices. International service-learning programs are often held during scheduled vacation periods within an institution. International service learning is typically for undergraduate students, yet graduate students can provide support through serving as a program coordinator or manager, which provides extra income or perhaps paid expenses in exchange for program support both before, during, and after the international service-learning experience.

Studying on a Graduate Student Exchange

There are few graduate student exchange opportunities because most study abroad offices that manage exchanges cater to undergraduate students. Graduate student exchanges require significant planning, and often include a lengthy application and selection process that may prolong the completion of coursework. In addition, graduate student exchanges often require students to gain permission from the program faculty to use course equivalencies to fulfill degree requirements, which includes understanding the courses offered by the graduate exchange partner during the timeframe when the student plans to enroll. Being able to obtain the course syllabus is critical so that faculty can approve courses in advance of the exchange. However, if a student is persistent, and has supportive faculty and administrative staff within the university, graduate student exchange can open up significant opportunities for field research and building an international network of scholars.

Engaging in International Field Research

International field research is an excellent way to support aspiring researchers in honing their project management and research skills. Due to the additional costs of international field research, graduate students and faculty members should be aware of funding opportunities that are available for field research. Ideally, a list of resources should be available to graduate students so that they are aware of scholarship and fellowship deadlines and requirements. Given the intensive planning process necessary to conduct research abroad, study abroad offices have the opportunity to develop workshops specific to graduate students who are conducting this type of research. These workshops can discuss the university systems in place that support students should anything happen in-country during the research (e.g., national crisis or health crisis of the student). Workshops can also highlight health and safety websites that graduate students should review to ensure that they are following the laws of the country in which they are conducting research.

Attending Conferences Abroad

In general, attending academic conferences helps socialize graduate students into their field of study and supports the development from student to scholar. Graduate students may present their own work or present the work they conducted as a graduate assistant under the direction of their faculty supervisor. Not only are conferences good for introducing students to the field and understanding the types of conversation and research happening in the field, conferences are also good for networking. Therefore, attending an international conference presents the opportunity to broaden a student's network in the field, which opens up the potential for international research partnerships or job placement.

Funding for international conferences is often available through the same venues as funding for domestic conferences (e.g., departmental or school funds, student union or student activities funds). If participating as a graduate assistant, there may be additional funds from the research project that can support attendance. International health and travel insurance may also be available to graduate students, as university employees. Similar to other international experiences, the study abroad office should be notified of international conference travel, in case something happens in-country during the time of the conference.

Tips for Graduate Students

It's never too early to start! Even before enrolling in graduate school, students can start asking questions about how international study is incorporated into the curriculum of their prospective programs. When financial aid is considered, prospective graduate students can ask about how their potential college or graduate school funds and/or coordinates international opportunities for students, such as researcher exchanges, conference participation, and faculty-led programs. Students should review the types of exchanges (found by reviewing the office of study abroad website) offered by the prospective universities and whether these exchanges are available to graduate students. The community engagement activities of the university also may highlight if international service-learning opportunities are offered.

In the first semester of a graduate program, students should map out their course requirements and consider if in their plan of study there is room for an international experience. After students have carefully considered—and mapped out—how they will complete their course requirements, they should consult with their academic advisor to discuss how much time is needed to properly plan for these opportunities. The academic advisor may also know about upcoming international conferences and how the university funds participation in these conferences.

Once the international opportunities have been identified, students should adopt a project manager mindset, listing all the tasks and deadlines related to these tasks, to clearly understand the "critical path" to obtaining an international education experience. In this process, it is especially important to understand if there are additional university requirements for participating in these activities, such as purchasing international health insurance, registering with the office of study abroad, or determining if tuition credits apply to study abroad courses. Prior to going abroad, students should clearly communicate their plans with their academic advisors and the study abroad office.

In order to make the most of the international experience, graduate students should adequately prepare their family, friends, and work colleagues for the level of communication that is feasible while the student is abroad. This preparation includes helping family understand the time differences and a reasonable timeframe for when the student is available to communicate, knowing where to access the graduate student's health insurance information, should the need arise, and having copies of all vital information (e.g., passport, credit card, health card, visa, etc.) in case needed.

Debriefing with family, friends, and colleagues is important to the learning process, as is journaling and self-reflection. While it may be tempting to not journal—due to limited time constraints in-country—journaling helps students process the intercultural communication issues they will encounter as well as provide a way to document the experience.

Getting enough sleep and exercise is also equally important to well-being. International travel at times can be exhausting. Exercise helps combat jet lag, while getting enough sleep helps students stay alert and aware of their surroundings so that the fog of jet lag does not impede learning (for more tips see Diversity Abroad, 2017).

Upon completion of the international experience, students may wish to ask if they can present their learning with others in the community, either through a brown bag lunch series, in classes, or during an advising group meeting. By sharing experiences of how to navigate the process and what was gained by this extra work, graduate students can cultivate a network of peers that can support other graduate students to pursue international opportunities.

Conclusion

There are many benefits to international education for graduate students, both at the individual, programmatic, institutional, and national levels. International academic mobility for graduate students can raise the profile of a program or institution, as well as build networks for international partnerships that support research on global problems. Through international education graduate students gain valuable cross-cultural communication skills; develop self-sufficiency during the research experience; and increase their prospects for future employment and career success. Although there are many barriers to graduate-level international education, especially considering the need for significant financial and personnel resources to support it, the long-term return on investment for institutions and students includes stronger international ties to the university and student, which increases global reputation both at the individual and institutional levels. This long-term return on investment may eventually lead to international research partnerships and increases in university world-rankings, and cultivate deeper connections with alumni.

References

Ackers, H. L., & Gill, B. (2008). *Moving people and knowledge: Understanding the processes of scientific mobility within an enlarging Europe.* Edward Elgar.

Ackers, L., Gill, B., & Guth, J. (2008). *Doctoral mobility in the social sciences* (Report to the NORFACE ERA-NET). University of Liverpool.

Altbach, P., & Knight, J. (2007). The internationalization of higher education: Motivations and realities. *Journal of Studies in International Education, 11*(3–4), 290–305. https://doi.org/10.1177/1028315307303542

Anderson Sathe, L., & Geisler, C. (2017). The reverberations of a graduate study abroad course in India: Transformational journeys. *Journal of Transformative Education, 15*(1), 16–36. https://doi.org/10.1177/1541344615604230

Avveduto, S. (2001). International mobility of PhDs. In *Innovative People: Mobility of Skilled Personnel in National Innovation Systems* (pp. 229–242). OCDE. http://www.oecd.org/dataoecd/33/49/2096794.pdf

Cubillos, J., & Ilvento, T. (2013). The impact of study abroad of student's self-efficacy perceptions. *Foreign Language Annals, 45*(4), 494–511. https://doi.org/10.1111/j.1944-9720.2013.12002.x

Dewey, J. (1933). *How we think. A restatement of reflective thinking to the educative process.* D. C. Heath Company.

Dirkx, J. M., Spohr, R., Tepper, L., & Tons, S. (2010). Adult learners and short-term study abroad: Formation or transformation? In *Proceedings of the adult education research conference* (pp. 122–127). Sacramento State University.

Diversity Abroad. (2017). *Pre-departure: Wellness.* https://www.powtoon.com/onlinepresentation/e59yFRERT5E/?utm_campaign=copy%2Bshare%2Bby%2Bnon%2Blogged&utm_content=e59yFRERT5E&utm_po=16262471&utm_source=player-page-social-share&utm_medium=SocialShare&mode=movie.

Dolby, N. (2007). Reflections on nation: American undergraduates and education abroad. *Journal of Studies in International Education, 11*(2), 141–156. https://doi.org/10.1177/1028315306291944

DuVivier, R., & Patitu, C. (2017). Effects of study abroad on graduate student dispositions, knowledge and skills. *College Student Affairs Journal, 35*(2), 15–28. https://doi.org/10.1353/csj.2017.0010

Farrugia, C., & Sanger, J. (2017). *Gaining an employment edge: The impact of study abroad on 21st century skills & career prospects in the United States.* Institute of International Education.

Jasinski, L., & Davis, C. W. (2018). Reflections from Brazil: Improving international research experiences for graduate students. *Transformative Dialogues: Teaching & Learning Journal, 11*(3), 1–7. https://kpu.ca/sites/default/files/Transformative%20Dialogues/TD.11.3_Jasinki&Davis_Reflections_from_Brazil.pdf

Knight, J., & Madden, M. (2010). International mobility of Canadian social sciences and humanities doctoral students. *Canadian Journal of Higher Education, 40*(2), 18–34. https://doi.org/10.47678/cjhe.v40i2.1916

Lightfoot, E., & Lee, H. (2015). Professional international service learning as an international service learning opportunity appropriate for graduate or professional students. *International Education Journal: Comparative Perspectives, 14*(1), 32–41. https://openjournals.library.sydney.edu.au/index.php/IEJ/article/view/7246

Luo, J., & Jamieson-Drake, D. (2015). Predictors of study abroad intent, participation, and college outcomes. *Research in Higher Education, 56*(1), 29–56. https://doi.org/10.1007/s11162-014-9338-7

Nguyen, D. J. (2016). *Does money really matter in doctoral education? Exploring the influence of financial considerations on doctoral student socialization* [Doctoral dissertation, Michigan State University].

Okahana, H., & Zhou, E. (2018). *Graduate enrollment and degrees: 2007 to 2017.* Council of Graduate Schools.

Posey, J. T. (2003). *Study abroad: Educational and employment outcomes of participants versus non participants* [Doctoral dissertation, The Florida State University].

Wikowsky, P., & Mendez, S. (2018). Influence of a short-term study abroad experience on professional competencies and career aspirations of graduate students in student affairs. *Journal of College Student Development, 59*(6), 769–775. https://doi.org/10.1353/csd.2018.0073

PART THREE

SUPPORTING GRADUATE STUDENTS BEYOND THE CLASSROOM

11

CONSIDERING GRADUATE
STUDENT MENTAL HEALTH

Carmen M. McCallum, Sarah Kurz, Emily J. Boerman, and Allison Boone

The discourse around mental health in higher education has historically focused on undergraduate students (Benton et al., 2003). However, mental health challenges are just as prevalent among graduate student populations (Hyun et al., 2007). A 2010 UCLA study of doctoral students found that 47% of respondents met the clinical criteria for depression based on self-reported survey responses (The Graduate Assembly, 2014). These findings align with a University of California, Irvine study that found 17% of graduate students reported having a serious mental health disorder (as cited in Willyard, 2012) and an American Psychological Association 2009 survey that reported 87% of psychology graduate students suffer from symptoms of anxiety, depression, and suicidal thoughts. Despite these alarming statistics, few studies have focused on graduate student mental health. Thus, we have limited knowledge of how graduate students with mental health concerns experience graduate school or navigate institutional supports that would best serve this population's needs.

The lack of emphasis on graduate students' mental health is concerning as there is an abundant amount of literature on the negative effect mental health challenges can have on undergraduate students. Research shows that mental health problems can affect undergraduate students' level of energy, optimism, dependability, mental ability, and academic performance (Eisenberg et al., 2007). Mental health concerns for undergraduate students have also been associated with lower grade point averages, dropping out of school, and the source of conflict in residential halls (Eisenberg et al., 2007). If mental health concerns can impede undergraduate students in such a significant way, then it seems reasonable to suspect that mental health concerns also similarly affect graduate students. A few studies have considered mental health challenges for graduate students (Eisenberg et al., 2009; Offstein et al., 2004); however, the range of mental health concerns, the full impact of those concerns on students' graduate school experiences, and the ways in which institutions can support graduate students remains unclear due to the limited amount of research in this area (Hyun et al., 2007; Turner & Berry, 2000). When scholars take an interest in graduate student mental health, they typically report numerical data indicating how many students struggle with mental health challenges (e.g., The Graduate Assembly, 2014). Rarely have scholars explored the lived experiences of graduate students with mental health challenges or inquired what supports they feel would be helpful as they navigate their journey.

This chapter reviews extant literature on graduate students' mental health in order to increase our understanding of how mental health challenges impact their school experiences. We will then illuminate the ways partici-pants in an empirical study suggested colleges and universities could support graduate students with mental health challenges as they navigate their degree programs. As we discuss our findings, we will highlight the applicability of our participants' suggestions and offer our suggestions for future research on graduate student mental health.

Graduate Student Mental Health

There is a growing mental health crisis in graduate education (Hyun et al., 2007; Turner & Berry, 2000). A recent study of 2,279 graduate students from 234 institutions found that over 40% suffered from at least one mental health condition, which is more than six times the rate found in the general population (Pain, 2018). Most graduate students reporting mental health challenges tend to report experiencing anxiety, stress, and depression (Pain, 2018). These findings amplify graduate students' mental health is a con-cern for all students; however, there are certain student populations who are particularly at-risk.

Nontraditional students, including those with families, people with disabilities, and ethnic minorities, are more likely to be impacted by mental health issues (Golberstein et al., 2008; Wexler, 2015). Women are more likely than men to experience increased levels of anxiety and stress (Mahmoud et al., 2015; Simonson et al., 2011; Wupperman & Neumann, 2006). This differential impact has been attributed to microaggressions, lack of belonging, as well as sexual and racial harassment experienced within departments and the larger college community (Burt et al., 2018; Smith et al., 2013; Williams & Williams-Morris, 2010). Clark et al. (2000) note high levels of negative race-related experiences cause students' emotional distress and weaken their sense of belonging in their graduate program. When students lack a sense of belonging, they become less academically engaged leading to difficulties completing their programs. Colleges and universities should be concerned about the cause of graduate student mental health challenges and the ways that institutions can support students as they navigate their programs.

Causes of Mental Health Challenges

A host of issues can be at the root of graduate student mental health disorders (Hyun et al., 2007; Kitzrow, 2003). Some students arrive to graduate school aware that they have mental health concerns that need to be attended to (Giedd et al., 2008). Others develop mental health concerns as a result of being in graduate school (Hyun et al., 2007; Kausar, 2010; Peluso et al., 2011; Rosenthal & Wilson, 2010). Graduate school norms such as isolation, academic work, finances, graduate assistantships, jobs, and funding have been identified as causing stress among students (Grady et. al., 2013; Oswalt & Riddock, 2007). Graduate school is also often emotionally, psychologically, and physically taxing (Djokić & Lounis, 2014). For many very bright students, graduate school can be the first experience with academic challenges that invoke stress, anxiety, and depression (Djokić & Lounis, 2014). The intersectionality of multiple roles, such as parent, student, employee, and so forth, often contributes to this stress (Dill & Henley, 1998). The intersection of student and professional identities and its concomitant stressors is one that many graduate students experience. The constant balancing act of managing both school and career often causes stress and anxiety in ways that potentially interfere with academic retention, persistence, and success.

Most anxiety issues have been reported to be related to negative thinking and poor coping mechanisms (DeVore & Pritchard, 2013; Eisenberg et. al., 2009; Simonson et al., 2011; Wupperman & Neumann, 2006). Current research suggests that cognitive-behavior interactions, negative thoughts associated with important relationships like that of an advisor and graduate student, are at the core of most students' anxiety (Mahmoud et al., 2015). Graduate students rely heavily on their academic advisor, and this relationship plays a large role in student success (Rosenthal & Wilson, 2010). Students with a negative advisor relationship are increasingly susceptible to stress and anxiety compared to other students (Rosenthal & Wilson, 2010). Graduate students in research focused or experimental programs are at a much larger risk of depressive symptoms compared to their peers in clinical/career-oriented programs (Peluso et. al., 2011). The advisor for graduate students in experimental programs seems to have a larger role in their students' research and success, thus the positives and negatives of the relationship greatly influence student academics and outcomes (Peluso et. al., 2011).

The Impact of Mental Health Challenges

Mental health challenges impact graduate students' academic performance, retention, and graduation rates (Eisenberg et al., 2009; Offstein et al., 2004). A study of undergraduate and graduate students with poor mental health found that depression significantly lowered students' GPA and those who experienced panic attacks reported spending more time on academic related tasks but achieving less productivity than students without mental health concerns (Eisenberg et al., 2009). These experiences lead to fatigue, burnout, depression, and guilt over prioritizing graduate school responsibilities over other life priorities (Offstein et al., 2004), resulting in students considering discontinuing their graduate programs (Eisenberg et al., 2009; Turner & Berry, 2000). If unaddressed, it is unlikely that many graduate students will be successful in their academic pursuits.

Mental health concerns such as anxiety and depression have also been found to lead to suicidal behavior (Garcia-Williams et al., 2014; Mahmoud et al., 2015). In a large epidemiological study of over 11,000 graduate students at 70 colleges and universities, researchers found 4% of graduate students seriously considered suicide in the last 12 months (Drum et al., 2009). Of those contemplating suicide, 90% had a specific plan. At Berkeley, 10% of the 3,121 graduate student respondents seriously considered suicide in the previous year and 0.5% had attempted suicide. Those with suicidal ideations are unlikely to pursue help due to the stigma of seeking mental health support, especially in graduate school (Eisenberg et al., 2009; Komiya & Gregory, 2001). The high percentages of graduate students considering suicide and the low probability that students will seek help warrants investigating ways of changing the culture of graduate school and being proactive about servicing students' needs.

Institutional Support

Graduate students rarely seek mental health support from their institution (Eisenberg et al., 2009; Lipson et al., 2016). They fear doing so will expose their vulnerabilities and possibly trigger faculty members, peers, and staff to perceive them as weak, incompetent, or different from other students in the program (Corrigan et al., 2001). This negative perception, they fear, will result in discriminatory behavior, further isolating them on campus (Corrigan et al., 2001; Link et al., 2004). Yet, in a study of mental illness in a university setting, 96% of faculty respondents and 84% of student respondents said mental illnesses are serious disorders that require attention, and that if students seek help, they can succeed in their academic pursuits (Becker et al., 2002). To address this disconnect, institutional leadership must work with students, faculty, and staff to reduce the stigma around mental health challenges and help provide services to those in need of care (Mahmoud et al., 2015; Moffit et al., 2014).

Historically, resources for faculty and graduate students outside of Counseling and Psychological Services (CAPS) has been minimal. Yet, technology is significantly changing the manner in which graduate students can be supported. With the aid of smartphones, text messaging, and apps, online communities have been found to provide meaningful mental health support for graduate students (Wyatt & Oswald, 2013). Students appear to be able to access online communities when support is needed and in a manner that is convenient to them, as university services are often not offered at convenient times. For example, texting with a provider rather than scheduling a meeting has been found as a useful tool by providers to stay in contact with graduate students, resulting in student success (Wyatt & Oswald, 2013). Institutions must look beyond the traditional model of meeting with CAPS staff and consider how graduate students can be supported utilizing technology.

Theoretical Framework

Mattering was used as the theoretical construct in this study (Rosenberg & McCullough, 1981). Mattering is the perception that we are important to others. The concept has seven key components:

1. *Attention*—feeling that oneself and one's actions are noticed by others.
2. *Importance*—feeling of being significant to someone who cares about you.
3. *Dependence*—feeling of being important because others are relying on you.
4. *Ego Extension*—recognizing that someone else is emotionally invested in you and what is happening with or to you impacts them.
5. *Noted Absence*—feeling that you are missed by someone.
6. *Appreciation*—feeling that you and your actions are valued by someone.
7. *Individualization*—being made to feel unique, special, and centered by someone based on how they regard your true self.

These feelings are deemed necessary for people to consider themselves to be healthy, happy, and productive citizens. Most importantly, it is the *perception* of mattering, rather than the actions of others, that matters most.

Those who feel like they do not matter are more likely to experience depression, stress, anxiety, isolation, and other forms of psychological pain (Rosenberg & McCullough, 1981). People with acknowledged mental health problems often feel as if they do not matter and that those around them also believe that they do not matter (Corrigan et al., 2001). In fact, Schlossberg (1989) argued that marginalization is the polar opposite of mattering. She also stated that anyone undergoing a significant life transition can feel marginalized, and when in a new situation it can make them feel invisible. Graduate school can be considered a significant life transition as those transitioning into and persisting through graduate school describe the experience as psychologically taxing (Djokić & Lounis, 2014).

Methods

The data from this study were drawn from a larger research project that explored the experiences of graduate students who identify as having mental health concerns during their graduate study. For the purpose of this chapter we have specifically analyzed the types of support participants stated would have been helpful or would be helpful as they continue to navigate their graduate school experience.

Eleven PhD/EdD and three master's students who identified as having mental health challenges were interviewed utilizing a semi-structured protocol. The majority of participants identified as White (7), while the remaining identified as African American (3), Asian (1), Hispanic (1), or Native American (1). One person did not identify. Participants' fields of study varied, with higher education as the most common followed by social science, library science, and education. Eight students indicated that they had mental health challenges prior to enrolling in graduate school, while six developed mental health concerns after their enrollment.

Students' Perspectives and Recommendations for Practice

Study findings highlight struggles graduate students with mental health challenges experience in graduate school. Considering their lived experiences and previous research on graduate student mental health, we have chosen to highlight three emergent struggles—developing relationships, resources and accommodations, and self-awareness and well-being. We will also offer suggestions for how advisors, departments, and institutions can meet the needs of this student population.

Developing Relationships

Developing relationships centers around graduate students' need for feelings of support and a sense of mattering. Students believed that developing strong relationships with peers, faculty, supervisors, and others in their network was essential to being able to succeed in graduate school. These relationships provided an opportunity for students to feel like they were not alone in their struggles, and that they were understood in whatever hardship, stress, discomfort, or mental health challenge they may have been experiencing. Participants identified peer support groups as essential components to belongingness during graduate school. When asked to give advice to other students who may be entering graduate school with mental health challenges, Jason, a student struggling with depression suggested

> Try to build those social connections with peers . . . because the social connections I've had since I've been in the PhD program have been more of a positive stress release than the more solo strategies. They're [peers] going through a lot of the same things you are even if they're in a different field. So, you can both talk through what you're doing to some degree. You can also hear what they've done in similar situations. And I know that's helped me a lot.

When Jason mentioned similar situations, he referenced occasions when his depression was interfering with his academic goals. For other students, having supportive faculty and supervisor relationships fostered their success. These relationships often went beyond academics and focused on developing work–life balance and handling stress among students. When students were not able to form a supportive relationship with their academic advisor, they sought mentorship elsewhere. When asked what advice she would give other graduate students with mental health challenges, Josephine, who identified as having post-traumatic stress disorder, depression, and a compulsive disorder offered:

> If you have a faculty member, mentor, or advisor [and it] is not working out, find someone who's gonna be supportive, not only of your intellectual work, but of your personal time. [They] forget as grad students that we put our job or our academic ambitions ahead of our personal time. And I think there needs to be a balance between the two. . . . Sometimes we're afraid to be proactive in our own recovery and health situations . . . your mentor can help with balance.

In addition to offering advice and assisting with work–life balance, peers, faculty, and staff were important in limiting isolation. Due to the nature of graduate work often being rooted in independent research, students often felt more mental health constraints during periods of isolation. Being a part of a community and in a network of like-minded and like-experience individuals helped to combat isolation. Steven, who stated he was overly stressed and suffers from depression, commented that isolation can be common in graduate school but for individuals with mental health challenges isolation can be immobilizing and cause greater harm to one's mental stability. He said,

> Make sure that you're not entirely in your own head, that you are finding outlets, whether it's friendships or counseling or whatever . . . make sure that you're open . . . and that you're not isolating or being all up in your own head . . . if I didn't have a cohort where I felt like I had some support, if I didn't go and seek some counseling, if I didn't have my own personal family support system and colleagues at work, I don't think I would have been able to maintain the degree of mental stability that I had.

Graduate students with mental health challenges need to be in supportive relationships with faculty and peers. To facilitate these types of relationships, departments should consider admitting students into programs utilizing a cohort model, a model that at least requires new students to take a 1st-year seminar together, or consistent community events. Research has shown that graduate students who are admitted into cohort models have enhanced feelings of support (Barnett & Muse, 1993), reduced feeling of loneliness (Norris & Barnett, 1994) and increased motivation to be academically successful (Bratlien et al., 1992). The opportunity to spend a significant amount of time with peers increases the opportunity for students to bond with one another during their graduate school experience. Institutions cannot assume that students will make the time to engage with one another outside the classroom thus the models suggested could provide an avenue for students to become better acquainted as they travel through the program. Once admitted, advisors can be helpful in building community and social networks by utilizing technology. Internet blogs, Facebook, Twitter, and other social media platforms have increasingly become popular to connect students and build community with graduate students who are often too busy to attend more traditional face-to-face departmental events (Wyatt & Oswald, 2013).

Technology can join students and faculty. The ability to connect anytime, anyplace can potentially increase opportunities for faculty and students to engage with one another without the hassle of driving to campus. Some students may still prefer to have face-to-face meetings. However, virtual meetings should not take the place of or seek to replicate face-to-face meetings.

Rather they should be viewed as another tool for relationship building and community creation. In addition, providing graduate students with a space where they can mingle, cocreate, and connect on a consistent basis can offer informal opportunities to develop community among themselves and fight isolation. These spaces could potentially include shared office space that is created with the intention of collaboration, or a department lounge where students can share a common place for both academic and personal connection. In distance learning programs academic advisors, faculty members, or administrators could designate a set day and time weekly where students know they can log on to a video conference room to chat and share ideas with peers and colleagues.

Resources and Accommodations

Resources and accommodations awareness refers to the need for graduate students to know that mental health counseling and resources are available to them on campus. Students in our study were often not aware of these types of graduate student resources offered. If they were aware of campus services, then they were not sure if they could access them or if they were only for undergraduate students. Students in our study believed that most graduate students are unaware of graduate student services. This point underscores the importance of such resources for students with mental health challenges. In discussing services, Kate, who experiences high levels of anxiety, said,

> I knew that there were services there because I had worked for a university for so long. But others may not know that there is a counseling center unless they were qualified for some sort of services. So awareness is important.

Similarly Ashley, who has depression, agreed. In addition to not knowing what counseling and other services were available, she believed the perceived cost of services and availability, or lack of availability, of services for graduate students becomes a barrier for those with mental health challenges. Throughout her interview Ashley raised the importance of informing students about the availability of resources and the cost of services, noting that most students are not aware that psychological services are much more affordable on college campuses than services in the community.

> [Institutions need to] highlight the resources . . . you get free sessions at the counseling center, and then [wellness] sessions, whatever ones you have to pay for, I think were $20 or $25. And you're not going to be able to get counseling for that price after you leave here, so definitely take advantage of it.

The stigmatization around utilizing university resources was also seen as another barrier. Many students in our study shared that they had mental health concerns but chose not to seek treatment due to fear of how they may be perceived by faculty and peers. When asked what advice he would like to give future graduate students entering graduate school with mental health challenges, Caleb, who suffers from depression and anxiety, emphasized the importance of utilizing resources before and when you need them. He said:

> Do not be afraid to seek counseling if you need it, medications if you need it, those kinds of things. . . . reach out for help if you need it and use your peers for support if you need it. There's no [shame] going to the disability office or accommodation office or whatever they call it at the college you're at. . . . this person needs one and a half times more on the test because they have ADD, or this person needs a quiet room because they have anxiety, and there's nothing wrong with asking for it. The problem comes in when you don't ask for it. You don't have to tough it out.

Despite being fearful of being discriminated against, most participants agreed that counseling and therapy were the most important resources for helping students combat mental health challenges. Joe, who suffers from anxiety, depression, and attention deficit disorder, utilized counseling services during his 1st year when he was having a difficult time. Having help on campus made the difference between him leaving graduate school and staying.

> I was really struggling with some health issues and issues with my home . . . I was having a lot of trouble in statistics. I would just have [left]—I just feel like I wasn't on the right path for success. I finally went to a therapist in graduate school . . . and that was like immensely helpful just to kind of dump on someone. Now I see a therapist on a regular basis on campus and it's been really—she's been really good to connect with.

Graduate students need to be aware of the resources available that can assist students with their mental health challenges. This information should be shared with students during orientation and throughout the academic year. Departments should be strategic in how they inform students about mental health services. Including information about services in admission packets is one way to begin the conversation and make it a normalized part of the graduate school experience. Previously, some students entered graduate school with mental health concerns. Knowing about services early on may help students strategize how they will address their mental health needs before coming to campus. Departments should also request that faculty put information in their syllabus about mental health services. This information can typically be obtained through the graduate school, faculty senate, or counseling office. Making the information readily available in every class is one way to normalize conversations about mental health and change departmental culture. Finally, academic advisors should intentionally ask students about their mental health and provide information about services during every visit. Although some students do not disclose, the recognition that the subject is not taboo may strengthen academic advisor–student relationships and encourage those who may be afraid to seek help and inquire about services.

Eliminating the stigmatization associated with mental health is a goal that all institutions should strive to achieve. Academic departments and advisors should work toward creating environments where faculty and students feel comfortable discussing mental health challenges. This requires providing training to faculty and resources to students around this important issue. Most faculty members are not trained to work with students around mental health concerns; however, institutions can provide faculty members with training to identify when someone is struggling so that they may refer them to the appropriate resources. Schreier (as cited in Gooblar, 2018) states that identifying when someone is struggling is easier than most people think. It really just requires paying attention. Educating faculty and students can go a long way in normalizing conversations around mental health and well-being, which is an essential step in promoting help-seeking behaviors.

Self-Awareness and Well-Being

While students are responsible for their own self-awareness, the development of how they cope with and come to terms with their own mental health limitations can be uncharted territory. For several students in this study, having the courage to prioritize mental health well-being and work–life balance required support from one's faculty or academic advisor. Faculty or academic advisors' support gave students permission not to feel guilty when investing in activities outside of their graduate school role. For those lacking support, achieving mental health well-being and balance was not a realistic goal. In this study, the culture of participants' departments was self-described as competitive. Neither students nor faculty were encouraged to achieve balance; therefore, balance or well-being was not a focus for anyone in the department. While discussing graduate school programs, Adam, who has anxiety, shared: "certain departments . . . I just know faculty may not be supportive . . . or certain programs where it's ultra-competitive, and people don't feel like they can be vulnerable [by asking for what they need for balance]." Leah, who has anxiety and depression, discussed how her work supervisor, who was also her faculty advisor, was not supportive and how she wished she would have thought about balance and well-being before entering the program.

> I don't get a lot of assistance. I get some pushback when I say that I need X night off for this semester. . . . I would just say really make sure that you're going to have enough time to take care of yourself, because that is not something that I considered when going into the program and I wish I had.

Other students discussed the need to have assistance in determining their limitations or triggers when it comes to dealing with their mental health challenges. Most students in our study developed mental health challenges during graduate school. Therefore, they were unaware of their triggers and were sometimes unable to be active on their research team or in classes because of it. These students recognized that it was their responsibility to figure out how to manage their mental health; however, they wish they felt more comfortable asking for what they needed in an academic setting. Adam offered this advice:

> They need to figure out what works for them to get them in control of their symptoms. I think mental health manifests itself in very unique personal ways for a lot of people. And so, if their symptoms are triggered a lot by certain content then they need to know that content is going to be a reoc-curring issue in classes. . . . I have to have something early in the morning to get me out of bed . . . if that's something that works for them, then they need to know that they need to find teaching assistantship in the morning. Because if they're going to do something at night that might not be the best decision for them, like their mental health . . . I'd recommend that they figure out what works for them to keep them in check. And then they just need to make sure [they stick to it] that's the way that they can try to maintain that normalcy in their lives when they're in graduate school.

Finally, students often expressed that seeking help early and often was a key to their success in combating and becoming self-aware of their mental health challenges and limitations while in graduate school. Nichols, who has attention deficit disorder said,

> So know what your limitations are and then work proactively around those. . . . Be proactive about whatever your limitations are. Talk to your faculty early. Go in and say, "Look, I have this diagnosis," or whatever and give them a letter, and just tell them, "I'm not asking for special treatment or anything like that. I just may need some support in terms of navigating this disability." . . . You have to be proactive, and it's been my experience most of the faculty will work with you.

Graduate students experiencing mental health challenges must be self-aware, learn their own triggers, and advocate for themselves for support from their academic advisors. However, higher education institutions also have a responsibility to provide students with the resources they need to accomplish these goals. University administrators and staff should consider well-being programming that is appropriate for graduate students. Often graduate students feel well-being programs are designed with only undergraduate students in mind. Offering well-being events that promote de-stressing and building the graduate school community should be highly considered in regular programming budgets. Programming that takes place before or after common graduate class hours or events that promote including family are just a couple of the ways this population could be successfully targeted to participate in graduate-specific university-sponsored wellness programming.

Conclusion

As universities bring on graduate students to not only take academic courses, but embody crucial roles within the university including teaching, staff, and administrative work, they must also prepare to take a stance that ensures the mental health needs of graduate students are met with concern and care. Graduate students must feel a sense of comfort and that they matter to the university for them to be successful in their academic endeavors. Institutions and advisors have an enormous opportunity to help connect students with proactive training, resources, professional development, and mentoring around graduate student mental health that can be useful to students and faculty as students attempt to navigate the graduate school experience. Helping to connect students to the correct and appropriate resources and providing faculty and advisors with adequate training early and often can help end the stigma around help-seeking and mental health challenges in graduate education.

References

Barnett, B. G., & Muse, I. D. (1993). Cohort groups in educational administration: Promises and challenges. *Journal of School Leadership*, 3(4), 400–415. https://doi.org/10.1177/105268469300300405

Becker, M., Martin, L., Wajeeh, E., Ward, J., & Shern, D. (2002). Students with mental illnesses in a university setting: Faculty and student attitudes, beliefs, knowledge, and experiences. *Psychiatric Rehabilitation Journal*, 25(4), 359–368. https://doi.org/10.1037/h0095001

Benton, S. A., Robertson, J. M., Tseng, W. C., Newton, F. B., & Benton, S. L. (2003). Changes in counseling center client problems across 13 years. *Professional Psychology: Research and Practice, 34*(1), 66–72. https://doi.org/10.1037/0735-7028.34.1.66

Bratlien, M. J., Genzer, S. M., Hoyle, J. R., & Oates, A. D. (1992). The professional studies doctorate: Leaders for learning. *Journal of School Leadership, 2*(1), 75–89. https://doi.org/10.1177/105268469200200107

Burt, B. A., Williams, K. L., & Smith, W. A. (2018). Into the storm: Ecological and sociological impediments to Black males' persistence in engineering graduate programs. *American Educational Research Journal, 55*(5), 965–1006. https://doi.org/10.3102/0002831218763587

Clark, R. A., Harden, S. L., & Johnson, W. B. (2000). Mentor relationships in clinical psychology doctoral training: Results of a national survey. *Teaching of Psychology, 27*(4), 262–268. https://doi.org/10.1207/s15328023top2704_04

Corrigan, P. W., Edwards, A. B., Green, A., Diwan, S. L., & Penn, D. L. (2001). Prejudice, social distance, and familiarity with mental illness. *Schizophrenia Bulletin, 27*(2), 219–225. https://doi.org/10.1093/oxfordjournals.schbul.a006868

DeVore, R. (2013). Analysis of gender differences in self-statements and mood disorders. *McNair Scholars Research Journal, 9*(7), 5–12. https://scholarworks.boisestate.edu/psych_facpubs/209/

Dill, P. L., & Henley, T. B. (1998). Stressors of college: A comparison of traditional and nontraditional students. *The Journal of Psychology: Interdisciplinary and Applied, 132*(1), 25–32. https://doi.org/10.1080/00223989809599261

Djokić, D. S., & Lounis, S. (2014). This is your mind on grad school: The state of graduate student mental health at UC Berkeley. *Berkeley Science Review, 26*, 44–48.

Drum, D. J., Brownson, C., Burton Denmark, A., & Smith, S. E. (2009). New data on the nature of suicidal crises in college students: Shifting the paradigm. *Professional Psychology: Research and Practice, 40*(3), 213–222. https://doi.org/10.1037/a0014465

Eisenberg, D., Downs, M. F., Golberstein, E., & Zivin, K. (2009). Stigma and help seeking for mental health among college students. *Medical Care Research and Review, 66*(5), 522–541. https://doi.org/10.1177/1077558709335173

Eisenberg, D., Gollust, S. E., Golberstein, E., & Hefner, J. L. (2007). Prevalence and correlates of depression, anxiety, and suicidality among university students. *American Journal of Orthopsychiatry, 77*(4), 534–542.

Garcia-Williams, A. G., Moffitt, L., & Kaslow, N. J. (2014). Mental health and suicidal behavior among graduate students. *Academic Psychiatry, 38*(5), 554–560. https://doi.org/10.1007/s40596-014-0041-y

Giedd, J. N., Keshavan, M., & Paus, T. (2008). Why do many psychiatric disorders emerge during adolescence? *Nature Review Neuroscience, 9*(12), 947–957. https://doi.org/10.1038/nrn2513

Golberstein, E., Eisenberg, D., & Golloust, S. E. (2008). Perceived stigma and mental health care seeking. *Psychiatric Services, 59*(4), 392–399. https://doi.org/10.1176/ps.2008.59.4.392

Gooblar, D. (2018, December 17). How to help a student in mental-health crisis. *Chronicle of Higher Education.* https://www.chronicle.com/article/How-to-Help-a-Student-in-a/245305

The Graduate Assembly. (2014). *Graduate student happiness and well-being report.* University of California-Berkeley.

Grady, R., La Touche, R., Oslawski-Lopez, J., Powers, A., & Simacek, K. (2013). Betwixt and between: The social position and stress experiences of graduate students. *Teaching Sociology, 42*(1), 5–16. https://doi.org/10.1177/0092055x13502182

Hyun, J., Quinn, B., Madon, T., & Lustig, S. (2007). Mental health need, awareness, and use of counseling services among international graduate students. *Journal of American College Health, 56*(2), 109–118. https://doi.org/10.3200/jach.56.2.109-118

Kausar, R. (2010). Perceived stress, academic workloads and use of coping strategies by university students. *Journal of Behavioral Sciences, 20*(1), 31–46. https://asset-pdf.scinapse.io/prod/2188512843/2188512843.pdf

Kitzrow, M. A. (2003). The mental health needs of today's college students: Recommendations and challenges. *NASPA Journal, 41*(1), 167–181. https://doi.org/10.2202/0027-6014.1310

Komiya, N., & Gregory, T. (2001). Predictors of attitudes toward seeking counseling among international students. *Journal of College Counseling, 4*(2), 153–160. https://doi.org/10.1002/j.2161-1882.2001.tb00195.x

Link, B. G., Yang, L. H., Phelan, J. C., & Collins, P. Y. (2004). Measuring mental illness stigma. *Schizophrenia Bulletin, 30*(3), 511–541. https://doi.org/10.1093/oxfordjournals.schbul.a007098

Lipson, S. K., Zhou, S., Wagner, B., III, Beck, K., & Eisenberg, D. (2016). Major differences: Variations in undergraduate and graduate student mental health and treatment utilization across academic disciplines. *Journal of College Student Psychotherapy, 30*(1), 23–41. https://doi.org/10.1080/87568225.2016.1105657

Mahmoud, J. S., Staten, R., Lennie, T. A., & Hall, L. A. (2015). The relationships of coping, negative thinking, life satisfaction, social support, and selected demographics with anxiety of young adult college students. *Journal of Child and Adolescent Psychiatric Nursing, 28*(2), 97–108. https://doi.org/10.1111/jcap.12109

Moffitt, L. B., Garcia-Williams, A., Berg, J. P., Calderon, M. E., Haas, A. P., & Kaslow, N. J. (2014). Reaching graduate students at risk for suicidal behavior through the interactive screening program. *Journal of College Student Psychotherapy, 28*(1), 23–34. https://doi.org/10.1080/87568225.2014.854675

Norris, C., & Barnett, B. (1994). *Cultivating a new leadership paradigm: From cohorts to communities.* Annual Meeting of the University Council for Educational Administration, Philadelphia, PA.

Offstein, E. H., Larson, M. B., McNeill, A. L., & Mwale, H. M. (2004). Are we doing enough for today's graduate student? *International Journal of Educational Management, 18*(7), 396–407. https://doi.org/10.1108/09513540410563103

Oswalt, S. B., & Riddock, C. C. (2007). What to do about being overwhelmed: Graduate students, stress, and university services. *College Student Affairs Journal, 27*(1), 24–44. https://files.eric.ed.gov/fulltext/EJ899402.pdf

Pain, E. (2018, March 6). Graduate students need more mental health support, new study highlights. *Science.* http://www.sciencemag.org/careers/2018/03/graduate-students-need-more-mental-health-support-new-study-highlights

Peluso, D. L., Carleton, R. N., Girdon, J., & Asmundson, G. (2011). Depression symptoms in Canadian psychology graduate students: Do research productivity, funding, and academic advisory relationship play a role? *Canadian Journal of Behavioral Science, 43*(2), 119–127. https://doi.org/10.1037/a0022624

Rosenberg, M., & McCullough, B. C. (1981). Mattering: Inferred significance and mental health among adolescents. *Research in Community and Mental Health, 2,* 163–182. https://psycnet.apa.org/record/1983-07744-001

Rosenthal, B., & Wilson, W. C. (2010). Mental health services: Use and disparity among diverse college students. *Journal of American College Health, 57*(1), 61–68. https://doi.org/10.3200/jach.57.1.61-68

Schlossberg, N. K. (1989). Marginality and mattering: Key issues in building community. In *Beyond the Box: Connecting Multiracial Identities, Oppressions, and Environments* (New Directions for Student Services, vol. 1989, no. 48, pp. 5–15). https://doi.org/10.1002/ss.37119894803

Simonson, J., Mezulis, A., & Davis, K. (2011). Socialized to ruminate? Gender role mediates the sex difference in rumination for interpersonal events. *Journal of Social and Clinical Psychology, 30*(9), 937–959. https://doi.org/10.1521/jscp.2011.30.9.937

Smith, J. L., Lewis, K. L., Hawthorne, L., & Hodges, S. D. (2013). When trying hard isn't natural: Women's belonging with and motivation for male-dominated stem fields as a function of effort expenditure concerns. *Personality and Social Psychology Bulletin, 39*(2), 131–143. https://doi.org/10.1177/0146167212468332

Turner, A. L., & Berry, T. L. (2000). Counseling center contributions to student retention and graduation: A longitudinal assessment. *Journal of College Student Development, 41*(6), 627–636. https://psycnet.apa.org/record/2000-12548-004

Wexler, E. (2015, November 15). How mental-health care entered the debate over racial inequality. *Chronicle of Higher Education.* https://www.stevefund.org/news-article-chronicle-of-higher-education-111915/

Williams, D. R., & Williams-Morris, R. (2010). Racism and mental health: The African American experience. *Ethnicity and Health, 5*(3–4), 243–268. https://doi.org/10.1080/713667453

Willyard, C. (2012, January 1) Need to heal thyself. *gradPSYCH, 10*(1) 28, https://www.apa.org/gradpsych/2012/01/heal

Wupperman, P., & Neumann, C. S. (2006). Depressive symptoms as a function of sex-role, rumination, and neuroticism. *Personality and Individual Differences, 40*(2), 189–201. https://doi.org/10.1016/j.paid.2005.05.017

Wyatt, T., & Oswalt, S. B. (2013). Comparing mental health issues among undergraduate and graduate students. *American Journal of Health Education, 44*(2), 96–107. https://doi.org/10.1080/19325037.2013.764248

12

EXPLORING THE ROLE OF GRADUATE STUDENT CAREER DEVELOPMENT IN HIGHER EDUCATION

How Resources Evolved

Jake Livengood

This chapter explores the role of graduate student career development in higher education across institutional types in the United States and offers recommendations for practice. This exploration addresses how career development resources evolved, especially how student needs have influenced graduate student service offerings. Graduate degree holders need a diverse set of professional and career-exploration skills that go beyond traditional research and discipline-specific competencies, especially for students to be successful in a variety of careers postgraduation. Recommendations for practice are included for institutions, departments, and graduate programs to support students' individual career choices.

The focus on graduate student career development has been growing exponentially. In a field-wide survey of graduate student services, more than half of 857 respondents, including graduate deans, college deans, graduate study faculty directors, and professional development program directors, indicated that they offer professional development services beyond the formal academic curriculum (Denecke et al., 2017). In 2018, the Graduate Career Consortium (GCC), the primary graduate student career development professional association in the United States and Canada, had

400 members at 164 institutions (GCC, 2019). Early on in this association's history, this organization held small meetings in a conference room for its members. Today, hundreds of professionals gather at an international conference. The growth in graduate career development is a byproduct of institutions acknowledging that the graduate student career experience is unique and requires specific resources and support.

A heightened focus on graduate student career development has been related to three main factors: increasing enrollment and degree options, changing demographics of students, and increasing amounts of graduate student debt. First, according to the 2019 National Center for Education Statistics (NCES) postsecondary enrollment report, graduate student enrollment has increased 39% from 2000 to 2017. Similarly, the total number of graduate degrees awarded has increased in this 10-year timeframe, especially with more online and hybrid offerings (Okahana & Zhou, 2018). Second, graduate student demographics have changed. The average age of graduate students has trended younger while the time-to-degree has become longer, especially for doctoral programs overall (National Science Foundation [NSF], 2008, 2018; Rockey, 2012). Since graduate students are trending younger overall, one could reason that these graduate degree holders are also less experienced with career search processes. Third, student debt is on the rise with average loan balances doubling for graduate students overall from 2000 to 2016 (NCES, 2018). Like undergraduate education, with increasing debt burdens, students may have a heightened focus on career outcomes and how a graduate degree can increase their earning potential overall.

Graduate student career services vary by institution. At some institutions, graduate career services are provided in a centralized career center, which also supports undergraduate students. An academic department or graduate college might provide these services either in addition to or in place of a centralized office. These varying access points can be confusing for graduate students. Therefore, this chapter offers practical recommendations for coordinated services and recommendations across and within institutions.

Graduate Student Career Needs and Challenges

Graduate student career needs and challenges will now be discussed for master's programs (nonprofessional) and doctoral students in all disciplines. In order to provide the best guidance possible, university administrators and faculty must first understand the specific needs of their graduate students. Compared to undergraduate students, much less is known about graduate student career needs although institutions are developing services in

TABLE 12.1
Overall Graduate Student Career Development Needs and Challenges

Doubts about adequate experience for future career
Fear of making a mistake with next career step after graduation
Struggle with nonlinear process of career searching
Navigating competitive job market
Pursuing a variety of positions concurrently

response to student feedback and growing demand (Denecke et al., 2017). Table 12.1 highlights frequent graduate student career development needs and challenges overall.

Graduate students often struggle with career decision-making and can feel lost with how to navigate this process (Denecke et al., 2017; National Academies of Sciences, Engineering, and Medicine, 2018; Thiry et al., 2015). This is understandable given the complexities of deciding about career, its nonlinear process, the increased cost of education, and a competitive job market. The confluence of these factors contributes to students wanting to feel confident that their academic training has prepared them for the labor market, but they may doubt that they have adequate professional experience for a future career (Fuhrmann et al., 2011; Sinche, 2016; Thiry et al., 2015). Each institution must, therefore, create a supportive ecosystem for mentorship and career decision-making. This is not the sole responsibility of a faculty advisor, academic department, or student services division; rather, it must come from a collaborative perspective (Fuhrmann et al., 2011; National Academies of Sciences, Engineering, and Medicine, 2018).

Many graduate students may lack certainty of next career destinations, so they explore multiple options (Sinche, 2016; Thiry et al., 2015). At the doctoral level, many pursue both academic and nonacademic positions at the same time as they near degree completion. This approach is used in order to keep one's options open in a competitive job market, which is present for most industries, especially the academic profession. The needs for master's students can be quite different than those of doctoral students, so the following sections explore the needs of different degree types. It is important to note that this information is general across these degrees and that the individual student will have their own needs and concerns.

Master's Student Career Needs and Challenges

This section focuses on nonprofessional master's programs, as the needs of professional programs are uniquely specific to each discipline. Table 12.2 summarizes the specific career needs and challenges of this group.

TABLE 12.2
Master's Students (Nonprofessional): Frequent Career
Development Needs and Challenges

Quick turnaround from start to finish in programs that last 1–2 years
The decision to continue education to a doctorate or other degree
Feeling unqualified for some positions that require additional experience or training while also feeling overqualified for positions that require only an undergraduate degree

Master's students' needs may depend on different attributes, such as degree type and duration of time between bachelor's and graduate education. For example, a master's student enrolled directly after undergraduate education may be conducting a full-time career search for the first time or may be rebooting an unsuccessful career search. The student's career needs are to become familiar with how to conduct a successful full-time job search process, including use of campus resources and connections, the role of job search websites, and networking both within the academic institution and via personal connections. However, not all master's students enter graduate education directly from a bachelor's program. Many people work full-time after undergraduate and return for a master's degree in order to either change career direction or to boost credentials for advancement in their current profession. This person has transferable skills from past work experience but may not know how to connect current academic program and experiential opportunities (e.g., internships, student club involvement, or projects) as a pathway to future career goals.

Most master's programs require 1 to 2 years of study. This length of time can be a boon or hindrance for the student. For students enrolled in 1-year programs, the career development timeline is accelerated because students may need to begin job searching during their first semester on campus. Though the other programs are 2 years in length, students may feel like they only recently started their program while now needing to think about their future job search.

The master's degree could be the conclusion of an academic journey for some students, but a continuation for others. In some fields, a master's degree may function as the terminal degree (e.g., Master of Fine Arts). On the other hand, some fields require doctorates as terminal degrees to be eligible for certain positions. Many master's students may question if they should pursue continuing education to a doctorate or other degree. This need can create a feeling of being "in between" academically and professionally. The needs for this student are to explore what it is like to be a doctoral student and what it takes to be successful in doctoral education.

Some master's students aspire to positions that have a master's degree required and doctorate preferred designation. This circumstance can lead a master's student to feel unqualified for some positions requiring additional experience or training. Conversely, some master's students are interested in positions that only have a bachelor's degree required designation. In similar circumstances, employers may view someone as not being a good fit or being overqualified for positions that require only a bachelor's degree.

Doctoral Student Needs and Challenges

The needs of doctoral students can add complexity to career development. The doctorate is typically a terminal degree, typically with a longer time commitment and additional layers of programmatic rites of passage. Table 12.3 summarizes the specific career needs and challenges of doctoral students and Figure 12.1 visually represents this process.

Doctoral Career Needs Overall

Doctoral enrollment overall has increased 28.5% from 1997–2017 (NSF, 2018). In turn, more doctoral graduates are competing for academic and nonacademic positions. During the same time period, there has been an increase in industry or business sector positions, while growth in academic

TABLE 12.3
Doctoral Students: Frequent Career Development Needs and Challenges

Overall:
- Deciding upon a myriad of options with the interest and expectation of being a faculty
- Should a student pursue additional postdoctoral training?

For nonfaculty paths:
- What career paths exist that are not tenure-track faculty?
- Making the cultural transition to nonacademic positions
- Identifying and translating research, experience, and skills to nonacademic settings

For faculty paths:
- Choosing an institutional setting that matches interests: What balance of teaching, research, and service is preferable?
- Establishing own research separate from advisor
- Obtaining research funding
- Preparing for and selecting courses to teach independently

Figure 12.1. Doctoral students: Frequent career development needs and challenges for career choice.

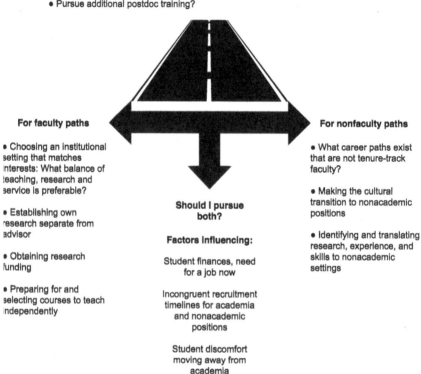

Overall Challenges:

- Deciding upon a myriad of options with the interest and expectation of being a faculty

- Pursue additional postdoc training?

For faculty paths

- Choosing an institutional setting that matches interests: What balance of teaching, research and service is preferable?

- Establishing own research separate from advisor

- Obtaining research funding

- Preparing for and selecting courses to teach independently

Should I pursue both?

Factors Influencing:

Student finances, need for a job now

Incongruent recruitment timelines for academia and nonacademic positions

Student discomfort moving away from academia

For nonfaculty paths

- What career paths exist that are not tenure-track faculty?

- Making the cultural transition to nonacademic positions

- Identifying and translating research, experience, and skills to nonacademic settings

positions remains flat (NSF, 2018). As there is increased competition for employment postgraduation, students have felt pressure and urgency to more broadly explore career options after graduation.

Historically, there has been a faculty-focused view of doctoral career paths postgraduation (National Academies of Sciences, Engineering, and Medicine, 2018). From this vantage point, faculty train doctoral students as future faculty with a significant emphasis on the research function. As competition has increased for faculty roles and career options for doctoral graduates have evolved, some faculty still view the only role of doctoral education as training future faculty (Fuhrmann et al., 2011; National Academies of Sciences, Engineering, and Medicine, 2018).

A student's advisor or program faculty mentors may not be comfortable or familiar with how to help a doctoral student navigate a nonacademic search (National Academies of Sciences, Engineering, and Medicine, 2018; Schlosser et al., 2011). Even though the faculty may support students seeking a nonacademic position, it is an unrealistic expectation to think that advisors or faculty should be all-knowing about how to search for careers in every discipline. Instead, students need mentors and supporters to inform them when they lack critical knowledge of career options.

One such question is whether to pursue postdoctoral training (Sinche, 2016; Vick & Furlong, 2016). Students may hope to keep the academic pathway open and a postdoctoral position may be one option to do so. A hypercompetitive academic job market forces some doctoral students toward postdoctoral training as they prepare to apply for faculty roles (Bodewits et al., 2018). The need for a postdoctoral position varies depending on the cultural norms of each academic discipline and availability. Another primary consideration is the function of the postdoctoral position because it may take the form of a primarily research or teaching position. However, across disciplines, it is common for doctoral students to feel uncomfortable moving away from their research or the potential of not working in a faculty role. After all, doctoral education requires a huge investment in time, financial resources, and emotional energy, so this question is certainly understandable. Additional training via the postdoctoral pathway is viewed by some doctoral students as a way to buy additional time to decide about the overall question of academia or another path or to have additional time to enhance one's credentials for the faculty search, including additional time to publish and boost other skills for faculty applications (Bodewits et al., 2018).

Doctoral Needs for Nonfaculty Pathways

Doctoral students are often confused about how to pursue nonfaculty career options. It is understandable that this feeling exists, especially when not knowing where to get help and if the students' advisor is not comfortable, supportive, or familiar with this process. Therefore, doctoral students need to know what options are available to them. This information can be found via national data, including the Council on Graduate Schools Career Pathways Project, the NSF Survey of Doctorate Recipients (NSF, 2018; National Center for Science and Engineering Statistics, 2018), and Sinche's Survey of Doctoral Careers in the book *Next Gen PhD* (Sinche, 2016).

Career outcomes data help students expand their mindset of potential career pathways in both academic and nonacademic settings. Data can inform ways to network with alumni for informational interviews or career conversations to learn about various options. Gathering this data is challenging so a variety of methods are recommended, including surveys and web scraping (Hoffer et al., 2019). Students can also gather data individually by searching for alumni via institutional alumni network programs/databases and social media platforms. This is a recommendation for the institution as a whole and can be accomplished through departments, centralized career offices, or institutional research.

Doctoral Needs for Faculty Pathways

Academia has its own unique culture that can shape a doctoral student's future interests. When those interests are not aligned with similar cultures to the academy, students need to explore and define organizational culture and the audience that they are trying to reach for a future next step after graduation. Students have been embedded for many years in an environment that rewards and values contributions to research (publications and conference presentations), but one's future interests may not reward or value those aspects to the same extent or at all. For example, a doctoral student applying to management consulting positions would need to emphasize a broader skill set of leadership and presentation skills rather than focusing on the contents of their publications.

A variety of faculty roles, including tenure and non-tenure track positions, research-focused positions, and teaching-focused faculty, are available in academe. For students following a faculty pathway, students need to define their desired balance of research, teaching, and service and the related institutional types that match that interest. The challenges and needs present for doctoral students in this regard will depend on the institutional type that they are attending and the experiential background of faculty in one's department and institution. For example, a student attending a research institution may not be as familiar with the process of searching for and obtaining a more teaching-focused position.

As doctoral students progress in their own research, they have the need of establishing their own contributions separate from their advisor. This derivation can be challenging for many as they define and demonstrate the distinction. A related concept is the student's need to obtain their own research funding, including how to write grants, where to seek funding, and how to maintain one's own research interests while also obtaining funding that may or may not closely align with that topic.

Professional Skills Gained in Graduate Education for Postgraduate Success

Graduate degree holders need a diverse set of professional skills beyond research and discipline-specific competencies. The majority of doctoral graduates across all disciplines report that their degree prepared them for success in nonacademic and academic settings. This trends upward as graduates gain additional experience, including humanities doctoral graduates and STEM fields (Okahana & Kinoshita, 2018; Okahana et al., 2018). In addition, the doctorate provides relevant training for jobs both inside and outside of academia (Okahana & Kinoshita, 2018; Okahana et al., 2018; Sinche, 2016). However, identifying, translating, and marketing these skills can be difficult for many doctoral graduates, which has given rise to many professional and career development programs for them.

The skills and attributes necessary for success in a postgraduation workplace are similar across academic and nonacademic settings for both STEM and humanities doctoral alumni (Okahana & Kinoshita, 2018; Okahana et al., 2018; Sinche, 2016). The importance of specific skills for success may vary depending on the population. However, eight core skills have been identified for postgraduate success of master's and doctoral students: communication, leadership, teamwork, mentoring, writing, teaching, job search, and networking skills (Denecke et al., 2017). On a broader level, the skills and attributes identified for graduate student success are: persistence, initiative, attention to detail, achievement/effort, analytical thinking, independence, innovation, stress tolerance, adaptability/flexibility, dependability, integrity, leadership, cooperation, concern for others, and social orientation (Okahana & Kinoshita, 2018; Okahana et al., 2018; Sinche, 2016). Institutions can use these skills and attributes as goals for career and professional development programming.

Recommendations to Support Graduate Student Career Development

Recommendations focus on individual-level support for graduate student career decisions and development and institutional-level collaboration and commitment to facilitate career exploration and development.

Individual-Level Support for Graduate Students: Becoming a Skill Translator

Graduate students often struggle with how to articulate their experiences and broader nontechnical skill set (Sinche, 2016). University administrators and faculty can offer professional and career development programs to address this challenge and help graduate students translate skills from academic to nonacademic settings. Career assessment, exploration, and decisions are ultimately the student's responsibility. However, departments can support this area by providing opportunities for skill development in both academic and nonacademic settings. By doing this, departments normalize the importance of career exploration while emphasizing important tools for those individual choices.

Students may have experience in nontechnical or nonacademic areas in their graduate training, but they may use different terminology. Training is recommended to help students learn about the related terminology that is used for their desired career path and target audience for the job search. Departments and institutions can offer workshops to help students broaden awareness of such skills. For example, skills workshops at the Massachusetts Institute of Technology help graduate students with this process. Table 12.4 is used to highlight the different terminology that is used in academic versus nonacademic settings.

Individual career advising appointments and workshops can help graduate students reframe and identify their skill set and provide a confidence boost in making the transition from academia to nonacademic settings. Departments can also integrate professional skills into the curriculum or through other experiences, which are further outlined at the end of this chapter.

TABLE 12.4
Skill Similarities Between Academia and Nonacademic Settings

Academic Settings: Graduate Programs	*Outside of Academia*
Teaching	Training
Conference presentations	Oral communication skills
Publishing	Written communication skills, report writing
Collaboration	Teamwork
Passing comprehensive exams, dissertation/thesis	Adaptability, creative problem-solving, conflict negotiation
Research (quantitative or qualitative)	Analytical ability
Mentorship (Example: Undergraduate Researcher)	Supervision, leadership, management

Individual-Level Support: Importance of Self-Assessment

This step is important for graduate students to generate filters for career decision-making. If one looks inwardly to assess their skills, values, interests, and strengths, then they can more accurately define personal characteristics needed for successfully choosing a match with a career path. There is little feedback provided in a career search—and it is often binary in nature (e.g., you either move on in a hiring process or you do not). Defining success, therefore, is a crucial step. Campus career services provide expertise in this area and typically offer self-assessment guidance and individual career advising. At the graduate level, free online career planning tools have been developed, including MyIDP (Individual Development Plan) for science students, ChemIDP for Chemistry students, and ImaginePhD for social sciences and humanities students.

Design thinking is an additional approach for career exploration and decision-making. *The New York Times* bestseller *Designing Your Life* (Burnett & Evans, 2016) emphasizes reframing the career exploration and decision-making process by incorporating process-oriented approaches. Design thinking emphasizes being active (or prototyping like a designer) and trying out various roles that are less resource and time intensive. Departments and institutions can create prototyping opportunities for students to try on new roles and explore various career options. This could be from faculty, administrators, or student service advisors to help students connect with alumni for a career conversation or an experience (e.g., employer site visits or career treks, an internship, 3-day leadership program, substitute teaching, or shadowing an alumna at a workplace). Design thinking reframes the binary mindset that many graduate students have regarding career decisions—that one should either be all in on a career pathway or move on from it. This reframe focuses on brief prototypes that inform one's career decisions while also gaining additional skills along the way.

Institutional Level: Providing a Collaboration and Commitment to Facilitate Career Exploration and Development

Career support is best provided using a collaborative approach with faculty, staff, alumni, and employers (Allum et al., 2014; National Academies of Sciences, Engineering, and Medicine, 2018). An institutional and department culture should be established that values diverse career paths tailored for an individual student's interests, values, and skills. When navigating one's career search, graduate students require support from academic departments (including faculty) and student services to look inwardly and become more of an expert in themselves and look outwardly to see what other trails have been blazed regarding pathways. Recommendations in this section include (a) providing tailored career services, (b) suggestions for collaboration with campus resources and employers, and (c) gathering department career data.

Career support is best done when it is student-centered and tailored for specific needs and challenges. Students typically engage in career exploration when they see the need or seek clarity. This need could be present prior to admission to a graduate program or even after graduation. Because the moment of identified need can arise at any moment, it is even more important for the entire campus community to support the career needs of students via referrals and navigation of services available. The Council of Graduate Schools and the National Endowment for the Humanities have developed career specific resources for units to consider adopting.

Embedded career exploration activities are recommended both in and out of the curriculum to help students explore options (National Academies of Sciences, Engineering, and Medicine, 2018). Career activities should be varied to provide multiple engagement points throughout the degree and match different styles of student learning. Most offerings combine departmental and institutional offerings (Denecke et al., 2017). Career activities could include for-credit internship programs, departmental and campus career seminars, alumni and employer guest speakers, faculty and staff sharing of their own nonlinear career path, and networking events like career fairs. Units should consider offering a variety of opportunities that include varying levels of time and resource commitment. For example, many graduate students cannot commit to a full summer internship, so some industries have developed a competitive 3-day leadership program where students can apply to become more familiar with career paths or industries.

One challenge for graduate career services is under which purview should these responsibilities fall. While many departments would like to offer in-depth career services offerings for their students, the financial and personnel resources may restrict the unit's ability to do so. Instead, much of this work falls to the institutional career services office that likely has responsibility for undergraduate and graduate students. One viable option would be for departments to collaborate with institutional career services to offer tailored services.

Collaboration with campus resources is key to supporting and encouraging students. In order to most effectively help graduate students' career and professional development needs, an ecosystem of support, compassion, openness to diverse career paths, and collaboration is needed from faculty, staff, and fellow students (Denecke et al., 2017; National Academies of Sciences, Engineering, and Medicine, 2018). Referrals to relevant services are vital between faculty and staff, and training should be provided regarding campus career services. Departmental faculty and staff may not have the time, comfort, or knowledge base to effectively create student-centered career exploration opportunities. Therefore, it is recommended that academic departments help students connect with key campus services, such as the career office and alumni relations. Collaboration can take many forms, including linking campus services to departmental webpages, following and sharing campus resources and articles on social media, inviting guest speakers from career services to courses and departmental events at key points throughout the degree—from orientation to comprehensive exams and as graduation nears.

Collaboration with employers provides another key perspective for career support. This will help a department and its students know of shifting job market needs and enhance career exploration activities and pathway information. Collaboration with employers can take many forms related to career exploration, including an employer or alumni advisory board to provide a feedback loop and inform programmatic changes, participation in career events, guest speakers at a class, sponsorship of a student organization or class project, serving as an internship site, and distribution of jobs and internships.

Departmental career data should be collected and results should be communicated to prospective and current students. Career outcomes data at the department level helps with admissions, retention, and career exploration (Allum et al., 2014). It is important for institutions and departments to collect data regarding graduate career paths so students know what options may be present. In their recent survey of graduate student data collection methods, Hoffer et al. (2019) conducted a survey of 130 U.S. institutions. More than 87% of respondents said that graduate career data was used to inform career guidance. Students may not know where to start their career search. If students are feeling lost about where to go after graduation, this data serves as a starting point for their career search and exploration. Graduate career data is most frequently collected each year through a survey of graduates, web-based secondary data collection via LinkedIn, and social media (Hoffer et al., 2019).

Gathering and sharing graduate career data is a challenging endeavor. Limited budgets, staff resources, low response rate, and finding graduates are main challenges (Hoffer et al., 2019). Because of these challenges, it is recommended to use a collaborative approach. For example, staff resources can be shared with offices of institutional research to partner with departments and career offices to develop and distribute surveys.

Conclusion

Graduate students face challenging, highly individualized career choices. In order to provide the best guidance possible, university administrators and faculty must first understand the specific needs of the students that they serve and then provide supports at the individual student and institutional levels. Recommendations to implement targeted individual career development support include providing help for students to become skills translators from academic to nonacademic settings that match an employer audience and incorporation of self-assessment for students to become an expert in themselves and what they want in a career. Institutional career support should be collaborative from faculty, staff, alumni, and employers, embedded in and out of the curriculum to provide a variety of exploration opportunities, and emphasize career data of alumni.

References

Allum, J. R., Kent, J. D., & McCarthy, M. T. (2014). *Understanding PhD career pathways for program improvement: A CGS Report.* Council of Graduate Schools.

Bodewits, K., Gramlich, P., & Giltner, D. (2018, March 26). *The autopilot postdoc.* http://blogs.nature.com/naturejobs/2018/03/26/the-autopilot-postdoc/

Burnett, W., & Evans, D. J. (2016). *Designing your life: How to build a well-lived, joyful life.* Alfred A. Knopf.

Denecke, D., Feaster, K., & Stone, K. (2017). *Professional development: Shaping effective programs for STEM graduate students.* Council of Graduate Schools.

Fuhrmann, C. N., Halme, D. G., O'Sullivan, P. S., & Lindstaedt, B. (2011). Improving graduate education to support a branching career pipeline: Recommendations based on a survey of doctoral students in the basic biomedical sciences. *CBE—Life Sciences Education, 10*(3), 239–249. https://doi.org/10.1187/cbe.11-02-0013

Graduate Career Consortium. (2019). *About.* https://www.gradcareerconsortium.org/about.php

Hoffer, T., Stewart, D., Bradburn, N., & Knepler, E. (2019). *Progress and pitfalls in tracking U.S. doctoral career paths.* http://www.norc.org/Research/Projects/Pages/progress-and-pitfalls-in-monitoring-stem-doctoral-degree-holders-career-paths.aspx

National Academies of Sciences, Engineering, and Medicine. (2018). *Graduate STEM education for the 21st century.* The National Academies Press.

National Center for Education Statistics. (2018). *Trends in student loan debt for graduate school completers.* https://nces.ed.gov/programs/coe/pdf/coe_tub.pdf

National Center for Education Statistics. (2019). *The condition of education: Postbaccalaureate enrollment.* https://nces.ed.gov/programs/coe/indicator_chb.asp

National Science Foundation. (2008). *Doctorate recipients from U.S. universities: Summary report 2007–08*. https://wayback.archiveit.org/5902/20160210221155/http://www.nsf.gov/statistics/nsf10309/content.cfm?pub_id=3996&id=8

National Science Foundation. (2018). *Doctorate recipients from U.S. universities: 2017* (Special Report NSF 19-301). Author.

Okahana, H., & Kinoshita, T. (2018*). Doctoral career pathways. Closing gaps in our knowledge of doctoral career pathways: How well did a humanities PhD prepare them?* Council of Graduate Schools.

Okahana, H., & Zhou, E. (2018). *Graduate enrollment and degrees: 2007 to 2017.* Council of Graduate Schools.

Okahana, H., Zhou, E., & Kinoshita, T. (2018). *Doctoral career pathways. Closing gaps in our knowledge of doctoral career pathways: How well did a STEM PhD train degree recipients for their careers?* Council of Graduate Schools.

Rockey, S. (2012). *What we've learned about graduate students.* NIH Office of External Research. https://nexus.od.nih.gov/all/2012/06/27/what-wevelearned-about-graduate-students/

Schlosser, L. Z., Lyons, H. Z., Talleyrand, R. M., Kim, B. S. K., & Johnson, W. B. (2011). Advisor–advisee relationships in graduate training programs. *Journal of Career Development, 38*(1), 3–18. https://doi.org/10.1177/0894845309358887

Sinche, M. V. (2016). *Next gen doctoral: A guide to career paths in science.* Harvard University Press.

Thiry, H. Laursen, S. L., Loshbaugh, H. G. (2015). "How do I get from here to there?" An examination of PhD science students' career preparation and decision making. *International Journal of Doctoral Studies, 10*(1), 237–256. https://doi.org/10.28945/2280

Vick, J. M., & Furlong, J. (2016). *The academic job search handbook* (5th ed.). University of Pennsylvania Press.

13

FINANCIAL MATTERS IN GRADUATE EDUCATION

Phil Schuman, Salome Aluso, and David J. Nguyen

As a graduate program coordinator, I (Nguyen) often field many questions from prospective and current students related to financial matters. Some questions that I have received include: "how much is the stipend? Is that enough to live on in Athens, Ohio? How much is rent? What percentage of students take out student loans?" After students matriculate, I often overhear students during class breaks asking each other about other financially implicated questions about graduate student life, such as, "are you going to the National Association of Student Personnel (NASPA) conference?" or "How many students do you have to recruit for your dissertation study?" While the conference name may be interchangeable, what remains constant is that many graduate students are interested in attending professional and scholarly conferences during their tenure as graduate students. Furthermore, conducting research is an expensive endeavor that many students are unaware of until it comes time for conducting the study. Discussing these types of events are important for socializing students to graduate student life and their field of choice (Duran & Allen, 2020; Gardner & Barnes, 2007; Signal et al., 2021). The immediate follow-up to the conference question is: "how are you going to pay for that?" Financial questions loom large for many students that pay for their education.

Generally speaking, graduate students piece together their financial picture through multiple sources of financial support, including fellowships, assistantships, and personal sources (e.g., loans, family contributions). Financing graduate education is a "complex matter" involving both tangible ("cost, price, personal income, multiple types of assistantships, and fellowships") and intangible factors ("personal attitudes toward, understanding of, and psychological approaches to acquiring and using money"; Nettles & Millett, 2006, p. 71).

Fellowships are often considered top prizes in graduate education. These institutional financial awards typically provide a tuition waiver and pay individual student fees in exchange for no or few work expectations (Nettles & Millett, 2006). *Assistantships* typically come in three forms: teaching, research, and administrative. Research assistantships allow students to work with a faculty member to gain research skills by working on the faculty member's research agenda. Teaching assistantships include teaching responsibilities that may be in the form of classroom support or teaching a class section. Administrative assistantships are where students work for an on-campus office such as career services. Due to assistantships being packaged differently, they vary in level of tuition coverage, stipend amount, and other financial elements such as health insurance. Finally, personal funds involve a student's personal savings, familial support, and student loans. The 2018 Survey of Earned Doctorates (SED) (National Science Foundation, 2018) found that students mostly commonly funded their doctoral education using research assistantships (33.0%), fellowships (25.3%), teaching assistantships (21.5%), and own resources (15.2%). As illustrated in Nguyen's first chapter, although there is variation across discipline and field (see chapter 1, this volume), students rely on institutional support for their financial stability.

Numerous studies have focused on the critical role of financial support and its relationship to important outcomes, such as the decision to enroll in enrollment decisions (Heller, 2001; Malcom & Dowd, 2012; Perna, 2004), time-to-degree (Abedi & Benkin, 1987; Ehrenberg & Mavros, 1995; Maher et al., 2004; Nettles & Millett, 2006), attrition (Berelson, 1960; Gardner, 2007; Lovitts, 2001; Nettles & Millett, 2006; Strayhorn, 2010; Zhou & Okahana, 2019), persistence decision (Mendoza et al., 2014), and socialization (Larson et al., 2019; Nguyen, 2016; Signal et al., 2021). In short, these studies show that money matters in graduate education. In this chapter, we first discuss research on the effects of finances on graduate students lives, then we highlight suggestions for what graduate students should know, and then we conclude with recommendations that departments and institutions should consider in matters of graduate student financial well-being.

Finances and Graduate Students' Lives

Like undergraduate students, there is not a common way to classify graduate students. For example, some have families, while others have been working for years and have decided to return. Similarly, there is wide variation in how students pay for their graduate education. Though some students have a "fully-funded package" they may also take on additional student loan debt to supplement living and personal expenses, while others can draw on familial support (Nguyen, 2016). These scenarios show that there is not a one-size-fits-all approach to the typical graduate students.

On average, graduate students earn approximately $18,700 per academic year (National Center for Educational Statistics, 2019). For some students, this stipend does not include a tuition scholarship, meaning that student loans will feature prominently in funding their graduate student experience. In cases where student loans are cost prohibitive or unavailable (e.g., like for international students), students may turn to secondary jobs, known as "side hustles," to support their graduate education. Students take on these secondary jobs, which can be unknown to their faculty or violate their fellowships or assistantships contracts, and can take away time from studying, researching, or completing tasks necessary for degree completion.

Many graduate students are in a state of financial fragility, as they may have stopped their careers to pursue additional education or have entered graduate school directly after their undergraduate programs. Fifty-seven percent of students say they would have trouble getting $500 in cash or credit to address an emergency should something happen (Trellis, 2018). Due to the lack of emergency funds, a significant event requiring financial resources such as a medical emergency or car trouble may cause a student to shift their priorities away from school. Research reports indicate that graduate students worry about meeting monthly expenses and feel stressed about their finances. Thirty-eight percent of both master's students and doctoral students worried about meeting their monthly financial expenses. Overall, 60% of master's and 55% of doctoral students felt stressed about their financial position (Trellis, 2018).

Financial circumstances and graduate student quality of life are closely intertwined (Acker & Haque, 2015; Rogers et al., 2016; Wilcox et al., 2019). The financial challenges have prompted graduate students to wonder "whether the financial reward [after completion] compensate[s] for the poor lifestyle [now]" (Rogers et al., 2016, p. 1724). Within the past decade, more and more institutions are taking a closer look at the mental health and stressors of graduate students (Johns Hopkins University, 2013; University of California, 2015). The University of California-Berkeley and Johns Hopkins University have released lengthy reports about the experiences of graduate students. These reports show that students are more concerned about their financial situations than any other aspect of graduate student life.

A primary challenge with the financial lives of graduate students is that few studies have included or center the perspectives of graduate students.

Two recent examples of stakeholder groups paying less attention to graduate students' financial lives include when the U.S. Congress eliminated subsidized federal student loans for borrowing graduate students and the proposed "Grad Tax" that was being considered on tuition waivers. In the former situation, to curtail arguments around the "debt ceiling" Congress eliminated the type of student loans where graduate students did not accrue interest on their loan balance while enrolled. The policy implementation effect led to borrowing students taking on more debt at the conclusion of their programs (Belasco et al., 2014; Webber & Burns, 2020). With the Grad Tax situation, U.S. Congress was discussing how to tax the waiver as income to graduate students rather than having a more lenient tax provision as is currently the case. These events highlight how graduate students can be viewed as "pawns" in legislative battles.

Financial circumstances and considerations for graduate students are a by-product of financial knowledge, financial stress, and financial well-being. Research studies on the financial knowledge of college students consistently demonstrate low financial knowledge (Montalto et al., 2019; Shaulskiy et al., 2015). While undergraduate students are different from graduate students, the samples that include graduate students also illustrate low levels of financial knowledge (Chen & Volpe, 1998). In turn, these low levels of financial acuity can directly shape their graduate student experience by inducing financial stress and concerns, which translate into increased absenteeism from work (MetLife, 2012), act as distractions while at work (American Institute of Certified Public Accountants, 2013), and cause employees to spend at least 3 hours each workweek thinking about or handling financial problems (PricewaterhouseCoopers, 2014).

In addition to how finances can affect their academic performance, graduate students begin to frame their existence more from a survival standpoint or one where people delay important milestones in emerging adulthood like financial independence (Acker & Haque, 2015; Cornwall et al., 2019). Participants in Cornwall et al.'s (2019) study of stressors for early-career doctoral students reported "financial stress related to transitional issues like finding acceptable accommodation, paying medical bills, and maintaining an income stream in the absence of a scholarship" (p. 375). In a study by Acker and Haque (2015), they found that doctoral students were struggling financially and these challenges led to poor living conditions that detracted from their educational studies. Finally, the institutional studies mentioned earlier in this chapter highlighted the financial challenges, including having to live with family, living more than an hour away from campus, and scraping together funds to make monthly ends meet. Graduate programs, departments, and colleges need to do a better job of educating or at the very least being open to discussing the financial matters of graduate education.

What Students Need to Know

Before diving into what specific things a graduate student should know about their personal finances, it is important to remember that every student's financial situation differs. Though students may compare stipend amounts, students may have more or less access to various financial resources to support their lives as graduate students (Nguyen, 2016). Personal finance is aptly named because it is specific to an individual's or family's financial situation and what works for them may not be best for another individual and/or family. In regard to specific financial knowledge, the following list details what is most important for graduate students to know and consider:

How Are You Going to Fund Your Graduate Studies?

As mentioned earlier, there are a variety of ways that students can fund their graduate education. These different forms include but are not limited to assistantships, in the form of research, administrative, and teaching; fellowships; both institutional and national awards; personal funds; and loans. Whether a graduate student completes an assistantship or takes out a loan, each funding method can profoundly shape the graduate student experience. Furthermore, the funding amount varies significantly across the forms which may require a student to live off-campus (Acker & Haque, 2015). Since this factor has been shown to be of great importance, students should consider *how* they are going to fund their education and *how much* the stipend is and for *how long* the funding is being offered. What we mean by this statement is that assistantships, for example, come in varying types, as well as varying lengths, such as 9-month, 10-month, and 12-month contracts, and durations, such as 2-year, 4-year, and 5-year packages.

Think About Your Student Loan Repayment Plan

For students opting to pay for their graduate education through student loans, a student must consider the different repayment options. For full-time graduate students, undergraduate student loans may not need to be paid if they are financed by the federal government through the federal Stafford Loan program. In some cases, loan balances may not accrue interest because you are a full-time graduate student. This only applies to subsidized undergraduate student loans. Subsidized graduate student loans were eliminated through the Budget Control Act of 2011. Accordingly, graduate students borrowing through federal U.S. lending programs will be subjected to interest accruing.

Paying for Your Life as a Graduate Student

Graduate school can be a frugal living experience. Though students may receive a stipend and tuition waiver, they may have additional costs such as institutional fees, living expenses, and health insurance. These finances add up: 32.1% of graduate students report their finances as being traumatic or very difficult to handle (American College Health Association, 2019). When students feel stressed about their finances, it is possible they may take on additional consumer debt to support their lives. It is important to be aware of how short-term financial choices may impact important future transactions such as purchasing a home and ability to meet financial demands.

How Will You Deal With Upcoming Expenses in Graduate School?

Life continues while in graduate school and can be marked with circumstances that alter your financial stability. For example, your car can break down, your phone could fall out of your pocket and break, and your computer could magically decide to stop working one day. While credit cards are the source of funds for these types of emergencies, if at all possible you should build up an emergency fund—about $1,000—before starting school. Whether it is through a summer job, a school-year job, or money from a previous full-time job, work to create a $1,000 emergency fund to help you in school. Furthermore, the emergency fund will decrease the amount of borrowed student loans, save on credit card interest rates when charging it, and provide you with a sense of financial assurance that if something happens, things will work out and that you will not have to spend the next several years paying it off on a credit card.

Create a Budget

Creating a budget will be a key to your time as a graduate student. While many know that they are supposed to budget, it does not necessarily mean that they are doing it. While there is no recommended percentage allocation for spending in graduate school, it is still important for you to figure out where your priorities lie, how much money you have in your bank account(s), and what you are willing to spend per month across several different categories. Not only will it help you save money while in school, it will also create a reasonable standard of living that will be much easier to translate once you have a full-time job. The people that struggle the most are those that inflate their lifestyle while in school and then do not have the income to support that same standard after they graduate from grad school.

Supporting the Financial Challenges of Graduate Students

In recent years, more institutions have begun to provide resources to help students with their financial questions, although the majority have placed the emphasis on assisting undergraduate students. In many cases, graduate students are harder to locate with information because graduate students are more localized to where their academic program is, rather than the entire campus like undergraduate students (Golde & Dore, 2001). In addition to the location of graduate students, many have unique financial situations that may require greater financial acuity to help graduate students make better financial choices.

Additionally, it is important to remember that the support needed for students when it comes to finances is not just in the form of financial education, but also in the form of assistance toward financial stress. For example, Americans cite finances as one of their top sources of stress. If not addressed properly, this stress could play a role in distracting a student from being able to complete their degree or delay their completion date. For students with families this financial stress could lead to relationship issues, which would increase the likelihood of distractions from degree completion. Regardless, any presence of financial stress increases the likelihood of mental health issues, which severely limits a students' ability to focus on their education.

Recommendations

To better support graduate students financially or when making financial decisions, it is important that key stakeholders such as institutions, departments, and faculty take a more active role and employ better strategies that influence students' financial decisions and well-being. The following are some practical considerations for stakeholders that can be used to guide graduate students toward effective financial behavior and attitudes.

Program/Department Level: Showing Students the Costs of Living

Graduate programs are in a unique position to ease financial concerns of students by being transparent about the financial aspects of graduate education. For example, graduate programs can survey their students about where they live in relation to their campuses. During recruitment events or further communications, the programs can share with prospective students about the costs of living, where many students live, what students do for fun, and some of the sample events that the graduate program and institution may offer. In addition to furnishing this information, programs can use social media and electronic communications to facilitate roommate connections that may help defray living costs. Another suggestion would be for programs to set up peer network systems that would allow students to connect with another student as they undergo the application and matriculation processes. Graduate programs can use these experiences to not only help with program recruitment but also to share lived financial realities for students.

Program/Department Level: Encouraging and Supporting Students to Access Scholarships Outside the Department/Institution

With most graduate students relying heavily on assistantships or loans to finance their graduate education, additional scholarships or fellowships can help lessen their financial burden. Graduate students may have additional financial expenses outside of school such as caring for family members or pets, life changing events such as planning a wedding, or medical expenses that may put a strain on their income (which is mostly the monthly stipend). Therefore, having access to external scholarships as an additional source of income during this period could help them finance their education better and reduce the stress that comes with worrying about everyday financial decisions. Moreover, it also lessens the burden of institutions/departments on having to support the financial needs of graduate students.

There are various ways that graduate students can access external scholarships. Basic internet searches can lead one to a list of scholarships/ fellowships for graduate students. The important thing is to make sure that you meet the eligibility criteria for the scholarship or award one is applying for, and make sure that you work on the application and provide all the required documents on time to be considered for the scholarship. An example of one of these scholarships is the American Association of University Women (AAUW) scholarship award that targets non-American women pursuing graduate education. Women who apply for this scholarship should demonstrate that their research has a focus on the advancement of girls or women and are eligible for a $12,000 research award per year. A graduate student who wins this award can use these funds as an additional means of financing their graduate education. Graduate student advisors and faculty should take the opportunity to expose students to the knowledge of the existence of these opportunities and highly encourage them to apply for these scholarships.

Institutional Level: On-Demand Online Education

Many institutions who provide financial education use an online platform and/or website to assist their program. Online platforms and websites are beneficial because they provide 24/7 access to financial education for students. In the case of graduate students, this is critical as their unique schedules and potential inability to be able to meet during regular hours could prevent them from accessing financial education if it is only offered during the day.

Online education is great because it also allows for the user to be able to choose what content is most relevant to them and get the answers they need. The only issue is that if they do have additional questions based on what they have learned, they may be unable to get answers immediately. Still, for those who may not feel comfortable talking to someone about their financial situation the ability to learn on their own could be worth that downside.

When I (Schuman) first began presenting information online to our students at Indiana University we presented everything as topic-based. This meant that if a student had a question about credit or budgeting or student loans they could just click on a link and get the information they needed. While that worked for some, those students who did not know what they needed to know about finances or had questions that were more situation-based rather than topic-based had less of a chance to find what was most necessary for them.

As a result, we ended up building our own financial literacy platform designed to teach students what they needed to know based on who they were as a student. In the case of graduate students, we built a few different courses: one for graduate students in general, one for students in medical or dental school, and one for students who considered themselves to be financially independent. For these graduate school courses, we built modules specific to the following issues:

- funding graduate school
- creating a student loan repayment plan
- funding a lifestyle while in graduate school
- working while in school
- managing coursework with a family
- managing coursework with a full-time job

- buying versus renting a house
- opening your own practice
- dealing with financial stress

We have been able to keep up with the demands and interests of students regarding their finances by using online delivery. For an institution wanting to address financial education with their graduate students, online is highly recommended.

Institutional Level: Financial Wellness and Literacy Sessions/Programs

At the institutional level, financial literacy and wellness education could be a valuable resource in helping graduate students ascertain necessary knowledge and skills that could be transferable to their own financial decisions. The sessions could potentially target graduate students' financial needs and challenges such as budgeting, saving, and appropriate money management skills. These financial literacy sessions have the advantage of teaching students how to gain control of their own finances, especially students who could be struggling with student loans and high credit card payments. Furthermore, these literacy education programs could help graduate students plan appropriately for their future by learning skills that would help them understand their finances, the choices they have based on their income, and how to make healthy financial decisions such as using credit cards wisely.

Indiana University launched the MoneySmart platform which contains information on a variety of financial topics such as money management, budgeting, loan repayment options, and podcasts with a range of financial topics. Through this platform, students can easily access financial knowledge as needed. The University of Alabama Birmingham has established the Institute of Financial Literacy program through their School of Business. Through this program, students, faculty, and community members can access programs, materials, and financial counseling to enhance their financial well-being. In 2016, the University of South Carolina Upstate offered a 5-week Lunch and Learn series that focused on financial education topics such as personal finances, insurance protection, individual investing, retirement plans, and estate planning. These sessions were free for students.

The previous examples highlight that institutions understand the importance of providing financial education to their students. By doing so, students get the message that the institution values their financial well-being, and this helps impact their financial decisions. In addition to this, the skills learned will be of value to students long after they leave the institution. Institutions therefore need to create and provide different avenues and resources that would help students access financial education.

Institutional Level: Debt Letter

Since 2012–2013, Indiana University has been issuing "debt letters" to its student borrowers. These letters inform students how much they have borrowed up to that point in their academic career, their projected repayment upon graduation, and information about resources on campus that will help them with any financial questions they may have. These debt letters were started as a result of student focus groups where they indicated they had no idea how much money they had borrowed or—in some cases—that they had borrowed at all. These letters provide an opportunity for students to understand their current debt situation and allow for them to respond by adjusting their borrowing for the upcoming year so that it is more efficient relative to their financial situation.

The simplicity—and potential effectiveness—of the debt letter has caught on among states around the country. Currently, there are 13 states across the United States that require aid-granting institutions to provide debt letters to their students (Ascendium Education Solutions, 2020). And while there is research that indicates the debt letters themselves do not lead to decreased debt (Darolia & Harper, 2018), that same research does indicate that the issuance of them leads to more frequent contact with financial aid offices.

A recommendation for those interested in issuing debt letters is to do a thorough review of how the letter is crafted to maximize the likelihood that recipients will read it. There is research available that shows how humans read letters and websites; utilizing the findings available could increase the likelihood that the letters will be understood. In addition, it is important to pilot the letters with a specific group of students before you implement them university-wide so that you can get feedback and tailor the letter to better fit the needs of your students.

The bottom line is that debt letters provide a very simple way to communicate financial information to students and can spark students to be reactive and proactive in regard to their debt.

Institutional Level: Emergency Financial Aid Resources

Due to the ever-changing economy, fluctuations in the funding of higher education, rising costs in healthcare, and other disasters such as the COVID pandemic, graduate students face financial setbacks that could affect their mental health and academic performance and can make a student drop out of school. For some graduate students, the COVID-19 pandemic affected their summer internship plans, which created a ripple effect because they lost their source of income for the summer months when they were not getting a stipend from their departments. This in turn affected how they would meet their basic needs such as housing, paying bills, transportation, and so forth. Universities can help students going through sudden financial hardships by creating emergency financial grants for their students.

While student financial needs may vary when experiencing a crisis, institutions need to be better prepared to assist their students. If students need food, the institution should have a food pantry or other resources that will help the student access food. If the students lack housing, there should be temporary housing that can be provided until the student can work out their situation. Some universities such as Ohio University also have emergency microgrants for students who may be facing financial hardships or emergency situations. In addition to this, international students at this institution can access financial assistance through the International Students Emergency Relief fund that was created to aid international students facing financial hardships during the COVID-19 pandemic.

Conclusion

This chapter is not intended to be a one-size-fits-all approach to financial support for graduate students. Instead, we outline the challenges that many may face, while offering smaller, potentially cost neutral recommendations to help graduate students live their lives, while also helping them to become more financially capable and perceive more financial stability.

References

Abedi, J., & Benkin, E. (1987). The effects of students' academic, financial, and demographic variables on time to the doctorate. *Research in Higher Education, 27*(1), 3–14. doi.org/10.1007/bf00992302

Acker, S., & Haque, E. (2015). The struggle to make sense of doctoral study. *Higher Education Research & Development, 34*(2), 229–241. doi.org/10.1080/0729436 0.2014.956699

American College Health Association. (2019). *Graduate/professional student reference group executive summary fall 2019.* https://www.acha.org/documents/ncha/ NCHA-II_SPRING_2019_GRADUATE_AND_PROFESSIONAL_REFER-ENCE_GROUP_EXECUTIVE_SUMMARY.pdf

American Institute of Certified Public Accountants. (2013). *AICPA survey: Money stress taking toll on many Americans' waistlines, friendships, sleep.* http://www.aicpa. org/press/pressreleases/2013/pages/aicpa-survey-money-stress-taking- toll.aspx

Ascendium Education Solutions, Inc. (2020). *Definitive guide to debt letters.* https:// www.attigo.com/definitive-guide-to-debt-letters

Belasco, A. S., Trivette, M. J., & Webber, K. L. (2014). Advanced degrees of debt: Analyzing the patterns and determinants of graduate student borrow- ing. *The Review of Higher Education, 37*(4), 469–497. https://doi.org/10.1353/ rhe.2014.0030

Berelson, B. (1960). *Graduate education in the United States.* McGraw-Hill.

Chen, H., & Volpe, R. P. (1998). An analysis of personal financial literacy among college students. *Financial Services Review, 7*(2), 107–128.

Cornwall, J., Mayland, E. C., van der Meer, J., Spronken-Smith, R. A., Tustin, C., & Blyth, P. (2019). Stressors in early-stage doctoral students. *Studies in Continuing Education, 41*(3), 363–380. https://doi.org/10.1080/0158037X.2018.1534821

Darolia, R., & Harper, C. (2018). Information use and attention deferment in college student loan decisions: Evidence from a debt letter experiment. *Educational Evalu- ation and Policy Analysis, 40*(1), 129–150. doi.org/10.3102/0162373717734368

Duran, A., & Allen, E. (2020). Exploring how professional associations socialize student affairs graduate students and new professionals. *Journal of Student Affairs Research and Practice, 57*(2), 132–147. https://doi.org/10.1080/19496591.2019.1625779

Ehrenberg, R. G., & Mavros, P. (1995). Do doctoral students' financial support pat- terns affect their times-to-degree and completion probabilities? *Journal of Human Resources, 30*(3), 581–609. doi.org/10.3386/w4070

Gardner, S. K. (2007). "I heard it through the grapevine": Doctoral student socialization in chemistry and history. *Higher Education, 54*(5), 723–740. doi. org/10.1007/s10734-006-9020-x

Gardner, S. K., & Barnes, B. J. (2007). Graduate student involvement: Socialization for the professional role. *Journal of College Student Development, 48*(4), 369–387. doi.org/10.1353/csd.2007.0036

Golde, C. M., & Dore, T. M. (2001). *At cross purposes: What the experiences of today's doctoral students reveal about doctoral education.* Pew Charitable Trusts.

Heller, D. E. (2001). *Debts and decisions: Student loans and their relationship to gradu- ate school and career choice.* Lumina Foundation for Education.

Johns Hopkins University. (2013). *Committee on the future of PhD education: Final report.* http://web.jhu.edu/administration/provost/docs/FinalReport_Commit- teeOnPhDEducation .pdf

Larson, J. B., Nguyen, D. J., Opoczynski, R., & Vizvary, G. (2019). Designing a pro- fessional development group for leader learners enrolled in graduate education. *Journal of Leadership Studies, 13*(2), 73–76. https://doi.org/10.1002/jls.21644

Lovitts, B. E. (2001). *Leaving the ivory tower: The causes and consequences of departure from doctoral study.* Rowman and Littlefield.

Maher, M., Ford, M., & Thompson, C. (2004). Degree progress of women doctoral students: Factors that constrain, facilitate, and differentiate. *Review of Higher Education, 27*(3), 385–408. doi.org/10.1353/rhe.2004.0003

Malcom, L. E., & Dowd, A. C. (2012). The impact of undergraduate debt on the graduate school enrollment of STEM baccalaureates. *Review of Higher Education, 35*(2), 265–305. doi.org/10.1353/rhe.2012.0007

Mendoza, P., Villarreal, P., & Gunderson, A. (2014). Within-year retention among PhD students: The effect of debt, assistantships, and fellowships. *Research in Higher Education, 55*(7), 650–685. https://doi.org/10.1007/s11162-014-9327-x

MetLife. (2012). *10th annual study of employee benefits trends: Seeing opportunity in shifting tides.* http://benefitcommunications.com/upload/downloads/MetLife_10-Annual-EBTS.pdf

Montalto, C. P., Phillips, E. L., McDaniel, A., & Baker, A. R. (2019). College student financial wellness: Student loans and beyond. *Journal of Family and Economic Issues, 40*(1), 3–21. https://doi.org/10.1007/s10834-018-9593-4

National Center for Education Statistics. (2019). Table 5: Percentage of graduate students receiving federal financial aid and, among recipients, average amount received (in constant 2016 dollars), by selected enrollment and student characteristics: 2003–04, 2007–08, 2011–12, and 2015–16. *Trends in graduate student financing: Selected years: 2003–04 to 2015–16.* https://nces.ed.gov/pubs2019/2019485.pdf

National Science Foundation (2018). *Doctorate recipients' primary source of financial support, by broad field of study, sex, citizenship status, ethnicity, and race: 2018.* https://ncses.nsf.gov/pubs/nsf20301/data-tables/#group5

Nettles, M. T., & Millett, C. M. (2006). *Three magic letters: Getting to PhD.* The Johns Hopkins University Press.

Nguyen, D. J. (2016). *Does money really matter in doctoral education? Exploring the influence of financial considerations on doctoral student socialization* (Publication No. 10144608) [Doctoral dissertation, Michigan State University]. ProQuest Dissertations and Theses Global.

Perna, L. W. (2004). Understanding the decision to enroll in graduate school: Sex and racial/ethnic group differences. *Journal of Higher Education, 75*(5), 487–527. doi.org/10.1080/00221546.2004.11772335

PricewaterhouseCoopers. (2014). *Employee financial wellness survey.* http://www.pwc.com/en_US/us/private-company-services/publications/assets/pwc-employee-financial-wellness-survey-2014-results.pdf.

Rogers, M. E., Creed, P. A., Searle, J., & Nicholls, S. L. (2016). Coping with medical training demands: Thinking of dropping out, or in it for the long haul. *Studies in Higher Education, 41*(9), 1715–1732. https://doi.org/10.1080/03075079.2014.999318

Shaulskiy, S., Duckett, K., Kennedy-Phillips, L., & McDaniel, A. (2015). Exploring differences in college student financial wellness by institution type. *Journal of Student Affairs Research and Practice, 52*(3), 250–261. https://doi.org/10.1080/19496591.2015.1035382

Signal, S., Nguyen, D. J., Amey, M., & Perkins, R. (2021). Supporting poor and working-class students' access to professional development during doctoral programs in education. In G. Martin & M. S. Ardoin (Eds.), *Social class supports: Programs and practices to serve and sustain poor and working-class students through higher education* (pp. 298–310). Stylus.

Strayhorn, T. L. (2010). Money matters: The influence of financial factors on graduate school persistence. *Journal of Student Financial Aid, 40*(3), 4–25. https://ir.library.louisville.edu/jsfa/vol40/iss3/1/

Trellis Research Student Financial Wellness Survey. (2018). *Student financial wellness survey.* https://www.trelliscompany.org/wp-content/uploads/2019/03/SFWS-Spring-2018-Summary.pdf

University of California Berkeley. (2015). *Graduate student happiness and well-being report.* Author.

Webber, K. L., & Burns, R. (2020). Increases in graduate student debt in the US: 2000 to 2016. *Research in Higher Education, 62,* 709–732. https://doi.org/10.1007/s11162-020-09611-x

Wilcox, M. M., Barbaro-Kukade, L., Pietrantonio, K. R., Franks, D. N., & Davis, B. L. (2019). It takes money to make money: Inequity in psychology graduate student borrowing and financial stressors. *Training and Education in Professional Psychology.* Advance online publication. https://doi.org/10.1037/tep0000294

Zhou, E., & Okahana, H. (2019). The role of department supports on doctoral completion and time-to-degree. *Journal of College Student Retention: Research, Theory & Practice, 20*(4), 511–529. doi.org/10.1177/1521025116682036

14

ENGAGEMENT IN GRADUATE STUDENT ORGANIZATIONS AND PROGRAMMING

Matthew Couch and Kerry M. Hodak

Involvement in out-of-class activities is a critical component of a holistic college education, contributing to students' achievement of many of the cognitive and developmental outcomes colleges are expected by accreditors, government agencies, and the general public to facilitate (Keeling, 2006). Countless studies based on the experiences of undergraduate students have reached consistent conclusions about the benefits of significant levels of involvement (Gellin, 2003; Terenzini et al., 1996; Wolf-Wendel et al., 2009). However, graduate education is structured differently from undergraduate education where students often are more disciplinary or field bound and may not even attend classes in another building on their graduate campus (Golde & Dore, 2001). Given the amount of intense time commitment graduate students invest into their program, they may no longer have the time, interest, or need for activities that may ultimately detract from their more focused academic pursuits (Gardner & Gopaul, 2012). Cocurricular involvement for graduate students is therefore not typically well-promoted, nor are significant resources often allocated for out-of-class engagement beyond academic events (Gardner & Barnes, 2007). Some institutions have challenged the notion that graduate students do not want or need cocurricular opportunities, and their efforts have been met with enthusiasm from grateful participants longing for interdisciplinary social opportunities, personal and professional enrichment, and family programming.

In this chapter, we begin by describing the theoretical background for the importance of cocurricular involvement for graduate students. We then offer some best practices for student organizations and intentional programmatic offerings as effective means of graduate student engagement. We also provide commentary on appropriate resources for fostering engagement for this population and explore some of the unique challenges and considerations when tailoring thoughtful programmatic experiences.

The Importance of Graduate Student Involvement

In 2011, the Association of American Colleges & Universities (AAC&U) engaged educators, employers, and accreditors to develop a set of principled learning outcomes for undergraduate education. In spite of the specialization that defines most graduate programs, these recommended outcomes can be further developed in the postbaccalaureate sphere, and they are tied in measurable ways to high-impact practices in the university cocurriculum. Among these outcomes are intellectual and practical skills, such as critical thinking, oral communication, teamwork, and problem-solving. Personal and social responsibility outcomes are also emphasized, including intercultural proficiency, ethical reasoning, and civic engagement (AAC&U, 2011). These fundamental learning outcomes of a 21st century college education have been demonstrated to occur in cocurricular settings, making the role of these out-of-class experiences vital to holistic student development (Astin, 1996; Gellin, 2003).

Practitioners who design and support purposeful cocurricular environments have relied heavily on the body of research that began with Astin's (1984) theory of student involvement. The key postulate of Astin's theory is that the amount of a student's learning and personal development is directly proportional to the quantity and quality of their involvement. Innumerable studies have sprung from Astin's foundational work applying student involvement theory to the experiences of students of various demographics and institutional settings, and the existing literature generally depicts the construct of involvement as quite helpful in the achievement of positive student outcomes (Kuh et al., 2008; Pascarella & Terenzini, 2005; Zacherman & Foubert, 2014). In their scan of the student involvement literature, Gardner and Barnes (2007) commented on the lack of known studies centering the graduate student experience, and that gap in college impact scholarship still has yet to be adequately addressed. However, the tenets of student involvement theory and related constructs like sense of belonging hold a great deal of relevance for postbaccalaureate students.

Astin (1984) derived his theory by examining the ways in which students' precollege characteristics, or inputs, interact with the college environment to produce various outcomes. Outcomes like student development, satisfaction with college, learning, persistence, and degree completion are as desirable for graduate students as they are for undergraduates. To assume that students entering graduate programs with various inputs—which may include habits of high involvement formed at previous stages of their education or career—could not benefit from interactions with purposefully designed environments in order to reach these outcomes is to ignore the applicability of Astin's framework to any level of education. Whether a graduate student matriculates directly after completing an undergraduate degree or rejoins the academy after time spent on career, family, military duty, or other commitments, that student brings unique inputs into the environment, and their prospects for degree completion can be improved through engagement with peers in cocurricular settings. Peer interaction contributes to sense of belonging, which has a powerful effect on positive educational outcomes (Strayhorn, 2012).

Sense of belonging to a group or community promotes overall wellness and personal motivation (Strayhorn, 2012; Wolf-Wendel et al., 2009). Though some graduate students may find this belonging among cohort members through classroom interactions, cocurricular involvement provides students with the opportunity to make connections with peers and to develop deeper affiliations. Belonging is a prerequisite for building self-confidence and realizing one's potential (Maslow, 1943)—developmental tasks that pertain to graduate students seeking a sturdy foundation in an often lonely and competitive environment. Compounding the difficulty in achieving self-confidence is a graduate student's tendency to suffer from imposter syndrome, hindering that student's ability to perceive and accept their own success (Parkman, 2016). A related concept is *mattering*, which is a person's feeling that he or she is noticed, thought of as important, and relies on others (Schlossberg, 1989). Schlossberg suggested the concept of *marginality*, defined as the feeling that one does not matter to others, as the antithesis of mattering. She found that experiences of marginality can result in feelings of depression and insecurity.

The idea that graduate students may find themselves marginalized at their institutions is not farfetched, even if they possess privileged social identities. This sense of marginalization is compounded by a student's own feeling as an imposter in a challenging academic program. When colleges gear their cultural norms and programmatic offerings almost entirely to undergraduate students, graduate students who may be interested in engagement at the institution may think twice about whether or not they are welcome to do so. Further, feelings of isolation that can result from faculty and peer power dynamics within graduate programs can contribute to feelings of marginalization. Scholars have measured the differential experiences of diverse student groups' achievement of sense of belonging, and although specific results have varied, previous research has consistently supported the notion that cocurricular student involvement contributes to the belonging that makes student success so much more possible (Strayhorn, 2012).

Graduate Student Organizations

Among the most well-researched cocurricular activities is participation in clubs or student organizations. Significant statistical correlations have been found between hours per week spent participating in student organizations and public speaking ability, interpersonal skills, and leadership skills (Astin, 1993). Foubert and Grainger (2006) suggested that involvement in student organizations has strong association with establishing and clarifying purpose, educational involvement, career planning, life management, and cultural engagement. Participation in clubs and organizations has also been connected with increased skill development, personal growth, and satisfaction with the college experience (Abrahamowicz, 1988; Astin, 1993). Student organizations provide an important access point for graduate students to establish peer connections, develop vital personal and professional competencies, and work toward establishing the sense of belonging that is so important to retention and degree completion. As Gardner and Barnes (2007) noted, "Graduate students' involvement in organizations and associations allows them to engage with their peers and faculty in ways that contribute to their socialization to the norms of graduate school" (p. 371).

Though most institutions support a student organization community for all students that consists of many different types of groups, including recreational, spiritual, social, and service-based organizations, graduate students often prioritize groups that are closely aligned with their academic discipline, issue-oriented, or identity-based. Recognizing the benefit of students finding small communities of peers who share a common interest, many institutions have developed policies friendly to the origin of new clubs. Establishing a low threshold for minimum membership numbers, structuring a relatively expedient registration process, and offering attractive resources available only to registered organizations are all strategies colleges have employed to foster growth and diversification within their student organization communities. As a result, since the early 2000s, many institutions have experienced what Levine and Dean (2012) referred to as a *mitosis* of student organizations—or a phenomenon in which groups based on broad concepts split into multiple distinct but related clubs. For example, an Accounting Club splits into separate undergraduate and graduate groups. From there, the Graduate Accounting Club may continue to exist but also give rise to an African American Graduate Accounting Club and a Latinx Graduate Accounting Club. As long as enough students are interested and the missions of these niche organizations do not duplicate one another, their existence can represent an opportunity for belonging and community to be built at an accessible level.

Where most graduate student organization involvement is encouraged is at the college or department level. Many departments support graduate groups that enable members to socialize, build out-of-class relationships with faculty advisors, and explore their academic discipline more dynamically than they may be able to in a curricular setting. These types of organizations are particularly vital to the socialization of students whose identification with the university may not yet extend beyond their own department. Another popular student organization setting for graduate students is in activist or issue-based groups, including graduate student government organizations. Graduate students seeking shared governance experience that could prepare them better for institutional service when they join the ranks of the faculty find value in the opportunity to represent their constituents in policy-making settings. Even students who are not planning on academic careers are drawn to the opportunity in student government to advocate for their peers on issues that may have particular importance to them or to the life of the college, such as graduate employee compensation, mental health resources, social justice, and public safety. Other activism-oriented student organizations provide an outlet for students interested in taking action on social justice issues that may pertain to their specific field of study or their life experiences. Finally, identity-based organizations chartered either broadly for graduate students—such as a Black Graduate Student Caucus or a Chinese Graduate Student Association—or developed with a more specific audience in mind—like an Association of Graduate Women in Engineering or an LGBTQ+ Graduate Students in Business organization—help peers support each other based on their deeper understanding of shared social identities. This type of peer interaction helps students find solidarity and achieve a powerful sense of belonging.

Graduate Student Programming

Akin to broad-based programs targeted at large segments of the undergraduate population, graduate students need institutional support and facilitation of programmatic opportunities for their particular interests. According to research by the Council of Graduate Schools (2010), the program environment is critical to student success. Broad-based programs engaging students across disciplines are critical components of an environment that enhances students' completion of their degrees. Graduate students benefit from "campus-wide efforts to bring students together across disciplines and within the department for academic and social interaction" (Council of Graduate Schools, 2010, p. 49). Additionally, professional development programming is specifically addressed as a critical aspect of promising practices.

Within this context, there are specific areas of programming that institutions should pursue to enhance graduate education: enrichment, social, and family. A few general principles apply to programming for graduate students, and we move now into a set of recommendations for best practices.

First, be sure that presenters understand the audience to whom they are presenting. Even if a nutrition workshop has information for individuals at many stages of life, using an example that implies that graduate students are undergraduates living on their own for the first time will lead to graduate students disengaging from the workshop (Paynter & Barnes, 2015). Acknowledge to the graduate students that the event is designed for them. Second, for any event in the evening or on weekends that would be of interest to a graduate student's friend, partner, or roommate, allow students to bring a guest for free or very low cost. Graduate students are less likely to attend an event afterhours on campus if they are not able to include that person in the activity. This is reflective of two characteristics of graduate students—limited time and a social support network beyond the university. Third, the timing of events is critically important. Weekend and evening programs can be successful with greater scheduling flexibility at those times. It is also important to vary when programs are offered. However, there is a critical mass of graduate students who will have the flexibility to attend events during working hours. Weekday events hosted in the morning or lunchtime generally work well.

Fourth, determine multiple methods of communication about the activities offered to graduate students, and do not assume that one method will meet everyone's needs. Although many graduate students may be close in age, the overall population is cross-generational. Therefore, using only one communication strategy geared toward one generation will miss more graduate students than the same strategy focused on traditional undergraduates. Establish an opt-out email list that includes all graduate students. Ensure that all communication through that list is curated based on graduate students' needs and interests. Create an online home where most, if not all, programming is captured on a calendar. Finally, select the type and number of social media outlets that can be properly managed to ensure consistent engagement.

Fifth, ensure that student input is used in developing and refining any programming. Graduate students may serve on a programming committee and engage in planning and executing programs. Another option is an advisory group of graduate students or a graduate student government that provides regular input to staff responsible for planning and implementing programming. In any circumstance, conduct evaluations, and use that feedback to improve recurring programs or to develop new ones. A brief discussion of exemplary programs for the critical areas follows.

Enrichment Programs

Enrichment programs are focused on the interests and needs of graduate students in the areas of professional and personal development. Table 14.1 provides a list of examples of professional and personal development programs. Note that these types of programs should be repeated on regular cycles as resources permit, such as weekly, per term, annually, or biannually.

Social and Family-Friendly Programs

Social and family programming provides opportunities for graduate students to engage with each other and build a community, which addresses many students' sense of isolation. Whether students have their own children, a younger sibling, mentor a child, care for elders, or live in a multigenerational household, family-friendly programming provides a fun experience for students and their guests of all ages. The programs are best designed as free or low-cost opportunities for students to network, experience various offerings within the local community, enjoy programs on campus, and have fun. Table 14.2 provides a list of various social and family-friendly programs. If events take place off campus where parking fees occur, providing transportation from

TABLE 14.1
Examples of Professional and Personal Development Programs

Professional	*Personal*
Academic Job Search Series*	Stress Management
Nonacademic Job Search Series**	Financial Management
Etiquette Dinner	Physical Health Programs
Mentorship Programs	Cooking Classes^
Writing Workshops	Candle Making^
Cultural Competency Education	Glass Blowing^
Skill Building Workshops***	Painting^

*CV Development; research, teaching, and diversity statements, cover letters, interviewing, negotiation
**Resume development (conversion from CV), cover letters, interview skills, negotiation
***Time management, project management, public speaking, conflict management, effective communication, overcoming imposter syndrome
^These programs may also be considered social

TABLE 14.2
Family and Social Events

Type of Events	Examples
Quiz Nights	
Happy Hours	
Speed Dating	
Picnics	
Group Outings:	
	Local sporting events
	Cultural attractions
	Zoos
	Museums
	Parks
PhD Comics:	
	Creator
	Panel with cast and crew
	Workshops
	Screenings of the *PhD Movies*
Afternoon Movies	
Performing Arts:	
	Broadway series
	Disney on Ice
	Ballet
	Concerts
	Theater productions
Roller Skating	
Ice Skating	
Craft Events:	
	Pumpkin painting
	Holiday themed
	School spirit themes
	Seasonal

Type of Events	*Examples*
Football-Oriented Events:	
	Football 101
	Tailgates
	Game watch parties
Campus-Wide Events:	
	Homecoming
	Commencement activities
	Sibs and kids weekends
	Parent and family weekends
Ice Cream Socials	
Carnivals	

campus may increase participation. In addition to family-friendly-specific programs, providing free or low-cost babysitting services enables parents to enjoy a social engagement or enrichment event.

If an institution has family housing, partnering with the housing entity will help connect both residential and nonresidential students who have families, enhancing both groups' networks of support. While it is important for graduate student parents to interact with each other, this group of graduate students is much more open and appreciative of opportunities to engage with undergraduates who are also parents. Unlike in other types of programming, it is more reasonable to program for all student parents, including graduate, professional, and undergraduate. Overall, a mix of adult-only and multigenerational programming will develop a sense of community for the broadest population of graduate students.

Resources to Foster a Vibrant Graduate Student Experience

Although some activities and initiatives for graduate students may be student-driven, it is important for the institution to provide resources to facilitate graduate student engagement. Though funds are important, staff time and training are also highly relevant to successful graduate student engagement. The approach to supporting student organizations and graduate programming is often different yet related to support for undergraduates. If graduate students are paying an activity fee akin to undergraduates, apportion some of the funds specifically for use by graduate students for both graduate student organizations and graduate student-oriented programming. Clearly articulating that certain resources are for graduate students will enhance those students' use of those funds.

Student Organizations

For all student organizations, financial resources are important. If possible, provide at least the same level of financial support for graduate student organizations as for undergraduate organizations. Operating funds that are used to recruit new members or provide other organizational development opportunities such as leadership retreats will enhance the quality of experience for graduate students. Institutions that provide student organizations with funds to offer programs will enable graduate student organizations to better meet their mission while enhancing the overall community environment. Providing staff support to demystify the registration process as well as offering leadership development to graduate student organization leaders can enhance the persistence and success of an individual student organization.

Programming

Depending on the institution, responsibility for facilitating programming may vary. It may be the responsibility, individually or in combination, of a programming board, the graduate student government, individual graduate student organizations, the graduate school, or staff in an area of student affairs such as student activities. Most institutions will have a mix of student-driven and staff-driven programming. To ensure that programming has the intended effect, it is important to engage students and seek their input and feedback. Staff support is important since graduate students have more substantial demands on their time compared to undergraduates and therefore less time and motivation to fill in programming gaps at the institution.

Regardless of the budget for programming, it is critically important that those facilitating the events understand the population. Although some content may be very similar to an undergraduate program, the delivery or approach often needs to vary to ensure that learning outcomes for graduate students are met. Programs do not need to be expensive, particularly if the event is well tailored to the needs of graduate students. Though offering food at an event over the lunch hour will enhance turnout, a brown bag event will be just as successful if graduate students value the content of the program. Thoughtfully considering timing and understanding the various types of schedules graduate students maintain when scheduling events is also important. Identifying a segment of the graduate student population as the target audience will ensure a better attended event. For example, if the event targets students who are in programs that offer classes during weeknights, schedule the event on the weekend. Assessing events, particularly new ones, will assist in ensuring that learning outcomes and goals for student satisfaction are met. Graduate students are incredibly busy, often with competing priorities. Attending programs that are not perceived as beneficial will lead to disengagement. Overall, ensuring the programing is developed specifically for graduate students is the most important aspect for student engagement.

Challenges/Differences in Supporting Graduate Student Involvement

Although challenges for undergraduate students are well-known and studied, they are not always identical or realized in a similar way by graduate students. There are particular constraints common to graduate and professional students, some of which are more challenging than for undergraduate students. In this section, we highlight constraints common among graduate students.

Time

Graduate students are likely to have significant demands on their time (Demb, 2012). The rigors of a postbaccalaureate education require significant investment of time outside of the classroom setting. As undergraduates, these students may not have spent as much time preparing and focusing on academic material as what their graduate programs now require of them. Further, many students also balance graduate research, teaching, or administrative obligations of approximately 20 hours per week and/or other part-time or full-time employment. More graduate students than undergraduates will have family commitments including minor-aged children, a partner, and/or elder care. Therefore, it is important to consider when programs are offered. Many graduate students tightly control their calendars. Beyond ensuring that the content or purpose of the program is beneficial, it is important for students to know in advance how much time to allocate to the program or event. Going beyond the predetermined end time is perceived highly negatively by the graduate student population even if the content is perceived as beneficial.

Academic Program Pressure

Although some academic programs and faculty advisors understand the value of involvement outside of the classroom, library, and laboratory, there are still those who actively discourage their graduate students from cocurricular involvement. Therefore, it is important to ensure that programming is offered during times when students are able to participate if faced with this dynamic. Students may also want to know whether their involvement is reported to their academic program. For example, if a workshop focuses on obtaining a nonacademic job, a student whose advisor has an expectation that the student will pursue an academic job upon completion of a PhD may want assurances that her attendance at the program will not be reported back to the advisor and/or department. Although the culture may be shifting at many institutions with broader acknowledgement of the benefits of involvement for graduate students and the role of a PhD for nonacademic jobs, student fear of retaliation for involvement or pursuit of a "nontraditional" career path is both a potential obstacle to graduate student engagement and a factor to consider when developing holistic programming.

Cost

Most programs and engagement opportunities should be free or low cost for graduate students due to financial burdens (Kerlin, 1995). Connected to time constraints, graduate students have financial demands that are not as common in the undergraduate population. Some of these financial burdens include childcare, repayment of undergraduate loans, mortgages, and general living expenses. Many more graduate students do not receive regular or consistent financial support from their families. For international students, many are living on graduate assistantship income alone and may also be supporting immediate and extended family. The financial burdens on first-generation graduate students and those from low-income familial backgrounds may disproportionally affect those graduate students. Enabling graduate students to pay a student activity fee that is reasonable and that provides access to resources without further cost is a practice that will reduce opportunity costs and encourage participation. Further, if graduate students are paying a fee without programs designed specifically for them, work with the institution to redirect those resources to directly benefit graduate students.

Social Network

Unlike undergraduate students whose university community and support network is comprised primarily of other students, graduate students' social and support network may well extend beyond the confines of the university community (Council of Graduate Schools, 2009). Though some graduate students will opt to invite another student, in many cases, graduate students will be more likely to engage in activities on or off campus sponsored by the university if the graduate student is permitted to attend with a guest who is not a student. For example, if hosting a quiz night, only require the teams to be comprised of 50% students. Allowing for nonstudent guests will also help nonstudents understand the importance of graduate students' connection to the university community.

Challenges for Organizations Seeking Interdisciplinary Membership

Many graduate programs are insular (Strayhorn, 2012). It is challenging for graduate students to meet students outside of their program. Therefore, it is difficult both for students to find common, non-discipline-specific student organizations and for organizations to identify and effectively communicate with potential members. Organizing opportunities exclusive to graduate students such as involvement and resource fairs will assist students in connecting with student organizations outside of their department, program, or college. Creating programming with broad interdisciplinary appeal will also help to break down barriers and encourage graduate students to engage with others outside of their program. Resist hosting programs in spaces that will only attract students from specific fields. Work with multiple departments and facilitate shared orientation sessions about university-wide resources and opportunities with students from multiple programs.

Communication/Marketing

Be prepared to use multiple methods of communication to connect graduate students to specific opportunities. Establish a specific repository for graduate-specific opportunities such as a calendar that only lists programs and activities for graduate students. Graduate students do not have the time to figure out what will be relevant to them. Even if general offices such as a student wellness center, multicultural center, or student union says it serves all students, graduate students will perceive that "all students" means all undergraduates. Explicitly state that a program is being hosted for *graduate* students. To graduate students, the word "student" is often white noise because many have experienced or attempted to engage in an opportunity thought to include them only to find that it focuses on the needs and interests of undergraduates.

The source of the messaging to graduate students is also important. This is not to say that a centralized, all-graduate student email or other type of communication should be avoided. However, recognize that different graduate students may need to receive the message from specific sources. Some will more likely participate in an activity suggested by someone from their program or college. Other students are from programs or colleges that do not have dedicated staff for graduate students or are resistant to sharing engagement opportunities, and the student's only source of information is what is provided centrally. Develop a trusted brand for graduate student programming, which will help students make decisions to participate without needing to spend time deciding what will be worth their time.

Use multiple methods of communication and a reminder system. Do not just rely on social media or email; use both. With social media, only take on the number of platforms that can be maintained and updated regularly to ensure consistent engagement. Requiring registration or an RSVP for a program or activity heightens the importance to graduate students, which leads to higher turnout, even for free events. By collecting an RSVP, a reminder can be sent. Determine what additional platforms are used by graduate students specifically at your institution. You may also encourage word of mouth and have graduate student "ambassadors" who are trained to provide information to incoming students in their programs. Once a robust programming initiative is operating, encourage graduate admissions to include information about it to prospective and newly matriculating students so they are primed to seek out opportunities.

Conclusion

Just as it does for undergraduates, cocurricular involvement for graduate students can lead to positive educational outcomes. Institutions should be concerned about the comparatively low rates of graduate degree completion (Council of Graduate Schools, 2010) and be prepared to invest resources into fostering out of class engagement to help facilitate sense of belonging. Joining student organizations and participating in programs designed intentionally for graduate student audiences can help graduate students combat the loneliness and self-doubt that often leads to attrition. Whether working with a modest budget or a substantial investment in graduate programming, institutions can offer a balanced slate of social, enrichment, and family programs that will signal to their graduate students that they are cared for and enable them to make vital interdisciplinary social connections.

References

Abrahamowicz, D. (1988). College involvement, perceptions, and satisfaction: A study of membership in student organizations. *Journal of College Student Development, 29*(3), 233–238.

Association of American Colleges & Universities. (2011). *The LEAP vision for learning: Outcomes, practices, impact, and employers' views.* http://www.aacu.org/sites/default/files/files/LEAP/leap_vision_summary.pdf

Astin, A. W. (1984). Student involvement: A developmental theory for higher education. *Journal of College Student Personnel, 25*(4), 297–307.

Astin, A. W. (1993). *What matters in college? Four critical years revisited.* Jossey-Bass.

Astin, A. W. (1996). Involvement in learning revisited: Lessons we have learned. *Journal of College Student Development, 37*(2), 123–133.

Council of Graduate Schools. (2009). *PhD completion and attrition: Policies and practices to promote student success.*

Council of Graduate Schools. (2010). *PhD completion and attrition: Findings from exit surveys of PhD completers.*

Demb, A. (2012). *Daring the doctorate: The journey at mid-career.* Rowman & Littlefield.

Foubert, J. D., & Grainger, L. U. (2006). Effects of involvement in clubs and organizations on the psychosocial development of first-year and senior college students. *NASPA Journal, 43*(1), 166–182. https://doi.org/10.2202/0027-6014.1576

Gardner S. K., & Barnes, B. J. (2007). Graduate student involvement: Socialization for the professional role. *Journal of College Student Development, 48*(4), 369–387. https://doi.org/10.1353/csd.2007.0036

Gardner, S. K., & Gopaul, B. (2012). The part-time doctoral student experience. *International Journal of Doctoral Studies, 7*(12), 63–78. https://doi.org/10.28945/1561

Gellin, A. (2003). The effect of undergraduate student involvement on critical thinking: A meta-analysis of the literature 1991–2000. *Journal of College Student Development, 44*(6), 746–762. https://doi.org/10.1353/csd.2003.0066

Golde, C. M., & Dore, T. (2001). *At cross purposes: What the experiences of today's doctoral students reveal about doctoral education.* Pew Charitable Trusts.

Keeling, R. P. (Ed.). (2006). *Learning reconsidered 2: Implementing a campus-wide focus on the student experience.* American College Personnel Association; Association of College and University Housing Officers–International; Association of College Unions International; National Association for Campus Activities; NACADA: The Global Community for Academic Advising; National Association of Student Personnel Administrators; NIRSA: Leaders in Collegiate Recreation.

Kerlin, S. P. (1995). Pursuit of the PhD: "Survival of the fittest," or is it time for a new approach? *Education Policy Analysis Archives, 3*(16), 1–30. https://doi.org/10.14507/epaa.v3n16.1995

Kuh, G. D., Cruce, T. M., Shoup, R., Kinzie, J., & Gonyea, R. M. (2008). Unmasking the effects of student engagement on first-year college grades and persistence. *The Journal of Higher Education, 79*(5), 540–563. https://doi.org/10.1080/00221546.2008.11772116

Levine, A., & Dean, D. R. (2012). *Generation on a tightrope: A portrait of today's college student.* Jossey-Bass.

Maslow, A. H. (1943). A theory of human motivation. *Psychological Review, 50*(4), 370–396. https://doi.org/10.1037/h0054346

Parkman, A. (2016). The imposter phenomenon in higher education: Incidence and impact. *Journal of Education Theory and Practice, 16*(1), 51–60. https://article-gateway.com/index.php/JHETP/article/view/1936

Pascarella, E. T., & Terenzini, P. T. (2005). *How college affects students: A third decade of research.* Jossey-Bass.

Paynter, K., & Barnes, J. (2015, March). Teaching undergraduate students versus graduate students online: Similarities, differences, and instructional approaches. In *Society for Information Technology & Teacher Education International Conference* (pp. 67–71). Association for the Advancement of Computing in Education (AACE).

Schlossberg, N. K. (1989). Marginality and mattering: Key issues in building community. In *Beyond the Box: Connecting Multiracial Identities, Oppressions, and Environments* (New Directions for Student Services, vol. 1989, no. 48, pp. 5–15). https://doi.org/10.1002/ss.37119894803

Strayhorn, T. L. (2012). *College students' sense of belonging: A key to educational success for all*. Routledge.

Terenzini, P. T., Pascarella, E. T., & Blimling, G. S. (1996). Students' out-of-class experiences and their influence on learning and cognitive development: A literature review. *Journal of College Student Development, 37*(2), 149–162.

Wolf-Wendel, L., Ward, K., & Kinzie, J. (2009). A tangled web of terms: The overlap and unique contribution of involvement, engagement, and integration to understanding college student success. *Journal of College Student Development, 50*(4), 407–428. https://doi.org/10.1353/csd.0.0077

Zacherman, A., & Foubert, J. (2014). The relationship between engagement in cocurricular activities and academic performance: Exploring gender differences. *Journal of Student Affairs Research and Practice, 51*(2), 157–169. https://doi.org/10.1515/jsarp-2014-0016

15

DOING IT ALL BUT NOT ALL THE TIME

Shaping Work–Life Balance for Graduate Students

A. Emiko Blalock, Katy B. Mathuews, and Nicole Parker

In the past decade, graduate education in the United States has witnessed a significant shift. Students seeking graduate degrees today are more likely to work full-time, take classes online, or commute substantial distances to attend classes during evenings or on weekends (Blagg, 2018; Cassuto, 2015). Additionally, students are more diverse in race, gender, and nationality (Blagg, 2018; Okahana & Zhou, 2018), and degrees have become more diversified and professionalized (Schuster & Finkelstein, 2006). These shifts also mean the lives of graduate students lived outside their studies are often equally as important. Juggling family, work, romantic partnerships, and other social and community obligations along with graduate education is the norm (Espinoza, 2010; Grenier & Burke, 2008; Hopwood, 2010). Simply put, the type of student now seeking a graduate education at the master's and doctoral level is vastly different from 10 years ago.

Familial obligations are particularly pronounced for graduate students with children, and women in particular face an increasingly difficult task in attending to these multiple demands (Lynch, 2008; Sallee, 2013; Springer et al., 2009). Gender norms and ideal worker norms contribute to the narrative on work–life balance, influencing the discourse between graduate school experiences. Ideal worker norms, norms that indicate an individual, likely a man, is available to work at any hour from any location (Williams, 1989), have long been present in the field of academia (Lester et al., 2017; Nerad & Cerny, 1999; Sallee, 2016; Sallee et al., 2009). Today as more women with families attend graduate school, they are confronted

with these norms. For example, having a family makes it difficult to participate in activities expected in graduate school such as attending conferences
(Brown & Watson, 2010); and students who enroll part-time in order to
balance family and academics indicate they are made to feel less committed
and experience isolation from their departments (Deem & Brehony, 2000;
Nerad & Cerny, 1999). Thus, for women graduate students in particular,
the dominant discourse about devoting oneself to work is in conflict with
the narrative that many women are also expected to devote themselves to
taking care of home and family.

As diversity of graduate students has increased to include more working
parents, so has the modality of how graduate school is delivered. Graduate
students have flexibility in their coursework through online programs or
courses scheduled in the evenings, yet this same flexibility has also added
pressure to student-parents. The pressure to balance school and work and
family increases a graduate student's risk of stopping out of their programs
(Brown & Nichols, 2013). Also taking note of the change in course scheduling, Sallee (2016) reported "nearly all courses were offered in the late
afternoon and evening hours . . . [which] was problematic for students with
children, particularly those who could not rely on family for child care"
(p. 60). Furthermore, Lynch (2008) found students who "have a child feel
isolated and discouraged and reported lower levels of satisfaction in peer relationships" (p. 601). Thus, geographic isolation and lack of social community and networks compound a graduate student's ability to seek or achieve
work–life balance. To this point specifically for women, Lowe (2012) noted
"since child-rearing in today's society is still considered a woman's responsibility, [this] impacts women's social networks differently than men . . . and
has a significantly negative impact on the size of women's social networks"
(p. 3). A lack of a social network, thus, can lead to feelings of social isolation. These networks not only provide valuable information, but also provide
sense of community and commonality for graduate students facing similar
work–life balance issues.

An obvious counterweight to experiences of isolation is social communities that can often help graduate students thrive. Martinez et al. (2013) found
that social supports were important for both progressing through graduate-
level coursework, and also expressing personal feelings and tensions. The
social supports Martinez et al. (2013) highlighted were spouses, families, and
relatives who were nearby. Specific to marriage, Labosier and Labosier (2011)
indicated that while graduate school can strain marriage and other significant
relationships, it also provides perspective about what is and isn't possible.
These supports for graduate students, however, are found in personal and
familial spaces, which policies and organized programming from universities

may not be able to replicate. Regardless, colleges and universities, and the faculty and staff who interact with students, have been increasingly encouraged to be more intentional about offering resources and supports for graduate students to manage work–life balance (Brus, 2006). Unfortunately, it cannot always be left to the administrative leaders to ensure policies are in place to support graduate students with families. While some colleges are reported to have flexible policies and programs, studies indicate there is a reasonable lack of support or feelings of support for students (Brown & Nichols, 2013; Cox et al., 2016; Gardner, 2008; Gardner & Holley, 2011; Larson et al., 2019; Sallee, 2016; Turner & Thompson, 1993).

Without intentional actions from university leaders, graduate students have taken it upon themselves to advocate for changes in university policies to be more supportive of graduate students' work–life balance and schooling. One such example is noted from the University of Southern California, where graduate student mobilization led to substantial change, including establishing a family and medical leave program for new graduate student parents (Sallee et al., 2009). These types of institutional programming can further support students who may not have family or relatives close by. Institutional programming can take the form of cohort models or group advising, or other opportunities for graduate students to regularly connect. Other resources for graduate students exist within scholarship on the subject: de Casanova and Brown (2013) provide strategies for graduate student mothers to progress through their degrees; Springer et al. (2009) offer glimpses of initiatives designed to support the work–life balance of graduate students; and Sallee and Lester (2009) review best practices for the family-friendly campus, suggesting these kinds of policies at the university level are realistic to implement and extremely effective.

Family notwithstanding, there are also other aspects of individual experience that shape work–life balance. Many have reported on the mental stress and health of graduate students, as well as how social position and socioeconomic status can play a role in how students feel supported and provided for and connect to others in graduate school (Evans et al., 2018; Gardner & Holley, 2011; Prince, 2015). Indeed, mental health challenges emerge during undergraduate years. In a national survey of approximately 33,500 college students, 86% of respondents reported feeling overwhelmed while 61% reported feeling anxiety and 40% experienced anger or depression (American College Health Association, 2016). These results are similar to a previous study of graduate students in which nearly half of respondents reported experiencing emotional or stress-related problems. A statistically significant difference was noted in which women were affected by mental health experiences more than men (Hyun et al., 2006). Graduate student experiences with mental health symptoms are likely exacerbated given the myriad of commitments involving work, family, and commute time cited previously.

Considering these competing demands, how are graduate students finding the quintessential "work–life balance" ratio? In this chapter, we address how students seek to locate and define their own balance in work, life, and school. Thus, our use of the term *work–life balance* is focused on our own individual understandings and how we have developed a way to navigate and negotiate different aspects of our life that may sometimes be in competition. Although we present our understanding of work–life balance from our perspectives of women in academia, we also offer suggestions that we believe are applicable to many types of graduate students.

This chapter uses three vignettes to describe how we each shaped our own sense of work–life balance while in graduate school. These vignettes reflect three different experiences in graduate school. Katy worked full-time during her doctoral studies, Emiko left a career to be a full-time student with a graduate assistantship and eventually started a family as a student, and Nicole continued to work full-time and raise a family as she progressed through her master's degree. By describing our own experiences, we also emphasize that students enrolled in graduate school are often further in their careers, in different stages of family life, or potentially changing careers after having worked years as professionals. Our discussion focuses both on strategies for the individual as well as recommendations for institutions to support work–life balance. Finally, we end with a brief conclusion encouraging graduate students to recognize that there are many times work–life balance may not be possible. To this end, our overall purpose for this chapter is to highlight (a) how work–life balance can be shaped by gender; (b) how opportunities for work–life balance can be deeply personal and meaningful; and (c) how institutions of higher education can better foster work–life balance for graduate students.

Vignette 1, Katy: Planning for Work–School–Life Balance

When I embarked on a doctoral program while maintaining a full-time job, I knew I would have to be very structured and intentional in my approach to balancing my career, graduate work, relationships, and personal health. This method included establishing realistic expectations with my spouse, establishing an aggressive study schedule, and finding a few friends who could serve as a tight-knit community of support. I fully credit these strategies for helping me find balance while successfully completing my doctoral work.

Before embarking on my doctoral journey, I had a thorough conversation with my spouse to prepare for the next 4 years. I would likely need to devote some time to my studies every day and had already envisioned that with each new course syllabi I would immediately record all due dates and assignments into my calendar. I was clear about the support I would need in order to be successful, and clear with myself about which hours would be scheduled for work, studies, class-time, and personal time. This meant almost all of the household duties were allocated to my spouse, and I committed to devote hours for quality time together every day. With a clear understanding of my expectations and the constraints on my time my spouse was able to express his concerns and expectations, allowing us to create strategies that were sustainable to both of us.

To further maintain balance, I scheduled time before each class meeting to have lunch with a classmate or to sit quietly alone in a coffee shop. This helped ground me and created a barrier of calm between the stress of work and marathon weekend class sessions. My lunches were often spent with a few of the close friends I developed through my cohort-oriented program. The cohort arrangement was an invaluable community of support because despite how supportive my spouse, friends, or coworkers were, they simply did not understand on a visceral level what it was like to simultaneously juggle graduate work, full-time employment, and the many aspects of life. My close friends in the cohort helped sustain me as we encouraged each other through hardships, held each other accountable, and made each other laugh.

My planning and doctoral cohort community were tremendous assets when I had to navigate an unexpected and serious medical issue, which resulted in a major surgery and a long, uncomfortable recovery. As soon as I learned about my surgery, I immediately talked with my professors. I explained my circumstances and let them know my plans to continue my schoolwork as I recovered. I was unable to avoid missing two class meetings, but I did not miss a due date. I was able to plan to complete work before surgery and then, after a week totally focused on recovery, I was able to use my time off from work to not only keep up with my studies, but to get ahead. My faculty were very understanding during this time and my classmates offered to take notes for me while I was out.

Vignette 2, Nicole: Transitioning Between Parenting and School

Typing furiously, I glanced at the clock. If I didn't leave in 2 minutes, I would risk being late to my class's required Zoom meeting. Yet it was not as simple as shutting down my computer and driving home. Standing between me and my Zoom meeting was a drive to childcare, a pickup (sometimes done in

5 minutes, other times stretching to 20), driving home, and a furious dash to provide dinner for the kids—all in the next hour.

Almost an hour later, I settled my daughter Helen down next to me on the floor of my bedroom, her plate full of peanut butter and jelly sandwich and apples, juice pouch precariously balancing on the carpeted floor. With 5 minutes to spare until my Zoom meeting began, I scarfed my food while logging into my computer, careful to not get breadcrumbs between the keyboard spaces. The call started and within a few minutes Helen transitioned from eating to iPad entertainment, which caused the first little hiccup. The professor thought I was muted but talking to them, and called on me specifically, saying, "Nicole, I think you're muted and we'd love to hear what you're saying!" Unmuting, I shared that my daughter was right next to me and that I had been talking with her. This piqued Helen's interest, and for the rest of the Zoom call, she periodically leaned over, making sure her jelly-covered face was easily seen on camera, and waved vigorously to the group. My faculty members and classmates handled the situation well by acknowledging her each time (though she couldn't hear them through my headphones) and carrying on with the meeting.

Though I am sure I lost some important information having to adjust my attention to her every so often, answering her questions and keeping her focused elsewhere—even wiping up spilled juice (I should have seen that one coming)—that is what I had to do. I had to be in class, I had to be okay with some interruptions from her, and I had to balance both my need to be in class and my need to be a parent. I was able to participate in the class discussion much of the time, while also keeping Helen entertained. Not only is this balance an important tension to sit with, but how a parent is received on the end of such tensions makes all the difference. Had my professor asked me to make sure she didn't interrupt anymore or suggested that I leave the meeting to attend to her, I may have been risking my grade and missed the valuable connection that video meetings give to fully online degree programs.

Vignette 3, Emiko: Finding a Sense of Place

At the beginning of my 1st year as a doctoral student, I started a personal blog. To relocate from the Pacific Northwest to the Midwest for graduate school only knowing one soul (my husband who moved with me) was terrifying and exhilarating. A blog, I thought, might help me catalogue some of the new changes I was experiencing. I recently went back to read over my posts from this time period, and I was astonished at how many of them were about "my life" and not about school. There were several posts about home remodeling, camping trips, day excursions, cross-country visits for family and friends, and finally, the baby who was born. Looking at these posts now, I see a trail of breadcrumbs I left directing me how to find my own work–life balance through the act of finding a sense of place.

In a post from late 2014, just a few months after I moved and started my program, I listed the new sounds I heard: "Katydids and cicadas; AC units; Snow plows; Undergrads; Constant talk about how bad the roads are." This list grounded me in my new place and gave me audible sources of encouragement about what I moved to Michigan to do. At the end of my 1st year, I took up running, and one post illuminated how running became a part of balancing my life. "Almost all of the trees have dropped their leaves, and the sun was shining through the long sinewy branches of young oaks. I run now and just listen to my breathing and my foot-fall . . . a quiet meditation." This theme of meditation on place and landscape was powerfully present in many of my posts.

When I wrote about my schoolwork, I described my experiences as a biracial woman in graduate school, and how my racial identity also navigated two spaces in a similar way the work–life aspect of myself did. I wrote about what motivated me, even as I struggled to feel I fit into academia, "there might be someone who, like me, yearns to see a professor who looks like her." Even in these posts about race and gender, I always circled back to my place as Hapa, as Both, or what Maria Root wrote of as a place to resolve Other. This sense of place was found in writing with another woman who shared my racial origins, as we developed our own space to celebrate living on the borders of race and ethnicity. Even as I became more secure in my new home, and feeling comfortable with my doctoral cohort, woven between these posts about place and landscape, race and gender, were entries of feeling inadequate, of feeling overwhelmed, and of feeling the imposter.

Reflecting now on my blog, I see that finding a sense of place was tantamount to having balance during my graduate school experience. At the end of my 1st year, I wrote, "I am learning more and more how to manage, not so much balance, my life here in Lansing as a student." This management came through ensuring I was taking time for myself, re-rooting my identity within academia, carving out time to take a short adventures, deciding and committing to be a parent, and saying no to working past 7 p.m. a few times a week. By protecting my time I was able to flourish in my new landscape, appreciate the subtle changes of my surrounding area, and be captivated by the small-town life, student-life, and parent-life that I was now living.

Discussion of Vignettes

These vignettes illustrate how we each navigated our own challenges of balancing work, graduate school, and life. Though this chapter focuses on our experiences as women, even within this categorization there is heterogeneity. It is impossible, then, to offer a one-size-fits-all solution to achieving work–life balance in graduate school. However, a few themes emerge. We first provide concrete examples about work–life balance from our individual vignettes, then turn to how institutions can draw from our experiences to support work–life balance for graduate students.

First, we each incorporated mindfulness into our strategies to achieve balance. For Katy, this meant spending weekly time alone at a coffee shop or staying present while lunching with friends. For Emiko, the sounds, conversations, and details of place grounded her. Emiko's running practice and meditations on sensory experiences like katydids and cicadas helped anchor her to her environment. Nicole shared her experiences navigating the tension that comes from dueling responsibilities. She gave herself permission to acknowledge and accept these feelings as she remained steadfast in her studies.

Second, though each of us had our own approach, time management became an important practice. Katy identified with a very structured and disciplined method to scheduling and completing schoolwork. The act of creating the schedule helped reduce stress as the implementation of the scheduling helped her maintain a steady pace that ensured her required work was completed in a timely manner. Emiko chose to use her time in alternative ways by running and creating a personal blog. Though she acknowledged these activities took up time, the benefits were worth the cost. She was able to think clearly, focus in, and gain writing practice through these seeming distractions. As a parent, Nicole often found it essential to multitask, caring for her daughter while simultaneously navigating due dates and online course meetings. While Nicole's approach was certainly challenging, her role of mother and student, in addition to working full-time, often left her no choice. Martinez et al. (2013) found that graduate students with children had an easier time mastering time management because of the competing demands. Nicole's vignette illuminates this literature, and that "sources of stress were also sources of support," as witnessed in her delightful and stressful interaction with her daughter in class.

Third, we each mentioned elements of community. Katy took time to socialize with classmates and scheduled daily time with her spouse. Further, Katy's cohort experience provided a systematic community of support. Emiko recounted how she found community writing with a woman with the same racial origins. This experience allowed her to find community not just in her academic pursuits, but in the lived experience fostered by her intersectional identity. Even Nicole's narrative highlights community. Though her program is entirely online, the acceptance of her parental duties by her classmates and faculty created a welcoming community for working students. These vignettes also reiterate literature related to how important geographic location is for graduate students in forming community, making connections with cohort members, or being committed to our own personal families who were nearby (Blalock, 2019; Martinez et al., 2013).

Institutional and Faculty Support

In addition to individual efforts, there are many ways institutions can help students navigate their full schedules and lives. Indeed, as institutions welcome an increasingly diverse student population, it is imperative that they support the various challenges students face. These efforts can be reflected in faculty behavior, institutional policy, or curriculum structure. Faculty can be a tremendous support to students who are navigating strategies to find balance. With such full schedules and long lists of responsibilities, time is valuable and scarce. Faculty who provide detailed syllabi help students plan their workloads. Last-minute revisions to plans in the form of additional readings and last-minute assignments can put extreme pressure on students juggling work, families, and personal wellness. Likewise, a preplanned class schedule can help students navigate major or unexpected life events such as the birth of a child, personal medical issues, or incidents with housing or transportation. Establishing attendance policies to anticipate emergencies and special needs up front can help create an environment where the student feels supported. As such needs are built into the framework of the course that allow for the realities of contemporary graduate students, it helps alleviate intimidating conversations with faculty while also sending a message of empathy and support.

Further, as students face adversity, faculty can be empathetic and encouraging. Often when students approach faculty to discuss their challenges, they are not looking for special treatment, but for empathy and encouragement to continue to meet their challenges (Mathuews, 2018). For example, a jam-stained child may make a guest appearance in class, as Nicole humorously recounts. Though an exemplary case, Dr. Nathan Alexander of Morehouse College is an inspiration to see the classroom environment in new ways. Dr. Alexander gained notoriety when he not only welcomed a student's child into the classroom when the parents lacked childcare, but also offered to hold the baby during his lecture so the student could focus in class (Paul, 2019).

This example of a male teacher stepping up to support a male student and parent is an inspiration to view classroom environments in light of modern challenges and reiterates that the duties of parenting are not singular to one gender (Sallee, 2013).

Policies that speak to graduate student work appointments and parental leave can be particularly helpful. For example, Ohio University offers up to 6 weeks of paid medical leave for students with graduate appointments (Pittman, 2018). Duke University offers up to $5,000 in childcare subsidies based on financial need (Duke Graduate School, n.d.). Universities can also consider online or cohort-based programs to fit working graduate students' needs. Considering time of day for course scheduling can be helpful, but it can also be helpful to offer alternative time options for dissertation defense meetings. Even in weekend- and evening-oriented classes, graduate students often can only schedule defense meetings during normal business hours.

Colleges and universities can also attempt to be more aspirational about how their work–life balance programs (e.g., offered through human resources) and student organizations (see chapter 14, this volume) can provide support to graduate students. Many of these offices are aimed at faculty or full-time academic staff or administrators; however, these offices can also target graduate students. For example, how can these offices address the importance of community that Katy, Nicole, and Emiko shared? While this question may not be fully answered in this chapter, we suggest campuses consider where these offices are housed and how they are accessed by graduate students who are working full-time. The built environment of college campuses speaks volumes to what a campus values (Peachy & Baller, 2015). Thus, work–life offices might consider embedding representatives in specific colleges, providing services that target financial management for graduate students, and ensuring that mention of their services is included in course syllabi for graduate students who are too busy to attend orientation sessions.

Finally, all of our vignettes were composed from our identity as women, and as such reflect in part our gendered experiences: being spouses, mothers, caretakers, communal members. Lester (2013) noted that many institutions perpetuate work–life balance as a gender-laden experience, often emphasizing the event of pregnancy as a means to establish procedures for work–life balance. These kinds of policies indicate that work–life balance is a gendered experience, and moreover that women in particular must not only strive to find work–life balance, but the demands of a gendered society imply that rather than letting go of certain facets of life to take on graduate school, women must instead add on this element to their lives. Because of such normative societal expectations, campuses should consider how their policies reproduce gendered norms about family and parenting.

Conclusion

Graduate students who are balancing their education with lives and experiences beyond academia may face certain challenges in completing coursework and maintaining their own professional pursuits. Our chapter is an attempt to elevate real experiences of navigating and negotiating what work–life balance means in graduate school. As such, we described the background context for women in graduate school, and then offered personal vignettes of our own experiences in graduate school as full-time workers, partners, and mothers. These vignettes provided recommendations for personal and institutional actions for work–life balance in graduate students. Recommended changes are widespread on college campuses, from something as small as a lactation space, to something as large as shifting an entire campus culture to support and work–life balance for graduate students. Yet, campuses often fall short in their obligations to the increasing populations of working and parenting students, especially women, when they lack the supports they need to be successful. College campuses who wish to attract and retain graduate students with already full lives, especially those who identify as women, need to create an action plan to sustain and support this special population, taking a self-measure of the friendliness of their campus, class offerings, and culture to working mothers. Furthermore, any policies, procedures, or structures found to create barriers for such students should be actively named and goals set to eliminate these barriers.

Finally, we must note that the term and attempt at "work–life balance" is itself problematic; it often demands more from individuals who identity as women, it may require certain monetary resources beyond one's socio-economic position or social capital in order "gain" work–life balance, and it insists that such a balance can be achieved in a traditional and normative manner (e.g., ideal worker social norms). We seek to emphasize that each individual managing multiple aspects to their life may find their own sense of community, place, and family practices. However, it must also be emphasized that failing to have balance, or the perception of balance, can itself be a source to reevaluate our priorities as graduate students and acknowledge our limitations. This final vignette from Nicole embodies what our sense of "balance" is: both a planned and ambiguous journey to be in the moment; a possibility to create a third space where all aspects of our lives are acknowledged and cared for.

"Mama, will you read me one more book?"

Being a working mom graduate student is one of the hardest things I've ever done. I always looked from afar at other women, puzzling as to how they balanced it all. Halfway through my graduate degree now, I know how I am doing it: one day, sometimes one moment at a time. A moment that made little difference to me had a profound effect on my 4-year-old. We need to be able to give ourselves permission to be in the moment: to feel the impatience of needing to finish a paper; to wish that we could read for an hour longer with our child; to be confident in leaving our children with their other parent or caregiver for a few hours to focus on school, and to take a break from school to make memories together that will outlast the temporary rush of finishing a project.

References

American College Health Association. (2016). *Fall 2016 reference group: Executive summary.* http://www.acha-ncha.org/docs/NCHA-II_FALL_2016_REFERENCE_GROUP_EXECUTIVE_SUMMARY.pdf

Blagg, K. (2018). *The rise of master's degrees: Master's programs are increasingly diverse and online.* Urban Institute.

Blalock, A. E. (2019). *How forms of capital shape the teaching strategies of women in fixed-term faculty positions* [Doctoral dissertation, Michigan State University].

Brown, L., & Watson, P. (2010). Understanding the experiences of female doctoral students. *Journal of Further and Higher Education, 34*(3), 385–404. https://doi.org/10.1080/0309877X.2010.484056

Brown, V., & Nichols, T. R. (2013). Pregnant and parenting students on campus: Policy and program implications for a growing population. *Educational Policy, 27*(3), 499–530. https://doi.org/10.1177/0895904812453995

Brus, C. P. (2006). Seeking balance in graduate school: A realistic expectation or a dangerous dilemma? In M. J. Guentzel & B. E. Nesheim (Eds.), *Supporting graduate and professional students: The role of student affairs* (New Directions for Student Services, vol. 2006, no. 115, pp. 31–45). Jossey-Bass. https://doi.org/10.1002/ss.214

Cassuto, L. (2015). *The graduate school mess: What caused it and how we can fix it.* Harvard University Press.

Cox, B. E., Reason, R. D., Nix, S., & Gillman, M. (2016). Life happens (outside of college): Non-college life-events and students' likelihood of graduation. *Research in Higher Education, 57*(7), 823–844. https://doi.org/10.1007/s11162-016-9409-z

de Casanova, E. M., & Brown, T. M. (2013). Making it work: Success strategies for graduate student mothers. In M. Castaneda & K. Isgro (Eds.), *Mothers in academia* (pp. 191–199). Columbia University Press.

Deem, R., & Brehony, K. J. (2000). Doctoral students' access to research cultures-are some more unequal than others? *Studies in Higher Education, 25*(2), 149–165. https://doi.org/10.1080/713696138

Duke Graduate School. (n.d.). *Childcare subsidy.* https://gradschool.duke.edu/financial-support/child-care-subsidy

Espinoza, R. (2010). The good daughter dilemma: Latinas managing family and school demands. *Journal of Hispanic Higher Education, 9*(4), 317–330. https://doi.org/10.1177/1538192710380919

Evans, T. M., Bira, L., Gastelum, J. B., Weiss, L. T., & Vanderford, N. L. (2018). Evidence for a mental health crisis in graduate education. *Nature*, *36*(3), 282–284. https://www.nature.com/articles/nbt.4089

Gardner, S. K. (2008). Fitting the mold of graduate school: A qualitative study of socialization in doctoral education. *Innovative Higher Education*, *33*(2), 125–138. https://doi.org/10.1007/s10755-008-9068-x

Gardner, S. K., & Holley, K. A. (2011). "Those invisible barriers are real": The progression of first-generation students through doctoral education. *Equity & Excellence in Education*, *44*(1), 77–92. https://doi.org/10.1080/10665684.2011.529791

Grenier, R. S., & Burke, M. C. (2008). No margin for error: A study of two women balancing motherhood and PhD studies. *The Qualitative Report*, *13*(4), 581–604. https://nsuworks.nova.edu/tqr/vol13/iss4/4

Hopwood, N. (2010). A sociocultural view of doctoral students' relationships and agency. *Studies in Continuing Education*, *32*(2), 103–117. https://doi.org/10.1080/0158037X.2010.487482

Hyun, J. K., Quinn, B. C., Madon, T., & Lustig, S. (2006). Graduate student mental health: Needs assessment and utilization of counseling services. *Journal of College Student Development*, *47*(3), 247–266. https://doi.org/10.1353/csd.2006.0030

Labosier, C., & Labosier, A. (2011). Who are you married to? Balancing graduate school and marriage. *The Geographical Bulletin*, *52*(2), 87–91.

Larson, J., Nguyen, D. J., Opoczynski, R., & Vizvary, G. (2019). Designing a professional development group for leader-learners enrolled in graduate education. *Journal of Leadership Studies*, *13*(2), 73–76. https://doi.org/10.1002/jls.21644

Lester, J. (2013). Work-life balance and cultural change: A narrative of eligibility. *The Review of Higher Education*, *36*(4), 463–488. https://doi.org/10.1353/rhe.2013.0037

Lester, J., Sallee, M., & Hart, J. (2017). Beyond gendered universities? Implications for research on gender in organizations. *NASPA Journal About Women in Higher Education*, *10*(1), 1–26. https://doi.org/10.1080/19407882.2017.1285794

Lowe, J. (2012). Poverty and social networks: The role social networks play in economic immobility. *Crittenton Women's Union*, *31*.

Lynch, K. D. (2008). Gender roles and the American academe: A case study of graduate student mothers. *Gender and Education*, *20*(6), 585–605. https://doi.org/10.1080/09540250802213099

Martinez, E., Ordu, C., Della Sala, M. R., & McFarlane, A. (2013). Striving to obtain a school-work-life balance: The full-time doctoral student. *International Journal of Doctoral Studies*, *8*(1), 39–59. https://doi.org/10.28945/1765

Mathuews, K. B. (2018). *The working time-poor: Time poverty implications for working students' involvement* [Doctoral dissertation, Ohio University].

Nerad, M., & Cerny, J. (1999). Another look at women graduate students. *Council of Graduate Schools Communicator*, *32*(6), 1. https://www.education.uw.edu/cirge/wp-content/uploads/2008/02/widening.pdf

Okahana, H., & Zhou, E. (2018). *Graduate enrollment and degrees: 2007-2017* (pp. 1–82). Council of Graduate Schools.

Paul, D. (2019). A student brought his baby to class because he didn't have childcare. His professor lent a hand. *The Washington Post.* https://www.washingtonpost .com/lifestyle/2019/03/04/student-brought-his-baby-class-because-he-didnt-have-child-care-his-professor-lent-hand/?noredirect=on

Peachey, A. A., & Baller, S. L. (2015). Perceived built environment characteristics of on-campus and off-campus neighborhoods associated with physical activity of college students. *Journal of American College Health, 63*(5), 337–342. https://doi .org/10.1080/07448481.2015.1015027

Pittman, D. (2018). *President Nellis announces Parental Paid Leave program for graduate students.* Ohio University Ohio News. https://www.ohio.edu/news/archive/ stories_17-18_01_Paid-Parental-Leave-Graduate-Students.cfm

Prince, J. P. (2015). University student counseling and mental health in the United States: Trends and challenges. *Mental Health & Prevention, 3*(1–2), 5–10. https://doi.org/10.1016/j.mhp.2015.03.001

Sallee, M., & Lester, J. (2009). The family-friendly campus in the 21st century. In J. Lester & M. Sallee, *Establishing the family-friendly campus: Models for effective practice* (pp. 159–165). Stylus.

Sallee, M. W. (2013). Gender norms and institutional culture: The family-friendly versus the father-friendly university. *The Journal of Higher Education, 84*(3), 363–396. https://doi.org/10.1353/jhe.2013.0017

Sallee, M. W. (2016). Ideal for whom? A cultural analysis of ideal worker norms in higher education and student affairs graduate programs. In L. Wolf-Wendel, K. Ward, & A. Kulp (Eds.), *How ideal worker norms shape work-life for different constituent groups in higher education* (New Directions for Higher Education, no. 176, pp. 53–67).

Sallee, M., Zare, M. D., & Lester, J. (2009). From advocacy to action: Making graduate school family-friendly. In J. Lester & M. Sallee (Eds.), *Establishing the family-friendly campus: Models of effective practice* (pp. 141–158). Stylus.

Schuster, J. H., & Finkelstein, M. J. (2006). *The American faculty: The restructuring of academic work and careers.* Johns Hopkins University Press.

Springer, K. W., Parker, B. K., & Leviten-Reid, C. (2009). Making space for graduate student parents: Practice and politics. *Journal of Family Issues, 30*(4), 435–457. https://doi.org/10.1177/0192513X08329293

Turner, C. S. V., & Thompson, J. R. (1993). Socializing women doctoral students: Minority and majority experiences. *The Review of Higher Education, 16*(3), 355–370. https://muse.jhu.edu/article/644673

Williams, J. C. (1989). Deconstructing gender. *Michigan Law Review, 87*(4), 797–845 https://repository.law.umich.edu/mlr/vol87/iss4/3

CONCLUDING THOUGHTS

David J. Nguyen and Christina W. Yao

Graduate education continues to be a popular option for people seeking career advancement, career changes, or academic careers. In the fall of 2019, over 3 million people enrolled in graduate programs across the United States (National Center for Educational Statistics, 2021). People participate in graduate education as more jobs require advanced degree attainment for addressing employer demands. More students from diverse backgrounds (e.g., gender, race/ethnicity, socioeconomic) will continue to enroll, yet research demonstrates that institutions may not be well-positioned to support a diversifying graduate student population.

Competition for coveted spots in graduate degree programs persists. Despite the oversupply of academically qualified students, graduate program attrition rates hover around 50%, and in some disciplines, the percentage is worsening. To combat poor completion rates, an increasing number of postsecondary institutions are investing in supporting graduate student success beyond traditional measures of financial and advising support. In this volume, we have explored how developing support mechanisms inside and outside the classroom for graduate students can benefit this student population and their increasingly complex needs.

Current studies on graduate education identified advising, finances, student preparation, test scores, loneliness, lack of community, mental health challenges, and socialization experiences as contributing factors to why graduate students lengthen time-to-degree completion or leave their programs altogether (Abedi & Benkin, 1987; Berelson, 1960; Bowen & Rudenstine, 1992; Gardner, 2009; Gururaj et al., 2010; Lovitts, 2001; Nettles & Millett, 2006; Strayhorn, 2010). Many of these attrition factors relate to activities beyond the classroom. Graduate students' lives are messy and complicated, and their academic, personal, and professional lives are difficult to disentangle. These challenges can have significant ramifications such as distracting students from completing degree requirements, disrupting continuous enrollment, or needing to seek out specific resources for addressing mental health concerns. In addition, studies on graduate education tend to focus on unwinding the attrition puzzle, with an emphasis on factors leading to departure rather than persistence and completion. Thus, the purpose of this book was to present existing research alongside promising practices for graduate students that may provide a holistic and comprehensive approach to supporting the whole graduate student on the pathway to individual success and completion.

When we first started writing this book proposal, Christina and I did not ever anticipate what would become the COVID-19 pandemic and significant racial tensions transcending campus boundaries. Never in our wildest thoughts did we anticipate that campuses would be shut down overnight with no return date in sight. For some, being in graduate school served as a buffer or refuge from their home lives. Furthermore, we did not anticipate the increased escalation of hate and violence toward People of Color, particular Black people. Though these events happened beyond the traditional campus boundary, but have deeply affected and disrupted the lives and mental health of graduate students. Although graduate students are navigating what are called "unprecedented times," their struggles with the complexities of graduate education, including issues related to health, racial disparities, and time management, have been consistent and pervasive even before the pandemic arrived. Our hope is that the contributions from authors in this volume will provide continued guidance on supporting graduate students, especially as we continue to reimagine what graduate education can and should look like in post-pandemic times.

This edited volume brought together scholars and practitioners for an in-concert dialogue on how best to support graduate students' shifting identities while developing requisite skills and finding support beyond the classroom. In particular, this volume addressed the needs of today's changing student demography and offered ways to address challenges they may face inside and outside of the classroom. In the remainder of this chapter, we offer implications and future directions for research and practice of graduate student services.

Implication for Future Research Areas

Though graduate students spend a considerable amount of time engaging with academic activities, graduate students' lives are complex and often extend beyond academic spaces. However, much of the research about graduate students' lives and their socialization tends to focus on the academic side of the house. For this reason, more research is needed on how many of these outside considerations shape the graduate student experience.

For example, how might participating in a campus-wide graduate student organization shape a student's sense of belonging or formulate community with students beyond the disciplinary home? Many graduate students do not venture outside their academic department to find students holding similar social identities (e.g., LGBTQ+, Students of Color). Throughout this volume, we have encouraged readers to consider ways to traverse or even break down disciplinary boundaries in hopes of building a greater sense of community across students.

A second area for consideration is the availability and usage of such student engagement spaces. Several studies have considered the availability and usage of campus resources for undergraduate students (Banjong, 2015; Halstead et al., 2017; Nguyen et al., 2018), yet, much less is known about these aspects for graduate students. Having a better understanding of how graduate students navigate and make use of campus resources can provide an advocacy opportunity for graduate students. More often than not, graduate students are overlooked for campus services because there can be an inherent assumption that they are for undergraduate students. In actuality, many cases do offer similar or the same services to all students across campus. Perhaps lack of usage may be attributable to how these services are marked or marketed. More research is needed on this topic.

A third consideration for future research has to do with a needs analysis of graduate students. While many institutions conduct campus climate surveys that may occasionally incorporate feedback from graduate students, considering the needs of graduate students as being distinct from undergraduate students is necessary. Some campuses are moving to have graduate student senates and graduate colleges that handle the germane aspects of graduate students.

A final consideration for future research on supporting today's graduate students has to do with preparing students for career beyond the professoriate. Within this volume, we have included a chapter addressing career development needs of master's and doctoral students. However, this chapter should serve as a starting point. As the academic labor market becomes more constrained and produces fewer tenure-track openings and institutions continue to expand the number of students in graduate school, particularly doctoral students, the confluence of these events leads to a situation where competition will be further amplified and students must consider a range of career options. While there will certainly be anecdotes of successful students beyond highly ranked programs, research definitively shows that students graduating from elite programs have a more substantial shot at landing these coveted positions (Burris, 2004; Freeman & DiRamio, 2016).

Implications for Improving Practice and Supporting Graduate Students

In this volume, different authors considered how centering identities outside the primary purview of graduate education is necessary for advancing the field and support for graduate students. The demographics, such as first generation, socioeconomic status, and race and ethnicity, and online programs of graduate students continue to evolve and change rapidly though many of the same socialization tools and mechanisms remain intact. If graduate education wants to remain elite, then these practices should continue. These calls for inclusivity are imperative for the academy and fields may miss the opportunity to engage with new and novel ideas needed to enhance the existing disciplinary structures.

A second consideration for improving graduate education requires forward thinking on the types of academic and professional skills necessary for the future. In this volume, we have addressed some of the more traditional academic considerations, such as developing teaching capacity and scholarly voice. Encouraging graduate students to think more broadly about how teaching and voice can profoundly shape minoritized students, who may not have felt represented or heard during their undergraduate education. Thinking about how developing these skills can translate to pursuits outside the academy and can also benefit students. Another space where graduate students can learn how to communicate complex information is through participation in professional associations. Within graduate education, students often participate in professional association work as a networking opportunity or a place to share in-progress scholarly work; however, participating in these kinds of events can be particularly costly to students. While professional associations often rely on membership and annual conference fees, the costs for participation can be particularly high and in turn act as an exclusionary barrier. Graduate programs and institutions need to consider how they can support the professional development of their graduate students, as well as provide them with opportunities to engage in the type of research activities required for maximizing this learning experience.

A third area with implications for practice involves thinking about the complex lives graduate students live. A primary concern for institutions regardless of degree type involves the need for addressing student mental health concerns. Countless studies have taken up undergraduate student mental health. Though the number is growing, fewer studies have accounted for graduate students. Graduate education is largely an independent venture and one requiring considerable concentration. Consequently, graduate students may experience feelings of burnout, isolation, and even depression. More attention and resources need to attend to graduate students' mental health. Some ways institutions can address mental health is through creating student organizations or developing career services specifically for graduate populations. Though resources may be available on campus for graduate institutions, institutions need to take up the challenge to highlight for graduate students that work–life balance is needed and students should feel like they belong at an institution.

Parting Words

Throughout this volume, we have attempted to invite readers into a conversation about how best to support graduate students. As shared by the contributing authors, institutions of higher education must reconsider how to best support both in-class and out-of-class experienes for graduate students. In addition, it is imperative that institutions do not simply leave it to disciplinary silos to support students; otherwise, the status quo will continue. It is our hope that readers, especially graduate school administrators, student affairs professionals, faculty, and researchers, will engage with advice shared in the book to reimagine ways to better support today's graduate student population.

References

Abedi, J., & Benkin, E. (1987). The effects of students' academic, financial, and demographic variables on time to the doctorate. *Research in Higher Education*, *27*(1), 3–14. https://doi.org/10.1007/bf00992302

Banjong, D. N. (2015). International students' enhanced academic performance: Effects of campus resources. *Journal of International Students*, *5*(2), 132–142. https://www.ojed.org/index.php/jis/article/view/430

Berelson, B. (1960). *Graduate education in the United States*. McGraw-Hill.

Bowen, W. G., & Rudenstine, N. L. (1992). *In pursuit of the PhD*. Princeton University Press.

Burris, V. (2004). The academic caste system: Prestige hierarchies in PhD exchange networks. *American Sociological Review*, *69*(2), 239–264. https://doi.org/10.1177/000312240406900205

Freeman, S., Jr. & DiRamio, D. (2016). Elitism or pragmatism? Faculty hiring at top graduate programs in higher education administration. *Journal of the Professoriate*, *8*(2), 94–127.

Gardner, S. K. (2009). Conceptualizing success in doctoral education: Perspectives of faculty in seven disciplines. *Review of Higher Education*, *32*(3), 383–406. https://doi.org/10.1353/rhe.0.0075

Gururaj, S., Heilig, J., & Somers, P. (2010). Graduate student persistence: Evidence from three decades. *Journal of Student Financial Aid, 40*(1), 31–46. https://ir.library.louisville.edu/jsfa/vol40/iss1/3/

Halstead, V., Williams, J. R., & Gonzalez--Guarda, R. (2017). Sexual violence in the college population: A systematic review of disclosure and campus resources and services. *Journal of Clinical Nursing, 26*(15–16), 2137–2153. https://doi.org/10.1111/jocn.13735

Lovitts, B. E. (2001). *Leaving the ivory tower: The causes and consequences of departure from doctoral study.* Rowman and Littlefield.

National Center for Education Statistics. (2021). *Postsecondary certificates and degrees conferred.* https://nces.ed.gov/programs/coe/indicator_cts.asp

Nettles, M. T., & Millett, C. M. (2006). *Three magic letters: Getting to PhD.* The Johns Hopkins University Press.

Nguyen, D. J., Brazelton, G. B., Renn, K. A., & Woodford, M. R. (2018). Exploring the availability and influence of LGBTQ+ student services resources on student success at community colleges: A mixed methods analysis. *Community College Journal of Research and Practice, 42*(11), 783–796. https://doi.org/10.1080/10668926.2018.1444522

Strayhorn, T. L. (2010). Money matters: The influence of financial factors on graduate school persistence. *Journal of Student Financial Aid, 40*(3), 4–25. https://ir.library.louisville.edu/jsfa/vol40/iss3/1/

EDITORS AND CONTRIBUTORS

Editors

David J. Nguyen (he/him) is dean of University College and associate professor of higher education and student affairs at Ohio University.

Christina W. Yao (she/her) is an associate professor of higher education at the University of South Carolina.

Contributors

Salome Aluso (she/her) is a 4th-year doctoral candidate of higher education and student affairs at Ohio University. She holds an MS degree in applied linguistics from Ohio University. Aluso is passionate about topics that relate to international students' college experiences and is currently working on her dissertation proposal that explores international students' community engagement experiences.

Sonja Ardoin (she/her) is program director and associate professor of student affairs administration at Appalachian State University. She is proud of her first-generation college student-to-PhD educational journey. Ardoin studies social class, first-generation college students, rurality, and career preparation and pathways. She is also a contributor to the NASPA Center for First-generation Student Success advocacy group and CatalystFIRST program, the NASPA Faculty Council, and the AFLV Board of Directors.

Colin Ben (he/him) is an assistant research professor and lead of the online Master of Arts in Indigenous Education, and associate director of the Center for Indian Education in the School of Social Transformation at Arizona State University. He is a qualitative researcher who studies access and persistence of historically underrepresented graduate students, specifically American Indian students. His research agenda focuses on the intersections of access, Indigenous research methodologies, and higher education policies.

A. Emiko Blalock (she/her) is an assistant professor in the Office of Medical Education Research and Development in the College of Human Medicine at Michigan State University. Core to Blalock's research agenda is addressing problems of social inequity in the spaces where communities and education intersect. As a qualitative researcher, she leverages critical, narrative, and place-based methodologies and analyses, specifically those that elevate the individual and communal experience. These methodologies contribute to increased knowledge about why problematic phenomena occur and how to develop systemic solutions and interventions for such phenomena.

Emily J. Boerman (she/her), PhD, MSW, is a Leadership Teaching Fellow at Nazarbayev University in Nur-Sultan, Kazakhstan. Previously, she served in the international education field for 7 years supporting international students from recruitment through post-completion practical work experiences. Her research is in international education and organizational development within higher education organizations, undocumented students, and university students with siblings with disabilities.

Allison Boone Green (she/her) is a doctoral candidate in the Educational Leadership program at Eastern Michigan University, an instructor in the Department of Leadership and Counseling, and a facilitator for the leadership training organization, LifeLabs Learning. She previously served as a program manager for the University of Michigan's College of Literature, Science, and the Arts and Department of Athletics. Her teaching, research, and consulting activities focus on leadership education, experiential learning, women in leadership, and the impact of leadership development programs on women's leadership identity development.

Josefina Carmona (she/her/ella), PhD, serves as the Dean of the Health Sciences Division at New Mexico State University, Doña Ana Community College. She has served in various administrator capacities in higher education for over 20 years as well as taught as an adjunct in Chicanx studies and political science. Her research focuses on the role that academic legitimacy plays in the experiences of Chicanas/Latinas in pursuit of the professoriate as well as experiences of Chicanx/Latinx students, particularly at Hispanic Serving Institutions.

Matthew Couch (he/him), PhD, is the associate dean of students and senior director of student activities and student life orientation at Ohio State University. During more than 2 decades with Student Activities at Ohio State, he has worked with graduate and professional student programming, student governments, and support of a community of more than 1,400 registered student organizations, many of which comprise primarily or exclusively graduate students. He is also an adjunct instructor in Ohio State's College of Education and Human Ecology. He holds a BS in Psychology and Linguistics from the College of William and Mary and both an MA and PhD in Higher Education and Student Affairs from Ohio State University. His doctoral research was a phenomenological study of over-involvement.

Jennifer Donaghue, EdD, is executive director of International Education at George Washington University. Her international background includes study abroad in Spain and Portugal, and teaching experience in Japan. She directs the Office for Study Abroad and International Student and Scholar Services. She is active in Diversity Abroad and NAFSA, and presents frequently on issues of internationalization, diversity, equity and inclusion. She holds faculty positions in the GW Elliott School of International Affairs and the Graduate School of Education. She holds an MA from American University and a doctorate in education from The George Washington University.

Maria Dykema Erb (she/her) is the inaugural director of the Boston University Newbury Center. This Center was established to support the holistic success of first-generation undergraduate, graduate, and professional students. Erb was formerly the codirector for diversity and student success in The Graduate School at the University of North Carolina-Chapel Hill where she directed the Carolina Grad Student F1RSTS initiative. This initiative is for first-generation graduate students whose parents or guardians have not completed a postbaccalaureate degree. As a proud first-generation college graduate, Erb holds a BS in hotel administration from the University of New Hampshire and an MEd in interdisciplinary studies with a concentration in higher education, leadership, and counseling from the University of Vermont.

Crystal E. Garcia (she/her) is assistant professor of educational administration at the University of Nebraska-Lincoln. Her research critically examines the mechanisms by which minoritized college students experience campus environments, specifically focusing on campus climates and the role of student affairs in student experiences.

Lucas B. Hill (he/him) is an associate researcher and evaluator at the University of Wisconsin-Madison in the Wisconsin Center for Education Research (WCER). His research focuses on the role of multisector and multi-institutional networks in implementing systemic and collaborative higher education reform, particularly related to the preparation of future faculty, the adoption of evidence-based pedagogical practices, and broadening participation of underrepresented students in science, technology, engineering, mathematics (STEM) education. He earned his PhD in higher, adult, and lifelong education from Michigan State University.

Kerry M. Hodak, (she/her), JD, is an assistant director in Academic Partnership and Career Success in Student Life at The Ohio State University. Her primary work entails development of programs which engage the approximately 14,000 graduate and professional students at Ohio State as well as outreach to better connect graduate and professional students to services and programs both internal and external to the university. She also advises the graduate and professional student governments at Ohio State. Additionally, she works with the Association of Graduate and Professional Administrators (AGPA) and the Office of Postdoctoral Affairs at Ohio State.

Natali Huggins (she/her) is a PhD candidate in the higher education program at Virginia Tech. She holds an MPA from the National Experimental University of Táchira in Venezuela. She has several years of experience in higher education administration and internal audit. Her research expertise lies in diversity and inclusion in graduate education, particularly international and Latinx graduate students' persistence and development. She specifically focuses on supporting students in their transition, adaptability, and socialization to higher education in the United States.

Sarah Kurz (she/her) is a graduate student in the higher education PhD program at the University of Pittsburgh. She is passionate about research topics including diversity and equity in STEM education, college to career transitions, access and persistence in graduate level education, and graduate student mental health.

Jake Livengood (he/him) is associate director of career management at The University of Chicago Booth School of Business. He has worked in collegiate career services since 2005 in a variety of roles with graduate students, including career coaching, employer outreach, teaching, and leadership. His scholarship focuses on the effectiveness of career services. He earned his PhD in higher education from the University of Nevada-Las Vegas (UNLV).

Chelsea H. Lyles, (she/her), PhD, is the Associate Director of Broader Impacts for the Center for Educational Networks and Impacts, adjunct instructor in the school of education, and affiliate faculty for the Department of Engineering Education at Virginia Tech. Her research interests explore the intersections of (a) P–12 and higher education policy and finance, (b) academic labor, (c) graduate education, and (d) assessment of student learning. By critically examining these areas, she aims to illuminate adverse, systemic impacts of policies and practices on historically marginalized populations at the organizational level. Current research projects include a scoping review of service learning courses, measuring sense of belonging in electrical and computer engineering, and a qualitative study of boundary-spanning educators.

Meggan Madden, (she/her), PhD, is dean of academics at Principia College. In this role as chief academic officer, she is responsible for the internation-alization activities of the campus, including Study Abroad, International Student Programing and Services, and the internationalization activities outlined in Principia College's strategic plan. Her research examines policy frameworks and student experiences that broadly explores international higher education for development and exchange. This examination specifi-cally focuses on supranational and regional policy frameworks that impact access and inclusion for global student mobility. Her recent work focuses on student experiences with international education to understand institu-tional practices used to promote, fund, and support underserved students.

Katy B. Mathuews (she/her) is the senior director of administration at Ohio University Libraries in Athens, Ohio. She has held the positions of member-ship chair, vice president, and president on the Academic Library Association of Ohio's Executive Board. Her practical work focuses on academic library assessment, library outreach, and library spaces. Her higher education research focuses on working students' experience with time poverty and its effect on curricular and cocurricular involvement.

Carmen M. McCallum (she/her) is an associate professor at Eastern Michigan University. She has previously served as a faculty member at Buffalo State University and as an academic research specialist for the Provost Office of Undergraduate Education at Michigan State University. Her research interests include access and retention within graduate educa-tion; African American students and faculty; programmatic assessment and evaluation; and graduate students mentoring experiences. She is particularly interested in understanding how race, ethnicity, gender, and socioeconomic status influence students' academic and career paths.

Kim Nehls (she/her) was the executive director of the Association for the Study of Higher Education (ASHE) and a visiting assistant professor of educational psychology and higher education at the University of Nevada-Las Vegas (UNLV). Nehls has served as the ASHE executive director for 10 years. Her research explores the role of philanthropy and volunteerism in college and universities.

OiYan Poon, (she/her), PhD, is an associate professor affiliate in the School of Education at Colorado State University. Her research focuses on race, policy, college access and affirmative action policies, college curriculum, and critical pedagogies.

Carmen Rivera, (she/her), PhD, serves as the talent manager for organizational development for the Division of Student Affairs and codirector for the student affairs in higher education master's program at Colorado State University. She earned her PhD in higher education leadership and her research focuses on the leadership experiences of queer Chicana/Latina administrators. She worked for TRiO programs for over 13 years then worked in international education for several years. Additionally, she's a faculty member for the Social Justice Training Institute and a consultant in the areas of social justice and leadership.

Claire K. Robbins, (she/her), PhD, is an assistant professor and program leader for the higher education program at Virginia Tech. Her publications and current research projects explore equity, diversity, and inclusion in graduate education; student development, socialization, and learning; and critical perspectives on race and gender. In 2019, she and Rosemary J. Perez were awarded a grant from the Spencer Foundation to explore the role of graduate colleges in advancing equity, diversity, and inclusion in the context of state policy constraints.

Phil Schuman (he/him) serves as director of financial literacy for Indiana University and executive director of the Higher Education Financial Wellness Alliance. Since 2012, he has helped implement a peer-to-peer financial education program, launch an interactive financial education website (moneysmarts.iu.edu), and create a comprehensive financial education platform (MoneySmarts U) used by universities across the country. Schuman graduated with a BA in psychology from DePauw University and an MBA from Indiana University.

Jessica Solyom (she/her) is an assistant research professor in the School of Social Transformation at Arizona State University where she also serves as director of special projects for the Office of the Vice President for Social Advancement. Her work draws from Tribal critical race theory, Indigenous knowledge systems, and critical Indigenous research methodologies to inform culturally responsive schooling, pedagogy, curriculum, and practices as a tool to promote education equity and enhance the mental, social, and intellectual well-being of diverse communities. She previously served as associate director for the Center for Gender Equity in Science and Technology.

Francena F. L. Turner, (she/her), PhD, is a an interdisciplinary historian of education and the Council on Library and Information Resources (CLIR) fellow and Postdoctoral Associate for Data Curation in African American History and Culture for the University of Maryland Restorative Justice Project where her research is an alloy of African American History, Culture, and Digital Humanities (AADHum), oral history, and the University of Maryland Libraries. Her critical studies of Black women's higher education and activist scholars explore historical and contemporary issues of equity, agency, and thriving in higher education more broadly. She earned her PhD in History of Education from the University of Illinois, Urbana-Champaign. Her research has been published in *Gender, Work, and Organization and Women, Gender & Families of Color.*

HyeJin (Tina) Yeo, (she/her), PhD, is an equity-minded educator, critical scholar and activist. She received her PhD in Sociology of Higher Education from the University of Illinois at Urbana-Champaign, where she was awarded her Outstanding Doctoral Student Medal. She has investigated campus climates and racial microaggressions, inclusion excellence in STEM fields for the success of domestic and international students of color at predominantly White institutions (PWIs) and community colleges. Currently, she is taking the lead on NSF-funded research entitled the Center for Inclusive Computing (CIC) project at *Momentum*: Accelerating Equity in Computing and Technology at the University of California Los Angeles.

Eboni M. Zamani-Gallaher, (she/her), PhD, is professor of Higher Education/Community College Leadership and director of the Office for Community College Research and Leadership (OCCRL) at the University of Illinois at Urbana-Champaign (UIUC). She previously served as associate head of the Department of Education Policy, Organization, and Leadership and associate dean of the Graduate College at UIUC. Her teaching, research, and consulting activities largely include psychosocial adjustment and transition of marginalized collegians, transfer, access policies, student development, and services at community colleges. Currently she also serves as the executive director of the Council for the Study of Community Colleges (CSCC) the primary professional association for community college scholars.

Teaching *Gradually*

Practical Pedagogy and Classroom Startegies for Graduate Students by Graduate Students

Edited by Kacie L. Armstrong, Lauren A. Genova, John Wyatt Greenlee, and Derina S. Samuel

Foreword by Mathew L. Ouellett

"*Teaching Gradually* is a unique resource for graduate student instructors at all levels. In brief, highly readable chapters, the authors draw on the wisdom of their practice grounded in pedagogical research and the unique positionality of graduate students as teachers. Readers will find themselves returning regularly to this volume for field-tested discussions of teaching contexts as varied as discussions, labs, field experiences, and undergraduate research, with a welcome and timely emphasis on diversity and inclusion."—*Matt Kaplan, Executive Director, Center for Research on Learning and Teaching, University of Michigan*

"The most important reform of graduate education over the past 3 decades has been the increased preparation of graduate students planning careers in the professoriate in the teaching and mentoring of undergraduate students. Both inspiring and practical, *Teaching* Grad*ually* is a sophisticated work and evidence itself of how far the movement to prepare future faculty has progressed. This thoughtful, well-planned volume will be an indispensable companion on the journey to becoming a professor ready to engage today's students."
—*Leo M. Lambert, President Emeritus and Professor, Elon University*

"Grounded, engaging, and thorough! *Teaching* Grad*ually* provides a plethora of evidence-based strategies for any new (or even seasoned) instructor. The example teaching practices and professional development approaches apply across the disciplines, and are made even more powerful coming from graduate student teachers who understand that context best. The diverse voices and chapter formats make for an interesting read. An excellent resource for a college teaching course or for supervisors to read with their graduate students. Thank you for this book!"—*Donna Ellis, Director of the Centre for Teaching Excellence at the University of Waterloo (Canada) and Past President of the Professional and Organizational Development (POD) Network*

The Productive Graduate Student Writer

How to Manage Your Time, Process, and Energy to Write Your Research Proposal, Thesis, and Dissertation and Get Published

Jan Allen

Foreword by Chris M. Golde

This book is for graduate students—and others—who want to become more productive writers. It's especially written for those who want to:

- increase their motivation, focus, and persistence to move a project to completion
- overcome procrastination and perfectionistic tendencies
- reduce (or write in spite of) their anxiety and fear of writing
- manage their time, work, energy (and advisor) for greater productivity

The process or craft of sustained writing is not a matter that's taught to undergraduate or graduate students as part of their studies, leaving most at sea about how to start a practice that is central to a career in academe and vital in many other professional occupations.

"Unfortunately, few graduate students start their programs with well-established habits of writing. Instead, they figure it out on their own; often relying on strategies that sufficed during their undergraduate years. Binge writing. Procrastinating. Mired in perfectionist gridlock.

Those strategies, however, don't work for doctoral writing. What to do? Shed the old habits and develop new ones. Easier said than done, of course. Fortunately, there is help. This book will set you on the right course.

Jan Allen has seen it all. For decades she has brought her empathetic wisdom to help graduate student writers find their voices and their writing rhythms. This book is a pithy distillation of her wisdom. She serves it up in bite-sized chunks. Use it as an energy burst to start your daily writing time and set your new habits into place."—***Chris M. Golde***, *Assistant Director of Career Communities for PhDs & Postdocs, Stanford University*

What They Didn't Teach You in Graduate School

Second Edition

299 Helpful Hints for Success in Your Academic Career

Paul Gray and David E. Drew

Illustrated by Matthew Henry Hall

Foreword by Laurie Richlin and Steadman Upham

"Authors Paul Gray and David E. Drew's (2012) text is a well written, excellent read, that is insightful for those who are in the process of starting their academic career. From the start to finish, they provide the reader with a lot of useful tips to help one be more savvy and keen as an academic. Readers should enjoy this book because it is well organized and structured. Additionally, the chapters and hints are laid out in a way that is easy and pleasurable to read. The authors do a good job of describing terms and breaking larger concepts into smaller sections or over several tips to allow for the reader to get a better grasp of the overall ideas put forth. They also write in a clear, concise and, more importantly, a direct manner. In essence, Gray and Drew do not try to stump you, nor do they try to act as if they are leading experts. Rather, they sincerely convey their thoughts based upon their experiences as professors. The topics covered in this book are essential and useful because they walk you through several stages of what it takes to have a successful academic career, such as ways to complete your dissertation and effectively publish to working through your first job search and colleague relations. That said, if you are considering a career in the professoriate or currently in a PhD program, and would like a few helpful hints please consider reading this text."—**Derrick Gunter**, *NACADA*

Also available from Stylus

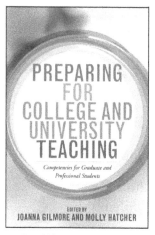

Preparing for College and University Teaching

Competencies for Graduate and Professional Students

Edited by Joanna Gilmore and Molly Hatcher

This book is a guide for designing professional development programs for graduate students. The teaching competencies framework presented here can serve as the intended curriculum for such programs. The book will also be an excellent resource for evaluating programs, and will be an excellent resource for academics who study graduate students.

This book presents the work of the Graduate Teaching Competencies Consortium to identify, organize, and clarify the competencies that graduate students need to teach effectively when they join the professoriate. To achieve this goal, the Consortium developed a framework of 10 teaching competencies organized around three overarching questions:

- What do graduate students need to achieve by the end of their graduate education to be successful teacher-scholars?
- What do graduate students need to understand about higher education to have successful careers as educators?
- What do graduate students need to do to be successful teachers during their graduate student careers?

"A framework of graduate student teaching competencies is exactly what we needed—and could not find in a single, integrated resource prior to this book—when developing our preparing future faculty program. With this volume, we now have a research-supported and actionable guide with which to justify, evaluate, and benchmark our program. *Preparing for College and University Teaching* will greatly benefit our preparing future faculty program—and the graduate students we serve."—**Kate Williams**, *Assistant Director, TA Development and Future Faculty Initiatives, Center for Teaching and Learning, Georgia Institute of Technology*

22883 Quicksilver Drive
Sterling, VA 20166-2019   Subscribe to our email alerts: www.Styluspub.com